THE COMPLETE
IDIOT'S
GUIDE® TO

Memes

by John Gunders, Ph.D., and Damon Brown

ALPHA

A member of Penguin Group (USA) Inc.

ALPHA BOOKS

Published by the Penguin Group

Penguin Group (USA) Inc., 375 Hudson Street, New York, New York 10014, USA

Penguin Group (Canada), 90 Eglinton Avenue East, Suite 700, Toronto, Ontario M4P 2Y3, Canada (a division of Pearson Penguin Canada Inc.)

Penguin Books Ltd., 80 Strand, London WC2R 0RL, England

Penguin Ireland, 25 St. Stephen's Green, Dublin 2, Ireland (a division of Penguin Books Ltd.)

Penguin Group (Australia), 250 Camberwell Road, Camberwell, Victoria 3124, Australia (a division of Pearson Australia Group Pty. Ltd.)

Penguin Books India Pvt. Ltd., 11 Community Centre, Panchsheel Park, New Delhi—110 017, India

Penguin Group (NZ), 67 Apollo Drive, Rosedale, North Shore, Auckland 1311, New Zealand (a division of Pearson New Zealand Ltd.)

Penguin Books (South Africa) (Pty.) Ltd., 24 Sturdee Avenue, Rosebank, Johannesburg 2196, South Africa

Penguin Books Ltd., Registered Offices: 80 Strand, London WC2R 0RL, England

Publisher: *Marie Butler-Knight*

Associate Publisher: *Mike Sanders*

Senior Managing Editor: *Billy Fields*

Acquisitions Editor: *Tom Stevens*

Development Editor: *Michael Thomas*

Senior Production Editor: *Janette Lynn*

Copy Editor: *Lisanne V. Jensen*

Cover Designer: *William Thomas*

Book Designers: *William Thomas, Rebecca Batchelor*

Indexer: *Heather McNeill*

Layout: *Ayanna Lacey*

Proofreader: *Laura Caddell*

John: To Lisa for picking up the load.

Damon: To Dr. Kevin Early for sparking my love of sociology.

Contents

Appendixes

Introduction

A meme is a simple concept—a cultural idea that gets passed on from person to person—but affects so many areas of our lives, from our religion and our dress to what we eat and how we communicate. In short, memes *are* culture. They are vastly important.

In this book, we break down the definition of a meme, how they are passed, what happens when they are active, ways in which multilayered memes can create societal shifts, protection against memes, and the nitty-gritty theories behind these cultural ideas.

Ideally, by the end of this book, you'll not only understand their importance but also recognize memes all around you. Don't be alarmed, however, because you've been let in on a secret: memes have been driving our society all along.

How to Use This Book

This book is divided into six parts:

Part 1, What Is a Meme?, covers the basics, including the definition of a meme, when they were first discovered, and why they are important. The two chapters also show the different parts of the meme and how each part is integral to how the meme will be received, passed, and understood.

Part 2, Pass It On: How Memes Spread, breaks down the process memes use to move so quickly through our society and help create our modern lives. The focus is on the three primary ways modern memes travel: word of mouth, internet, and marketing.

Part 3, Memes In Action, shows the direct impact cultural ideas have from conception to result. Pop culture, technology, philosophy, religion, sex, and politics are all built on memes, and our history is based on what ideas are accepted, taught, and dismissed.

Part 4, Complex Memes, gets into the heavier, multilayered memes, including the most recently defined meme classifications. The memes here can be made out of a smaller set of memes, hijack an existing meme, or remain dormant until it is revived by another idea. This part also discusses dangerous memes, from scams and hoaxes to memes that can literally kill.

Part 5, Defenses Against Memes, explains why we are susceptible to certain memes more than others. There are conscious ways to block an unwanted cultural idea from influencing our lives.

Part 6, The Theories Behind Memes, gets into the nitty-gritty, heavy concepts based on the meme theorists. Here are the classic ideas, such as the meme-related Darwinism, and more modern concepts and theories being touted today. We also look at some objections to meme theory.

We also have six appendixes for your reference. Appendix A is a glossary of common meme terms. Appendix B is a question-and-answer section to respond quickly to your basic meme questions. The next appendix gives you a hardy list of books and resources for further reading and research. Appendix D breaks down the seven most influential memes in history. Appendix E is a fun list of the biggest Internet memes. Finally, Appendix F contains interviews with a few of the people behind cultural ideas that consumed the world.

Extras

The more you know about memes, the more you'll realize how they interweave into our lives. Each chapter is sprinkled with interesting sidebars under the following headings:

DEFINITION

Check these boxes for definitions of meme or pop-cultural words that may be unfamiliar to you.

PASS IT ON

Here, you'll find tips, hints, and insights to help you understand memes.

INFECTION!

These boxes contain warnings about confusing or hard-to-understand details about memes.

HAVE YOU HEARD?

Check these boxes for fun, interesting tidbits, notable history, or trivia to share with friends.

Acknowledgments

John would like to express thanks to his family for enduring months of chatter about memes and for allowing him to test out ideas on them; to readers of *The Memes of Production* for answering questions and providing tips; and especially to Damon for inviting him onboard.

Damon would like to thank his family, his girlfriend, Dr. Parul Patel, and his favorite sociologist, Dr. Kevin Early, now director of criminal justice at the University of Michigan at Dearborn, for sparking his interest in social movements. And last, but not least, John for creating a fun, memorable co-author experience.

Trademarks

All terms mentioned in this book that are known to be or are suspected of being trademarks or service marks have been appropriately capitalized. Alpha Books and Penguin Group (USA) Inc. cannot attest to the accuracy of this information. Use of a term in this book should not be regarded as affecting the validity of any trademark or service mark.

What Is a Meme?

In Part 1 we start on our journey with a quick overview of the meme and the science of memetics. We explain that a meme is a unit of culture that can be spread by various means across and between societies, and that memes are much more complicated and important than just funny pictures of cats on the Internet (although they are memes, too). We learn that memes aren't just ideas: they are replicators, and their purpose is to copy themselves from host to host.

We then get slightly more technical and define what a meme is and explain why some things that look like memes aren't, and describe the different parts of the meme. We talk about the way that memes affect us and can control us, and the different methods by which memes spread.

Part 1 also introduces some terminology that will help with the descriptions in later chapters, and lays a basic framework for explaining the science and theory behind memes. We give a basic outline of the history of memetics and how the concept was invented, including a short discussion of how memetics is connected to Darwin's theory of evolution.

Learning About Memes

In This Chapter

- Defining a meme
- Why memes are passed along
- Memes beyond the Internet
- Reasons memes are important—and dangerous

Before the new millennium, calling something "viral" usually meant Yellow Fever or perhaps a nasty cold going around the office. It was a physical thing your body could catch—and something you definitely didn't want!

We've learned in the new Internet age, however, that something viral isn't necessarily related to our body or even a bad thing. It just means a concept that catches on. As you probably know, an idea can be viral, a video can be viral, a spiritual belief can be viral, and so on.

Before the word viral became modern and hip, there was already a term for these tidbits of culture passed along to others: memes. Sounds funny, doesn't it? But as you'll soon discover, the word *meme* (which rhymes with *dream*) means much more than just a video of a cat playing the piano on YouTube. Indeed, some scientists believe it ties into our very evolution.

So what, exactly, is a meme? In this chapter, you'll find out.

Definition

First defined by Richard Dawkins in his 1976 best-seller *The Selfish Gene,* a *meme* is a cultural unit of measure. It can be a thought, a phrase, a style, or any other cultural expression that can be imitated by individuals.

> **DEFINITION**
>
> A **meme** is a cultural expression that is passed on from one person or group to another person or group.

The basic idea is that learning could be seen as a unit of cultural information being transmitted by imitation.

Richard Dawkins

Earlier scientists, such as F. T. Cloak, discussed this concept in the early '70s, but Dawkins was the first person to expand on the theory and to establish the term "meme" to describe it.

An assistant professor at the University of California at Berkeley, Dawkins argued that evolution occurred not only on the physical level but also on the mental level. Families, organizations, and the culture at large survive because certain cultural ideas are passed on—and other cultural ideas are killed or blocked. These cultural ideas were called memes.

This fascinating argument was tucked into Dawkins's book on evolution, *The Selfish Gene.* The 1976 hit sold more than a million copies, making Dawkins a celebrity and initially popularizing the idea of a meme.

Mimicry

The Greek root of the word meme, "mimema," means something that can be imitated. Consider other words with their roots in "mimema," such as mimic, which means to copy, or mime, which describes a person mimicking an action.

If you think about it, despite individuality being so fashionable in our time, culture often changes based on mimicry. The latest hip lingo, popular baby names, or funny haircuts are all memes. A designer in the '60s—probably French—decided that bell-bottomed jeans were what his or her model should wear and created a meme that would influence the following generation.

We watch each other, consume, and adapt. When we take in a cultural idea and express it in some form, we are passing on a meme.

A Life of Its Own

So a meme is a simple idea that can be passed easily from person to person. But it's also a bit more than that. You may have heard someone describe a rumor or a story as having "a life of its own." That's a meme.

They might spread quickly and effortlessly, but they are not easily controlled. Someone might want to start a meme—a great new joke, say, or an advertising campaign (we talk about viral marketing in Chapter 5)—but nothing he or she can do will guarantee that the meme will survive. Of those that do, it's impossible to tell which will prosper and which will be forgotten within days. And some of the memes that do survive are not the ones we really want to (think of racism, for instance).

What Makes a Meme?

A meme is a unit of culture—an idea, a habit, a fashion, a tune—that travels around from person to person as if under some design of its own. But that still doesn't make it very clear. If a simple melody can be a meme, is a symphony? What about an entire novel? Maybe a way to clarify the definition is to determine what *isn't* a meme.

A Meme Must Be Original

Let's take a look at music. Musicians know that the notes D, F$_\sharp$, and A form the D Major chord, that this chord can be transmitted easily on a musical instrument or in print, and that it can be imitated easily on a different instrument or even by voice (provided you have three people to sing it). But D Major isn't a meme—it doesn't have enough originality or difference from other competing forms. A meme has to be recognized as an individual unit that is distinct and repeatable.

A Meme Must Be Digestible

What about the symphony? *Symphony No. 5* by Ludwig van Beethoven is certainly original and recognizable. But this time, the unit is too big. I can't pass on an entire symphony to my friends by whistling it, and the symphony has no specific "idea" that could be transmitted.

But there are parts of *Symphony No. 5* that are memes—the opening five bars, for instance. Those famous four notes in the repeated short-short-short-long form have been used as ringtones and referenced in songs and jokes and form one of the most recognizable themes in classical music.

We could say, therefore, that *Symphony No. 5* by Beethoven is a *meme-complex* (or a *memeplex*) because it contains a number of different memes—that is, different themes and passages that are familiar on their own.

DEFINITION

A **meme-complex** or **memeplex** is a concept that contains a collection of memes.

A Meme Must Be Easily Understood

Charles Darwin's famous book *On the Origin of Species* has been in print for 150 years, has been read by many people, and gave rise to an entirely new branch of biology—but it is not a meme. Like the symphony, a book is too complex a production to be passed from person to person through imitation.

But most people know and understand (at least, to a limited extent) Darwin's theory of evolution (if you don't, turn to Part 6 of this book, and we'll try to infect you with that particular meme!). They have not memorized an entire biology textbook and may not be able to recite specific passages from Darwin, but they will know the essential basis of the theory. It is this essence of the theory that is the meme. Plenty of biologists disagree about the details of the theory, but the core concept—natural selection through survival of the fittest—is an idea that can be passed on to other people.

HAVE YOU HEARD?

During World War II, BBC radio used the opening bars of Beethoven's *Symphony No. 5* to introduce its news service, because the dit-dit-dit-dah rhythm formed the Morse Code symbol for the letter V: V for victory!

In short, for something to be a meme, it has to be simple enough to be conveyed to others easily.

Types of Memes

As you can probably imagine, there are countless memes in the world. For the sake of argument—and to keep our sanity—we can say most memes fall into three broad categories:

- Physical
- Technological
- Personal

Let's take a look at each category.

Physical

Memes can fly fast when you're around someone else. Being in the vicinity of a particular action can make it, well, contagious. Again, we don't mean literally like a cold, but contagious as in we may have a desire to imitate it—conscious or otherwise.

For example, one person starts yawning in the room—and suddenly, you and everyone around you is yawning. Sure, there may be what scientists would likely call "environmental factors"—it's late at night, you woke up early that morning, and so on. Still, the idea that you *should* yawn probably didn't occur until you saw another person do it. In this case, yawning is a meme.

Want further proof? The next time you're with a group of people, try looking up at the sky or fixating on one particular object. Chances are other people will begin trying to see what you're seeing—and you would have created a meme (albeit a shallow one!).

Technological

Technology can also be used to create memes. New innovations, such as the Internet, can help memes move faster and even create new memes more quickly. The Internet pushed memes into modern lingo, but remember that memes aren't only about Web trends. They can be any cultural expression that is passed on to the masses.

For instance, "RickRolling," the practice of promising a particularly interesting Web link online but really sending the user to a music video from '80s crooner Rick Astley (we discuss Internet memes further in Chapter 4) was something that would not have taken off as fast nor would have been as possible in a previous age. RickRolling became a regular joke via e-mail, Internet boards, and social networking sites such as Facebook and Twitter. Without the Internet as a vehicle, RickRolling would have remained an inside joke among the creators. Instead, it became popular enough to be referenced and recognized in the 2008 Macy's Thanksgiving Day Parade—viewed by millions—although the RickRolling practice had started only a couple years earlier.

HAVE YOU HEARD?

How did America get RickRoll'd during the popular Macy's Thanksgiving Day Parade? The commentators announced a new float, and just as it came into view, Rick Astley himself emerged from the structure. The RickRolling song "Never Gonna Give You Up" blasted from the float, and Astley sung the first few verses.

RickRolling was an Internet meme during the 2008 program, but a majority of the huge audience still watched it on television. In other words, the Internet meme became a television meme within one broadcast. Better yet, the YouTube of Astley doing the television RickRoll, which itself was based on a YouTube video, became one of the most-watched clips on the site.

The same technological changes in meme transmission can be described when radio, television, or cinema first came about during the last century.

Personal

As we hinted earlier, memes do not have to be wide-sweeping ideas or changes to society as a whole. A meme can be a cultural trend or ritual within a family or a specific group.

A classic parable displays how a cultural meme can work within a family. In the story, a daughter asks her mother why she always cuts the ends off the pot roast before putting it in the oven. Puzzled, the mom says she does it because her mother did. The daughter asks her grandmother, and sure enough, the grandmother says her mother did as well. The daughter finally visits her great-grandmother, who laughs and says, "Well, me and your great-grandfather were poor, and we had the tiniest oven! The only way we could fit things in was to …"

Usefulness aside, memes can help establish those bonds within a group. In this way, a meme can become something that is not given lightly but instead as a connector or as a right of passage.

How Memes Are Passed

Memes move from person to person, and sometimes to a million folks at once, but they all must be passed via a certain communication line.

Three of the most prominent ways in which memes are passed are:

- Word of mouth
- The Internet
- Marketing

Let's go deeper into how memes are delivered to you.

Word of Mouth

Have you ever had no interest in a group but decided to buy its album based on a friend's glowing recommendation? We all have, whether it's a new movie, a new restaurant, or a new toothpaste—and for some of us, it's the only time we'll actually try something new!

INFECTION!

Memes are cultural ideas and are neither good nor bad—they just are—but the influence can be variable. For instance, the memetic idea of self-sacrifice can be attached to a revered icon like Jesus Christ as it can be to a terrorist who hates a particular race or group. The individual reaction to a meme makes the impact.

In this case, a meme is passed along via word of mouth. We're getting information and acting on it because it's coming from someone we trust. This is exactly how we have phenomena such as a little-known indie (independent) movie becoming a hit virtually overnight—people pass the meme, or the idea, that this movie is good to enough people, making it a success. It makes sense that some people, such as film critic Roger Ebert, would have a better chance of creating a movie-related meme that sticks—but it has to do with the number of people he can reach as much as it does his weight as a critic.

We discuss word-of-mouth memes more in Chapter 3.

Internet

The concept of memes may have originated in the '70s, but the mainstream idea really blossomed with the advent of the Internet. In fact, some people familiar with the term think it *has* to be related to the Internet—which is a mistake, of course, because the term was around before the Internet became mainstream.

HAVE YOU HEARD?

The Internet may be older than you think. The foundation of our modern-day World Wide Web was laid in the late '60s by the United States Department of Defense. It was called ARPANET, or the Advanced Research Projects Agency Network, and was built to facilitate quicker communication between government agencies.

Nevertheless, the Internet has become an awesome conduit for passing along memes quickly. First, one comment on Twitter, Facebook, or another social networking website is immediately and publicly available to every literate human being with access to a Web-enabled computer. Second, aforementioned social networking websites and other multimedia tools such as blogs and video upload services make it really easy for everyone to express themselves, making the Internet an excellent barometer for finding out the latest trends—and arguably making it the best meme tracker in the world.

The speed and ease of spreading an idea across the Internet has led to the rise of online games such as "blog tagging." An early and influential example of this was the "Friday Five" blog, which asked readers to answer five simple questions about their likes and dislikes, and put them on their own blog. With the rise in popularity of social networks such as Facebook and Twitter, these sorts of games spread quickly, often with particular users being "tagged" and thereby asked to continue to spread the meme. A relatively new innovation, the Internet is discussed in depth in Chapter 4.

Marketing

"Have It Your Way." "Coke Is It." "The Big Apple." Whether it's Burger King, Coca-Cola, or New York City, marketers and their respective clients live and die based on how successfully they can get you to accept and pass on their respective memes.

A marketing meme can be as simple as one of these slogans—or, collected together, can be as complex and multi-layered as a lifestyle. As an example, Playboy Industries has always tried to represent the intelligent, well-traveled male with a strong interest in the ladies. The iconic Playboy Bunny ears, sold on hats, belts, and other clothing accoutrements carry this cultural idea. Seeing the icon is one way the 50-year-old company continues to pass along its legacy, its idea, and essentially, its meme.

Marketing, advertising, and all their intricacies are broken down in Chapter 5.

Seeing Memes in Action

Moving from person to person or group to group is only half of the meme's purpose. A meme is a failure if it isn't actually implemented by the receiver.

> **PASS IT ON**
>
> Memes can die—such as when a fad goes out of style—and can be revived, can create new memes and eliminate others, and can do so many other things!
>
> When you're ready, you can take a peek at Part 5, where we talk about the more complicated ways in which memes function—although we recommend reading through the initial four parts first!

It may sound abstract right now, so let's run down a few ways we can see memes in action:

- Popular culture
- Technology
- Philosophy

- Sex
- Religion
- Politics

Here's a preview of what we'll be discussing in upcoming chapters.

Popular Culture

We may dismiss the impact of comedian Jay Leno or cringe at the thought of socialite Paris Hilton, but pop culture (which includes both of these icons) is a serious transporter of cultural ideas.

There are three great ways to see pop culture in action:

- Fashion
- Music
- Humor

These seemingly superficial memes actually mold our lives, although we might not recognize their importance as we're reacting to them. For instance, the poet William Shakespeare, now considered one of the greatest writers, was the equivalent of a soap opera producer during his time. His plays and performances, understandable by mainstream audiences, serve as an excellent view into the fashion and the humor—that is, the memes—of his lifetime.

We discuss popular culture a lot more in Chapter 6.

Technology

Technology doesn't just involve today's GPS, Twitter, and iPhones. Remember that technology is relative, and compared to human history, computers haven't been around that long!

When it comes to technology, there are three ways to break things down:

- Architecture
- Language
- Machines

Architecture, language, and machines are all logical systems that are understandable, sustainable, and most importantly, easily duplicated. For instance, children are expected to learn the spoken word from their family within the first year through daily repetition and continuous context. As we read later on, architecture, language, and machines aren't just ways to create and communicate but are also carriers of memetic ideas.

Chapter 7 has much more information on important technological memes.

Philosophy

There are always ideas we stand for—often shown by our actions, not our words—but philosophies are the common ideas that a group of people deem worthy of definition.

Our chosen philosophy is a reflection of at least one of these influences:

- Social norms
- Initiation
- Tradition

As a simple example, let's say you were born into a Roman Catholic family. It's your prerogative to become, say, a conservative Jew or a practicing Buddhist—but family tradition, as well as the norms created within your family, make you more apt to stay a Roman Catholic.

Philosophies are quite a complex subject, and in Chapter 8 we'll get into different ideas based on celebrity, charity, and causes.

Sex

Sex is part of everyday life—and, frankly, how most of us got here—but the act itself can be filled with fear, confusion, and most importantly, powerful memes.

The most popular reasons for having sex are:

- Procreation

- Pleasure

- Power

There are a myriad of other reasons, something that is explored by another long-standing human tradition: pornography. Understanding our sexual expression requires getting to know our darkest memes—those assumptions that drive humans together and apart. For more information on how memes influence sex, pornography, and intimacy, check out Chapter 9.

Religion

More wars in human history have been started because of religion than for any other reason. Did you ever ask why? Religion, of course, usually connects to the very personal beliefs in spirituality, but it also can represent a set of accepted rituals—and the rejection of other principles. It's no wonder that those defeated in war are often forced to convert to the victor's chosen religion.

PASS IT ON

Spirituality is a personal belief, while religion is an accepted practice and ritual. In other words, religion is a meme, but spirituality is not.

Religion comprises a major, controversial set of memes, and we discuss those further in Chapter 10.

Politics

The word "politics" often conjures images of slick candidates and false promises, which isn't inaccurate! However, politics can also apply to our smaller, more private lives; hence "office politics" and similar terms.

The same rules apply; a good meme will get you support, and a bad one could end your campaign. Political memes fall into three major areas:

- Slogans
- Soapboxes
- Partisan memes

Check out Chapter 11 to go a lot deeper into politics and the impact of its related memes.

The Least You Need to Know

- A meme is a cultural unit of measure; essentially, an idea that can be passed on to another person.
- Memes can be physical, technological, or personal.
- The most prominent ways to pass memes are through word of mouth, the Internet, and marketing.
- To be a meme, an idea must be original, digestible, and easy to understand.
- The Internet transformed memes and sped up how quickly ideas were passed.

The Science of Memetics

In This Chapter

- Where the term "meme" came from
- The parts of a meme
- How memetics relates to evolution
- The medium versus the message

Memes can seem vague because cultural ideas aren't as concrete as the physics of gravity or the logic in algebra, but there is an actual science behind them. In fact, once you read this book—and if we're doing our job as authors—you'll see memes all around you.

In this chapter, we dip our toes into the science behind cultural ideas, breaking down the composition of memes, how they evolve, and why the deliverer is as important as the message.

If you're ready to go into the deep end for the full history of memes and learn how a simple idea turned into a new science, check out Part 6. For now, let's get into the basics.

The History of Memes and Memetics

Although there had been some similar ideas around, the term "meme" was coined by zoologist Richard Dawkins in his 1976 book *The Selfish Gene*. Far from a book about cultural meaning, it was an attempt to explain genetic evolution to a general audience. Dawkins's view was that the "selfish" genes created organisms for the sole purpose of copying themselves. At heart, the behavior of all organisms can be reduced to ways of propagating their genes.

This is quite a controversial idea for many people, and we will look at some objections to the theory in Part 6. Dawkins proposed the idea of the meme as an analogy to the gene—a piece of cultural information that exists to replicate itself by jumping into a host's mind and causing it to spread the idea. Think about the last time you heard a new joke and couldn't wait to tell it to someone else. Was it you who wanted to spread the meme, or was it actually the joke itself—influencing all the mental faculties it could to make you think it was your idea?

As philosopher Daniel Dennett puts it, "A scholar is a library's way of creating another library."

PASS IT ON

Daniel Dennett is considered a major contributor to memetic studies. Best known for his 1991 book *Consciousness Explained,* Dennett argued that memes don't just behave like genes but that they also literally evolve. It made scientists look at memes as living, dynamic entities as opposed to abstract, static entities.

For more detail on Dennett's theories and other foundational studies, check out Chapter 21 on classic theories.

Of course, this makes it sound like the meme is some sort of conscious entity, planning strategies to get itself copied. It is nothing of the sort. Genes, Dawkins argued, are dumb replicators that replicate. And the miracle is that this activity at a microscopic level gives rise to all the complexity of chromosomes, cells, organs, and ultimately, us. Memes also replicate because that is all they can do, and the unique capacities of the human mind mean that those memes can spread from person to person and around the world.

The Basic Idea

Memes, as Dawkins envisioned them, are subject to what we call *universal Darwinism.* This principle indicates that the same forces that shape biological evolution—what we usually call "natural selection"—apply to entities other than just biological organisms.

> **DEFINITION**
>
> **Universal Darwinism** is the principle that natural selection does not necessarily have to apply only to organic evolution but can also describe equally well things as diverse as economics, linguistics, and computer algorithms.

Natural selection requires three things: variation, selection, and retention. Variation means that there will be slight differences between individuals within the same group of entities. Selection means that when these entities are subject to environmental pressure—diminishing resources, perhaps—only some will survive, and those that do will be the ones better suited to the conditions. Retention means that characteristics of a particular entity will be passed on to others. In organic evolution, this process is called heredity—characteristics of your parents are passed on to you—but retention can refer to any form of information transmission.

Memes are a good example of this. They demonstrate variation—think of the children's game Telephone (sometimes called "Chinese Whispers," "Broken Telephone," and "Whisper Down the Lane") in which a message is passed down a line of people, usually changing completely in the process. When you tell a joke, you most probably won't repeat it exactly the way you heard it.

Memes also demonstrate selection. In a busy world, many things compete for your attention: songs, advertising, news reports, and so on. You can't take notice of them all, so the most persistent or most interesting things get noticed, and everything else is ignored.

Finally, memes are retained. The things that get past our attention filters and impress us sufficiently get passed on. We repeat the joke, tell someone about the fabulous book we've just read, or alert someone about an important news item. Most of this book is devoted to explaining how these things happen.

Dissecting a Meme

A meme might be an (often simple) cultural idea, but it requires several components to exist:

- The memetic engineer
- The hook
- The bait

- The vector
- The host
- The memotype
- The sociotype

Here's a breakdown of the parts.

The Memetic Engineer

The memetic engineer is the creator of the meme itself. There are two important points to meme engineering.

First, the actual meme creation doesn't have to be a conscious act. For instance, a hip schoolboy might wear mismatched socks on accident, but because he's a trendsetter, others might be inspired to wear mismatched socks the next day. A meme is created.

Second, the memetic engineer doesn't even have to be human. Artists can be inspired by nature, so a sudden shift in climate (global warming) could change the technique of hundreds—and, in turn, create an entire series of memes. Imagine how Paul Gauguin's art techniques changed when he was in Tahiti, or how Hurricane Katrina affected the ideas of Gulf Coast artists.

The Hook

A common term in advertising, the hook is the connector that attracts us to memes.

HAVE YOU HEARD?

In pop music, the chorus is called the "hook." The biggest music hits have catchy hooks—a repeated refrain that attracts the listener.

A simple hook is, "Marijuana is a gateway drug." In other words, marijuana may have been found relatively harmless, but getting involved with it will automatically pull you into more harmful substances such as cocaine or heroin. The point here isn't whether this statement is true or not—but that memes, which are just ideas, don't have a political value themselves. The only goal is to entice others to believe in the same idea.

The Bait

The other side of the hook, the bait, is the desired result promised by the meme.

In the axiom, "Helping other people creates good karma," the bait is that being of benefit to your fellow humans will help you have a positive life. Of course, the hook is the implied opposite result—not helping others creates bad karma!

The Vector

A vector is the impartial medium used to transport the meme to others. Think of the vector as a carrier, or a messenger—such as a book or television show—delivering the cultural idea to the masses.

Have you ever been e-mailed a joke that, if you look at the top of the message, has a long series of e-mail addresses? It likely was mailed by one person to a set of friends, who in turn mailed it to their set of friends, and so on—passing along a meme (in this case, a joke). The vector isn't the funny person who started the conversation but the e-mail medium itself.

INFECTION!

Remember, people are not vectors because vectors are not alive. Instead, vectors are impartial media used to pass along the meme. As people, we cannot be impartial.

What about talking? In the case of, say, you telling someone a joke in person, you are the memetic engineer and the spoken words themselves are the vector. How we use them is separate from the impartial words because they have a concrete, established meaning. It's up to the deliverer and the receiver to put them into their own, nonobjective context.

The Host

If the vector is the medium used to pass along the meme, the host is the carrier that sent the meme in the first place. Think of the vector as mail and the host as the mail deliverer.

In recent years, obnoxious millionaire Donald Trump has become a reality television staple with his show *The Apprentice*. Contestants compete to get a job with Trump Enterprises, with one being kicked off each episode by Trump saying, "You're fired."

"The Donald" didn't invent the saying "You're fired," but he did it in such a crisp, New York accent that mainstream America began repeating it in his dialect. When it comes to this meme, Trump is the meme host and television is the meme vector.

The Memotype

The memotype is the actual expression of a meme. A well-worn fashion meme is, "Don't wear white after Labor Day," referencing the American holiday that marks the beginning of autumn. The memotype of this meme is simply that instruction—it might be termed slightly differently or in a different language, but the basic information is the same. For people in the Southern Hemisphere, where the seasons are reversed, the phrase, "Don't wear white after Easter" might be used, but it would be the same meme and would have the same memotype.

The Sociotype

The sociotype is the meme's expression within the social and cultural environment in which that memotype exists.

The sociotype is the way the meme is understood and enacted in a particular situation. Let's go back to the "Don't wear white after Labor Day" meme. For a large group of couture-conscious people, it means using more color during the fall and winter months. It also includes all those assumptions about fashion, etiquette, and of course the physical principles that mean that white clothing tends to reflect heat while darker clothing tends to absorb it. The sociotype also reflects regional differences—in countries such as Australia, this meme has little currency. The sociotype of that particular meme seems to be limited to North America.

HAVE YOU HEARD?

The terms memotype and sociotype are derived from similar words in organic evolution: genotype and phenotype.

Genotype is the specific genetic constitution of an organism—its genetic fingerprint. In memes, the equivalent is the memotype.

On the other hand, the phenotype is expressed in the observable characteristics of an organism—its physiology, appearance, and behavior. In memes, this is the sociotype.

Evolution

Because of meme theory's basis in Darwinism, we have to talk about organic evolution a little bit. If you want more information, see Chapter 21.

Genotype refers to the specific genetic constitution of an organism—its genetic fingerprint. It is analogous to memotype. Phenotype refers to the observable characteristics of an organism—its physiology, appearance, and behavior—and is analogous to the sociotype. The phenotype is strongly influenced by the genotype: I can't fly because my genes haven't seen fit to give me wings. But it, in turn, can affect the genetic makeup of a species.

Somewhere between 6,000 and 10,000 years ago, people in Europe started domesticating goats and cows and drinking their milk. This phenotypic behavior caused the genotype of these populations to change over time, making it easier for them to digest the lactose in the milk. In modern times, we can see that in countries where milk drinking wasn't a common part of the culture, the instances of lactose intolerance are much higher. In Africa and some Asian countries, for instance, lactose intolerance runs at about 90 percent of the population, as opposed to places in northern Europe, where it is as low as 5 percent.

The Internet and Modern Memes

The biggest change since Dawkins coined the term "meme" has been the rise of the Internet.

HAVE YOU HEARD?

According to Nielsen Online, more than 1.7 billion people have Internet access in 2010—compared to just 360 million a decade earlier. It means one out of every four people worldwide is online—a phenomenal number when you consider that the modern Internet is only a few decades old.

Mind you, the nature of the meme itself hasn't changed much, but the way that ideas are delivered and the types of memes available are dramatically different. Using the new terms, the memetic engineer (creator), the hook (enticing factor), the host (deliverer), the memotype (content), and the sociotype (social/cultural context) are the same. However, the bait (perceived reward) and the vector (medium) now are different: the Internet has become a dominant vector—a vector that creates new types of bait.

New Vector

The Internet enables memes to pass along more quickly than virtually any vector before it. In a nutshell, the Internet:

- Allows distribution to multiple parties

- Has a variety of delivery formats (text, video, and sound)

- Enables the memetic engineer to remain virtually anonymous or become famous overnight

- Ensures the survival of only the strongest memes

We will talk a lot more about the Internet and its impact on memes in Chapter 4.

New Bait

As the medium changes, so does the bait; that is, the reason we would accept a particular meme and reject another.

As a simple example, RickRolling only works because of the Internet. Let's break it down: the bait could be a new video clip of an important event, one that is enticing enough to cause the potential victim to lower his or her guard (or neglect common sense). The concept isn't new; people have been conning others for millennia, of course. But the specific con, RickRolling, could not have worked in a previous age. YouTube was launched in 2005, and before then videos had to be downloaded onto the computer to be viewed—forming another barrier to entry and giving the potential receiver another second to think about his or her foolish decision.

INFECTION!

Memes are more easily accepted if accompanied by the promise of a quick payoff, which is why grifters (con men) will tell the potential victim that the offer isn't going to last long—and that he or she will get paid fast.

We discuss the new bait created by the Internet throughout this book because the Web has influenced virtually every major meme category featured.

However, to really see how the Internet changed the bait on classic memes, check out Chapter 12 to learn about urban legends, conspiracy theories, the Nigerian Scam, and other naughty (and dangerous) cultural ideas.

The Least You Need to Know

- A meme requires seven elements: a memetic engineer, hook, bait, vector, host, memotype, and sociotype.
- The hook and bait are the attracting factor and the perceived reward of the meme.
- The memetic engineer creates the meme while the host initiates the delivery.
- The memotype is the actual expression of a meme while the sociotype is how a particular group applies the meme.
- The Internet has become a major vector, or deliverer, of memes.

Pass It On: How Memes Spread

In Part 2 we look at the way that memes spread. A replicator that doesn't replicate is a contradiction in terms, so the way that it spreads is the most important thing about a meme. This part devotes a chapter to each of the three main ways that a meme travels: word of mouth, the Internet, and viral marketing.

Word of mouth remains one of the most important ways in which memes travel. Whenever you recommend a new movie or band, gossip over the fence, and tell a friend about the latest fashion sported by your favorite celebrity, you are spreading memes. If enough people help those memes replicate, they might reach a tipping point and become a craze.

Because of its speed and convenience, the Internet is a powerful medium for spreading memes. In fact, many people who talk about memes are actually talking about Internet memes. Chapter 4 discusses the rise of video memes, as well as computer viruses and hoaxes.

Every marketer's dream is to have their product promoted by dozens, or hundreds, of willing allies. Chapter 5 looks at viral marketing, and the way in which advertisers try to use the power of memes to get their message across convincingly.

Word-of-Mouth Memes

In This Chapter

- Passing along information through words
- Memes as gossip
- Tipping points
- Memes lost in translation
- The power of celebrity memes

Think about the last time you changed your hairstyle or decided to pick up a new book. How did you hear about the new haircut or the new novel? While memes are often tied to modern communication such as the Internet, many cultural ideas are passed along the old-fashioned way: via word of mouth.

The funny part is that we often don't recognize when word of mouth is happening. Memes passed via word of mouth are those almost-hidden hints that drive our lives. They are the little influences that change the way we dress, the things we watch, and the decisions we make.

In this chapter, we take a look at how memes are transferred through verbal communication, why gossip and useful information aren't mutually exclusive, and ways in which a celebrity can create a seismic social shift.

Gossip

The modern view of *gossip* often conjures visions of older busybodies under hair dryers at the local salon or folks whispering to each other by the water cooler. The reality is that we all gossip in some form—and not necessarily maliciously.

In fact, gossip is a way to communicate to another about a public or private circumstance. The only difference between gossip and other communication is our own personal judgment.

Let's examine this further. Say there are rumors of a company merger, and you pass this information on to a fellow co-worker. It would be considered a legitimate concern, right? In another case, let's say there are rumors that an illicit affair is happening between two co-workers, and you communicate this information. Is this also a legitimate concern? It could be if the affair were happening between people in two conflicting departments or if the gossip recipient were interested in one of the co-workers.

Regardless, both the merger and the affair information are the same in the meme world. A meme is just a cultural unit of information passed on. There is no good and no bad.

Abstract world aside, we obviously have a general idea of what gossip is and is not. Let's break down the parts of memes that are considered gossip.

How do we separate gossip from other word-of-mouth ideas? It has a few unique attributes:

- It is passed on for personal gain.
- It is often misinformation masked as helpful information.
- It is a slightly skewed version of the truth.

Personal Gain

Self-interest is the number one trait of memes that are labeled gossip. The host, or communicator, of the meme has personal reasons for passing along the information. It's not just out of the goodness of his or her heart.

Helpful Information

Although the book focused on animals and genetics, Richard Dawkins's *The Selfish Gene* argued that even seemingly altruistic actions by living beings were committed for personal gain.

HAVE YOU HEARD?

Animals of all sorts have "alarm calls" in which one member of the herd will shout when a predator is in the group's area—one type of expression that is comparable to gossip among humans. In *The Selfish Gene,* Richard Dawkins gives several theories showing that this selfless act—drawing attention to oneself for the betterment of the group—is really a selfish move. One proposed theory says that it is better to warn the group, so it will become quiet and perhaps hide, rather than have the group act normally and attract attention to everyone—including the alarm caller.

For example, let's say a bird is lovingly feeding her chick. It's an arduous process, because the mother has to go hunt for food, partially digest or chew the food, and then drop the food in the chick's eager mouth. Sometimes she goes hungry because she has just enough food for her growing chick. On the surface, the relationship is all about sacrifice and love.

However, the mother has other, more selfish reasons to take care of the child before herself:

- Protection in later years
- Survival of its genes

First, the better the chick develops during its formative days—through positive nourishment and protection—the stronger it will be as a full-grown bird. Of course, as the chick grows older, the mother will become weaker with age. And the stronger the offspring, the better it can protect the elderly parent—not to mention, after a positive upbringing, having a reason to protect the parent at all!

Second, the better the chick develops, the more likely it will survive beyond its parent's life. It will ideally mate with one or more birds and eventually have chicks of its own—all carrying the parent's genes. In short, by making sure the chick survives, the parent has the opportunity to keep its genes alive—the closest thing to eternal life earthly creatures have.

Dawkins's theories were directly tied to how genes are passed on in the animal kingdom, but in *The Selfish Gene* he began to apply these theories to cultural ideas. One of its later chapters, "Memes: The New Replicators," became the origin of the name of this very book.

Partial Truth

The most dangerous—and, to the objective observer, humorous—part about gossip is that it often isn't completely true. More often than not, a kernel of truth is masked by layers of lies, opinions, or miscommunications.

INFECTION!

While we often think of gossip as a malicious act, it is a dangerous meme when passed along by either the informed or the ignorant. For the informed, the truth is consciously twisted for their own ends—to make you believe something's true to create a particular reaction. For the ignorant, the truth seems revealed, but the secondhand news often is skewed by the informed—which means the ignorant are essentially doing the bidding of the malicious and creating just as much damage!

The classic kids' game Telephone can show us much here. In this elementary school pastime, a dozen or more kids are lined up next to each other. The teacher whispers a short but complex sentence into the ear of the first child in line. The child then turns to the next child and whispers the phrase in his or her ear, and so on, until it reaches the final child. The last person says out loud what he or she was told—which, usually, is a strange, almost alien bastardization of what the teacher originally said!

The game proves that when it comes to humans, information is not objective. In most instances, we cannot passively take in ideas—memes—and pass them on without our own slight variation, twist, or addition. Everything we receive is colored by our life experience, opinions, and—in the case of gossip—our own personal agenda (conscious or not).

The Telephone game is a cute example, but misinformation can lead to clumsy urban myths, racism, xenophobia, and other memes with potentially hazardous results. We'll get into these examples in Chapter 19.

Tipping Points

In 2000, *The New Yorker* contributor Malcolm Gladwell released *The Tipping Point*. In *The New York Times* best-seller, Gladwell argued that social trends—from hipsters wearing Hush Puppies to smoking rates among teenagers—could be attributed to *tipping points.*

DEFINITION

A **tipping point** is the moment when a trend becomes popular among the mainstream. It is essentially when a meme becomes both public and viral.

Gladwell defined a tipping point as when a social idea becomes part of the social norm.

Gladwell's Theory and Memes

Although he rarely, if ever, uses the word "meme" in *The Tipping Point*, Gladwell identifies three types of individuals who serve as gatekeepers to tipping points:

- Connectors
- Mavens
- Salesmen

Gladwell says in *The Tipping Point* that these three types of people are required to make massive trends (or, in our terminology, memes) viral, although later critics argued that it was the potency of the meme and not the skills of the deliverer that differentiated the popular from the obscure.

Let's take a look at these three personalities.

Connectors

Connectors are individuals who are great at networking. Their communication and people skills are essential to creating a buzz. When it comes to memes, the connector is the equivalent of the host—the deliverer of the information. Based on Gladwell's perspective, these connectors instinctively know the right sociotype, or group of people, in which the meme would be most effective.

One simple way to see a connector in action is to observe a social network such as Twitter. The average person will communicate with family, co-workers, and friends. Connectors, however, will have an inordinate number of friends and followers—often of extremely different backgrounds.

Mavens

Mavens are people with a deep knowledge base—something that is both recognized and respected by the general public. Gladwell says these people like to be of service and provide people with the most reliable information. They could be considered the equivalent of a memetic engineer, recognizing patterns and ideas and creating memes.

INFECTION!

Malcolm Gladwell's tipping point theories aren't without detractors. The biggest criticism is how every major trend and its creators cannot be neatly compartmentalized into his categories. Gladwell's view may have changed the way many of us think of how and why memes flow, but it is more of an augmentation of the work from Dawkins, Dennett, and other forerunners as opposed to a complete revision.

If there is one area *The Tipping Point* revolutionized, it was the business world. According to the magazine *Fast Company,* Gladwell commands a reported $40,000 to speak to corporations. The book itself has sold more than a million copies over the last decade.

Traditionally, mavens will always command a crowd, often for a very specific reason—which is different than attracting a crowd for being famous. For instance, the billionaire Warren Buffett is a maven when it comes to investing. He speaks, people listen, and more often than not, they accept whatever meme he's propagating. However, Gladwell notes that our acceptance of such memes stems from the maven's specific knowledge base, which is why we don't care about Buffett's view on, say, breastfeeding or the death penalty.

Salesmen

Salesmen (which is Gladwell's term, but refers to people of either sex) are charismatic, persuasive folks with the ability to get the general public to see things their way. In the meme world, these would be the curators of the hook and the bait—the intended message and the implied reward.

Think of the crazy things we do today because of smart salespeople. Think about what people do for fun. For example, tie a long, elastic rope around your legs and jump off a high bridge, or post your thoughts in front of complete strangers in 140-character bursts. Every meme has a beginning, and according to Gladwell, salesmen convince the rest of us that the cultural idea is worth pursuing, believing, and spreading.

Social Shifts

Keep in mind that not every social trend has a tipping point, and not every meme is shepherded by mavens, connectors, and salesmen. In our interpretation, Gladwell's theory is focused on big social shifts, not little earthquakes.

For instance, let's say you and a friend decide to go on an annual trip. A few of your friend's friends hear about the trip, and because you are fine with them coming, they decide to tag along. A couple of *their* friends want to come, too, and so on, until it becomes a slew of people going on the annual trip. Now, you and your friend could be considered mavens, connectors, and salesmen (or hook and bait creators, memetic engineers, and hosts), but in this case, it really isn't that deep. The tipping point may have been when three different sets of friends decided to go, but you and your friend are only influencing a handful of people.

Compare your friendship trip to a cause such as the Lance Armstrong Foundation's Livestrong. Started by famous cyclist and cancer survivor Lance Armstrong, the Livestrong program has raised money toward cancer research for nearly a decade. The center of the fundraising effort is a simple yellow wristband with "Livestrong" written on the side. Sound familiar? With sales beginning in 2004, the dollar wristbands became a fashion statement within a couple of years. You could see them worn by other professional athletes, presidential candidates, and eventually average people on the street. With literally millions of wristbands sold, it would be nearly impossible to say which celebrity or notable figure created a tipping point with Livestrong—but the size of its impact definitely makes it worthy of having a tipping point at all.

PASS IT ON

The Livestrong phenomenon also touches on the Cult of Celebrity, which we'll talk about in Chapter 8.

Why Now and Not Before?

As Gladwell notes, timing is also an essential part of tipping points.

For instance, a worldwide charity such as the RED program to suppress AIDS in Africa may not have gotten word-of-mouth support if international travel via safer aviation, global awareness via the Internet, and other innovations didn't make us interested in other countries.

A tipping point only occurs if the audience itself is ready for the idea.

In a simple example, think about the popular website YouTube. There were video upload websites before it, such as eBaum's World, but YouTube happened to come at a time when camcorders dropped in price and social networks like MySpace became places to share videos. When it comes to memes, timing is everything.

Cultural Currency

The most powerful memes via word of mouth come from a well-known public figure. Regardless of the idea, we all invest a certain cultural currency in a meme deliverer's status.

Let's say you are walking down the street and bump into a person in ragged clothes, perhaps smelling of alcohol. He randomly recommends that you eat at a new French restaurant down the street. Do you ask the length of the reservation wait? Probably not.

In the same instance, if you bumped into a nicely dressed man, perhaps smelling of sweet cologne, and he gave you the same recommendation in a Parisian accent, then you're more likely to consider the suggestion.

HAVE YOU HEARD?

The Hollywood Stock Exchange takes "cultural currency" literally. This fun website puts a value on celebrities, and just like stockbrokers, players can trade investments.

The values vary based on actions. For instance, a number one movie would make Angelina Jolie's stock rise, while a scrape with the law might make another star's stock plunge. In other words, some stock changes are based on logic while others are based on public perception.

The Hollywood Stock Exchange is online at www.hsx.com. Playboy.com, Yahoo!, and other websites were inspired to offer their own twists on the concept.

The power of the meme is important, but the cultural currency—that is, the respect—the potential meme receiver has for the deliverer is just as crucial when it comes to word of mouth.

The Least You Need to Know

- A gossip meme isn't necessarily malicious, but it does imply personal gain.
- By nature, a meme passed along via word of mouth changes with each carrier.
- A tipping point is when a meme becomes public and viral on a grand scale.
- Tipping points do not happen until the mainstream public is ready for the idea.
- The word-of-mouth success of a meme depends on the cultural currency of, or respect one has for, the deliverer.

Memes and the Internet

In This Chapter

- The power of Internet images
- Internet memes versus other memes
- Videos spawning other videos
- Viruses—real and fake
- Why we donate online

The Internet has revolutionized the way we interact, learn, and adapt. In other words, the Internet has changed how quickly memes spread.

In this chapter, we look at how the Web has changed visual ideas, created new hazards with viruses, and made the world a smaller place.

Images on the Internet

Pictures can evoke feelings that words never could, but that's not anything new, right? Visuals go back to the prehistoric era, with cavemen (and women) scrawling on the walls with dirt, blood, and dung.

That said, two extremely significant changes occurred with the introduction of the Internet:

- Pictures could be easily spread.
- Pictures could function as blank memetic slates.

Easily Spread

When the camera was invented, the early models had an extremely long exposure time and a single print method à la the modern-day Polaroid. The former detail was the reason people looked so stoic in eighteenth-century pictures—they had to stand completely still for the duration of the shot—and the latter detail was the reason pictures weren't copied and handed out to friends and family as frequently as they are today. Even in later times, as negatives were created, the darkroom duplication process was much more involved than just sending a web link or attaching a digital photo.

INFECTION!

The Internet has made it easier to spread and modify images, but it isn't the only reason why there are more images than ever.

Keep in mind that we have digital cameras, affordable home computers, cheap hard-drive space, photo-editing software and other art programs, and so on. The Internet alone isn't responsible, but it did make the image meme-spreading process much easier.

For more information on the impact of technology on memes, check out Chapter 7.

The Internet, along with modern digital cameras, incorporates the very opposite system. An average camera can take a shot in less than a second, while the Internet—turning the photo into digital zeroes and ones—can pass along images in an even shorter period of time.

As a result, images have a certain disposability. Winter 2010 brought two worldwide catastrophes—a 7.0 earthquake in Haiti and an even more powerful one in Chile. In previous times, such as during a hurricane in Florida or a flood in Kansas, a limited number of pictures would run in the newspaper or in a magazine. Based on space constraints, editors would decide which pictures would resonate with readers the most. Certain pictures, such as soldiers raising the U.S. flag during the Battle of Iwo Jima, became unifying ideas and opinion creators. Today, with these two devastating earthquakes, we were overwhelmed with video, sound, and thousands of pictures. The *Boston Globe* alone featured more than 100 visuals from the Chilean disaster. It is harder to find a unifying picture to capture the moment, and it will probably be months—if not years—until we can sort through the bevy of memes to find "the truth" (if ever).

Blank Slates

Images on the Internet are less likely to have a singular purpose—some to the point where they become an empty memetic vessel as opposed to representing the set idea for which they were created.

In 2008, artist Shepard Fairley used an Associated Press photo of Illinois senator and U.S. presidential candidate Barack Obama to create a new image. Utilizing Obama's profile and a stark, Russian-style polarization with America's red, white, and blue colors, Fairley called the new picture "Hope." Posters were put up around the country. The iconic image inspired hundreds, if not thousands, of parodies as the presidential race peaked in November 2009. For instance, one featured *Sesame Street*'s Cookie Monster with one word: "Cookies." Adapting the photo became easier when several websites made "Hope Generators" so users could easily insert their own images.

> **HAVE YOU HEARD?**
>
> Launched in 2003, 4chan represents the very best and worst of the Internet: irreverent images; mocking of world events; extreme instances of racism, sexism, and other offenses; and purely genius-level creation of memes. Many of the most memorable Internet memes were coined by 4chan, including "LOLCats/I Can Haz Cheezeburger," "Dramatic Prairie Dog," and "O RLY?" to name a few.
>
> Reminiscent of the old-school bulletin boards that were popular pre-Internet, 4chan has only one rule: no child pornography. Otherwise, the discussion boards, mostly comprised of pictures and short videos, push the boundaries of humor and taste. It's not for the weak-hearted.

What does Obama have to do with Cookie Monster? Nothing. But, contrast the malleability of an image uploaded on the Internet to, say, a pre-Internet image such as the famous 1970s Farrah Fawcett swimsuit poster. A teenage-boy staple, the poster represents youth, sexuality, and beauty. Imagine if the poster came out today: within hours, it would be uploaded, modified, and spread throughout the Internet.

The Power of Video

Words have power, but some memes are best passed within the visual, audio, and—in some cases—kinetic strength of the video. Movies have been a wonderful meme platform for more than a century, although the Internet definitely increased the penetration and impact of this medium.

Viral Video Before the Internet

It may be hard to remember, but viral videos actually occurred before the Internet. Delivery methods such as e-mail and YouTube didn't create video memes, but they did speed up their dissemination.

Viral simply means an idea that catches on—a meme that survives and thrives through other people. It is not synonymous with the Internet.

HAVE YOU HEARD?

In the 2002 horror hit *The Ring,* an evil spirit will kill the viewer of a haunted video unless the viewer makes someone else watch the video. Talk about a viral video!

If we were to compare pre-Internet and post-Internet viral videos, the key differences are that pre-Internet videos …

- Spread slowly
- Offer a limited number of viewings

Let's break down these two differences.

They Spread Slowly

In one example, part-time animators (and full-time pizza delivery guys) Trey Stone and Matt Parker created a satirical short called "The Spirit of Christmas." The brash, hysterical videotape somehow got into the hands of Hollywood's elite and supposedly became regularly viewed by George Clooney and other major actors. The video eventually got to Comedy Central, which found the working-class duo and offered a production deal. The result was the hit show *South Park,* one of the longest-running animated series in history.

For an older example, let's look at the film *Reefer Madness.* Also known as *Tell Your Children,* the 1936 "educational" film was meant to show the dangers of marijuana. The movie shows the protagonist caving into peer pressure, taking a drag of marijuana and quickly going down a Jekyll-and-Hyde slippery slope. All the horror ends with murder. A bit much? Definitely. Unlike the satirical "The Spirit of Christmas," however, *Reefer Madness* was meant to provoke fear, not laughter—and it failed miserably. In fact, among all the fear-based sex, drugs, and rock 'n' roll public service announcements of the era, *Reefer Madness* is the only one still regularly watched—usually while people are getting high. It also is definitely the only one to inspire a musical.

In both cases, it took years—if not decades—to build up the cult following. Movie critics say *Reefer Madness* didn't even achieve its modern, vaulted status until the '70s, when recreational drug use became more acceptable in America and other countries. So the '70s idea, or meme, that casual drug use is okay turned a previously appropriate film about how casual drug use is *not* acceptable into a meme.

They Offer a Limited Number of Viewings

The natural question is, "How could a viral film truly be seen and actually spread pre-Internet, or for that matter, pre-VCR?" There are several ways:

- Film festivals

- Private viewings via 16mm film

- Public-access television

Ironically, the strength of some pre-Internet cult films grew because they were hard to access. For instance, the much-maligned Nazi epic and Jerry Lewis vehicle *The Day the Clown Cried*—yes, it was considered as bad as it sounds—wasn't officially released. Due out in 1972, the film's early critical reception and financing problems behind the scenes prevented its premiere. The original and perhaps only movie negative was rarely shown, while the only VHS copy is supposedly under lock and key in Lewis's office!

HAVE YOU HEARD?

For more than a decade, Roger Ebert, formerly of *At the Movies with Siskel & Ebert*, has hosted Roger Ebert's Film Festival. Also known as Ebertfest, the multi-day event features films rarely seen or forgotten.

Held annually every summer in Urbana, Illinois, Ebertfest has grown in popularity over the years—showing that there are still rare movies in a post-Internet world. More information is available at www.ebertfest.com.

In other words, their limited availability helps these memes to propagate.

The YouTube Revolution

Launched in February 2005 by Chad Hurley, Steve Chen, and Jawed Karim, YouTube changed how quickly memes could be passed in video form.

According to legend, the website was created so the founders could easily share video from a recent dinner party. Hurley, Chen, and Karim realized that it could be of value to other people.

YouTube obviously hit a sweet spot, because 18 months later Google bought YouTube for $1.65 billion.

YouTube changed the viral video concept in a couple of key ways:

- Virtually instant passing of ideas
- Mass public discussion

Here is how YouTube changed our lives.

Instant Passing of Ideas

YouTube enabled the nearly instantaneous passing of ideas. Have a new philosophical concept? Record a video of yourself discussing the idea and upload it to YouTube, and nearly the entire world can hear your perspective.

PASS IT ON

According to Google, people upload more than 20 hours of video to YouTube every minute. More than one billion videos are viewed every day. It is the fourth most-visited website behind Google, Yahoo!, and Facebook.

Prior to YouTube, new videos had to be viewed based on restricted television schedules, as attachments in e-mails, or via hand-to-hand passing of VHS tapes, DVDs, or another portable media.

Mass Public Discussion

Furthermore, YouTube expands the transformation of the meme itself. YouTube videos are rated on a five-star system, but viewer comments are connected below the video itself. Any ideas conveyed in the video are discussed, debated, and in many cases, transformed—as would be any meme passed along to another person. Compare this activity to a more passive, and much smaller, audience experience. Compare the thousands, if not millions, of viewers and commenters going back and forth on a YouTube page to, say, 100 people sitting in a traditional movie theater reacting to the entertainment. Discussions happen in both arenas, but the reach and impact of the idea within the YouTube video is much, much larger.

Memes of Memes

Memes can always spawn variations that take on a life of their own, but nowadays the most common example is with videos. Popular viral videos inspire similar videos that themselves become viral.

In July 2009, Jill Paterson and Kevin Heinz uploaded a video from their wedding—specifically, their walk down the aisle—when they came in dancing to Chris Brown's R&B hit "Forever." Quirky and original, the video was linked all across the Internet, garnered 3.5 million hits by the end of 2009, and even got the couple (and some of their entourage) onto several morning television shows.

Three months later, in October 2009, the NBC show *The Office* married two major characters—doing a parody of the Paterson/Heinz wedding video. It was one of the highest-rated episodes in the series, and the abbreviated wedding scene became an online viral video itself.

Clearly, the NBC episode wouldn't have been possible without the original wedding video (because it was the inspiration), but it also wouldn't have been understood without people themselves actually knowing the original wedding video. The first video had to be a particular tipping point; that is, seen and accepted by the mainstream, to successfully spawn other memes. Otherwise, this *The Office* episode and other similar ideas would seem random at best and at worst, confusing.

Viruses: Digital Memes

Computers have opened up our world to new ways of communicating—as well as new ways of being harmed.

Malicious Codes

Malicious codes, or viruses, can be considered the memes of the digital world (and, depending on your thinking, our personal memes could be the viruses of the real world). There are millions of different computer viruses, with the main commonality being self-replication.

Computer worms search for weaknesses in the system, comparable to a meme trying to find a way to reach another carrier. Spyware secretly relays your actions back to a host, enabling the meme creator to have more power in the future. Other malware erases the content of your hard drive—the equivalent to the toxic memes discussed in Chapter 17.

And, like traditional memes, the goal of the virus is to spread. The caveat is that to spread, virtually all computer viruses require an action on the user's part: opening an e-mail, downloading a file, clicking a link, and so on.

PASS IT ON

The first mass computer virus was 1982's "Elk Cloner," a relatively harmless practical joke that recited poetry on your computer. It spread through shared floppy disks. Programmer Richard Skrenta would later become a major figure in Silicon Valley, building the foundation for several well-used computer programs. When Skrenta unleashed "Elk Cloner," he was in the ninth grade.

Hoaxes and Fake Viruses

Ironically, the fear of catching an unstoppable, malignant computer virus can make people more susceptible to believing false information. Like seeing Elvis at the supermarket, your stomach exploding from ingesting pop rocks and soda simultaneously, and other traditional urban myths, computer memes with false information can create more chaos than an actual threat.

One excellent example is the Y2K virus. Like many fake virus memes, it was rooted in a truth: some short-sighted programmers hadn't prepared their programs for the new millennium, which meant some computers would have problems when the year no longer began with "19." Popular memes took it a step further, saying anti-government groups would release a computer virus—and come January 1, America would come to a standstill. As most of us now remember, there were very few hiccups on New Year's Day 2000.

Hoaxes and fake viruses tend to flourish during particularly historic moments. For instance, besides Y2K, two of the other most-discussed computer virus threats during the last decade, "WTC Survivor" and "Olympic Torch," occurred in the weeks after

America's September 11, 2001, attacks and the 2006 Winter Olympics, respectively. Fear seems to open people up to memes.

Philanthropic Memes

Giving—and not giving—can take the form of memes. A friend may say, "I never give to the homeless. They're just going to bum my change and buy liquor, not food. All of them are liars." Depending on your mood, social leaning, and other influences and preferences, you may take this idea to heart—and, at least the very next time, you may avoid eye contact with someone asking for help.

Reasons We Give

There are several reasons we decide to support causes:

- Seasonal pressure

- Guilt over another matter

- Personal meaning

For many people, holidays mark the time to give. In America, the season between Thanksgiving and New Year's Day is marked with an exponential increase in charitable donations. The equivalent is found in other countries during their respective holidays. This, in itself, is a meme: "Give during this particular time. Do not worry about giving during the rest of the year." It is passed on through observed behavior.

Another reason is guilt over another matter that you cannot change or don't want to address. Perhaps falling under the umbrella term "karma," the meme is to give to one cause to make up for your lack of giving in another. A third common reason, of course, is personal meaning: a relative passing away from a disease, a friend ailing from an addiction, or a similar example. In this case, you actually *become* a meme host, or advocate, prompting others to join the cause.

The Snowball Effect

While people are capable of altruistic acts on their own, there is a natural sense of inertia within a community. In other words, there is a tendency toward *groupthink*.

DEFINITION

Groupthink occurs when a crowd makes decisions that the individuals within the group would not commit to on their own. The group usually puts swift action over rational discussion and judgment.

The Internet shows this pattern, particularly through donating on social networks. Facebook pushes the social pressure to new levels, with "Causes" applications that send e-mails to all of your friends, advertise on your profile page, and push the cash requests to other social networks. Peer pressure has always been a factor, but the Internet allows it on a much larger—and faster—scale.

The Least You Need to Know

- Video memes existed before YouTube, but the website helped them proliferate.
- Videos will not be copied or referenced unless they have reached a mainstream tipping point.
- Viruses are real, but hoaxes tend to occur around major global events.
- There are millions of computer viruses. The main commonality is that they self-replicate.
- Societal pressure to donate is magnified through our online social networks.

Marketing Memes

In This Chapter

- Viral marketing
- Getting consumers to buy
- Grassroots movements
- Manufacturing memes
- Anti-ad campaigns

Think about your favorite toothpaste. When did you start using the brand? And why did you start? It could have been because your mom or dad gave it to you during childhood.

If we are to believe marketers, however, it was because of a smartly written print ad or a memorable TV commercial. Advertising is a multi-billion dollar industry for a reason.

Whether it's a snappy slogan or a Madison Avenue campaign, marketing has always been part of our world—and memes are often how information on services or products is passed along.

Viral Marketing

You might have heard about something going "viral." As we mentioned earlier, the definition of viral has, well, multiplied in recent years. Viral still means something contagious, but instead of something physical, the contagion is an idea.

Viral marketing is creating an idea interesting enough for people to tell others about it.

> **DEFINITION**
>
> **Viral marketing** is creating an advertisement or message so powerful that the recipient will tell everyone in his or her social circle about the product.

Why Viral Marketing Has Taken Off

The viral marketing concept—making advertising fodder for water cooler discussions—is a simple, seemingly timeless idea, but viral marketing truly took off in recent years because of several factors, including the following:

- The Internet
- Globalization through travel
- Social networking

Let's take a look at each of these.

The Internet

Like other meme-related trends, viral marketing has become more important with the Internet. Never before in history has a company been able to post something on a virtual wall and have billions access it at once. Think about the time before the Internet: if you read about a great product in the newspaper, you'd theoretically need to copy the page—or worse, cut it out and mail or fax it to a friend. If you saw something interesting on television, you'd have to record it the next time it happened to come on; and so on. The Internet is one massive collection of ideas accessible by anyone with a computer and a connection.

Globalization Through Travel

Globalization through travel has also made viral marketing faster. People are traveling more than ever, and at least in America, each younger generation is less likely to stay in their respective hometowns. Overseas flights can be booked literally within minutes—via the Internet, naturally—and, taking inflation into account, long-distance flights are as cheap as ever. Impressionable marketing travels more quickly because *we* travel rapidly and frequently.

Social Networking

Finally, any remaining gaps with globalization are filled with social networking. Through Twitter, we can be literally one degree away from Bill Gates, Oprah, and Barack Obama. Facebook, MySpace, and the social networks of the future will continue to keep ideas flowing faster.

HAVE YOU HEARD?

American pundits say President Barack Obama's Internet initiatives helped him secure the youth vote. Part of his platform was a "transparent government" in which citizens could see what his office was deciding. The initiative included a Twitter account, interactive menus at www.whitehouse.gov, fireside chats available via YouTube, and other online resources. His videos during the election created a viral buzz.

What does this mean for marketers? If an idea catches on, it's easier for it to spread like wildfire. It also, of course, means that there is much more competition for what ideas actually stick and get passed on.

Viral Marketing Before the 'Net

Viral marketing accelerated because of the Internet, but advertising companies have been aware of the power of memes since the 1950s.

Before the 1950s

To see how much modern advertising has changed, grab an old magazine from the 1940s (or earlier!) from the library, or better yet, catch an old television program on PBS—many of which had sponsorship ads in the actual show. Products would be described, not pitched, and the focus would be on the facts surrounding them.

Sex Sells

By the late '50s, however, as business psychology, demographics, and sociological studies came into vogue, major advertisers realized that a product could sell more if the advertising appealed to basic human needs, wants, and fears.

Sex, power, safety, and shock are just some of the ideas conveyed in modern advertising. The goal is to disturb you enough so that you *must* share the idea with someone else you know, and they in turn are equally touched and share it within their social circle—making the original ad viral.

Not the Product, but the Delivery

You might have noticed a switch here, though. It's important to realize that in modern advertising, the product or service doesn't have to be noteworthy to be viral. In fact, it often isn't a noteworthy product at all.

For instance, a classic Alka-Seltzer commercial has a middle-aged husband rubbing his belly, complaining, "I can't believe I ate the whole thing!" The agitated wife reminds him that, yes, he ate the whole thing, and perhaps he should have an Alka-Seltzer. Comedians were spoofing and consumers were spouting the husband's woeful line, particularly when the commercial came out in the '70s. "Why?" you may ask. Stomach-soothing antacids were a dime a dozen. In this case (as is often the case), the "sticky" parts are the setup and delivery, not the product—and when people say the husband's memorable line, the idea of the product is connected to it like a fisherman's reel.

How They Get You to Buy

Like any agile meme, modern advertising taps into our basest instincts:

- Fear
- Ecstasy
- Loneliness
- Jealousy

A successful advertisement arouses these feelings and compels you to either buy the product at the next opportunity or tell people in your social circle about the ad. Ideally, you will do both.

INFECTION!

The four emotional triggers aren't the only reasons you would buy a product. You could like a particular ketchup because of the taste, a jeans brand because of the fit on your body, and so on. It's important to remember that advertising isn't about trying to make you buy a product you're already loyal to—it's pushing for you to try a new product you haven't invested in yet.

Let's take a look at the various triggers advertisers use to get your attention.

Fear

Do you ever have an anxiety dream in which you have to give a presentation—and just when you are about to step onstage, you realize that you're in your underwear? (Interestingly, as more people talk about it, more people will experience the dream through suggestion, making it a nasty little meme.) When advertisers use fear as the bait, they want you to tap into the same feelings you had in your dream—and the only way you'll feel secure again is if you have the product or service on hand. To use an analogy, advertisers make you feel like you are naked and the product is your clothes.

Consider the erectile dysfunction advertisements that have become prevalent since the discovery of Viagra as well as the increasing number of older Baby Boomers. One particular television ad shows a 50-something man, and rather annoyingly, a significantly younger woman performing a mundane task. Then they both pause, look longingly at each other, and she leads him up presumably to the bedroom. The male announcer says, roughly, "Will *you* be ready when the time is right?" An overlay of the drug logo appears on the screen.

The fascinating part about this meme is that the bedroom ad isn't selling sex but is provoking fear. "Will I be ready when the time is right? I'm usually ready, but what if I'm not ready? Maybe I should check into this drug, you know, just in case." The meme grows from a suggestion to an order, feeding on whatever insecurity there may be for the male watching. It may also give the female watching a particular idea, too.

Ecstasy

Coined in the '60s, the axiom, "Sex sells" refers to our interest in anything related to intimacy. It is related to our instinct to procreate—despite not all intimacy being engaged in for the sake of procreation—and advertisers use this drive to focus our attention on their goods.

HAVE YOU HEARD?

Several scientific studies have observed the human body and its reaction to sedate, wholesome material versus provocative media such as swimsuit magazines and risqué ads. Even the calmest individual has a physical reaction to the racier stuff, including dilated pupils, increased heart rate, a flushed face, and most notably, heavy activity in the pleasure center of the brain.

It's noteworthy that the physical expression can't be helped, which some believe is an indicator of how we have a hard time psychologically resisting sexy pictures, advertisements, and multimedia.

Ecstatic marketing takes a rather humorous detour as it goes around the world. While many Western European countries such as France and Spain are historically comfortable showing skin in media, which is reflected by the advertisers, more relatively conservative countries such as the neighboring United Kingdom and America frown upon direct sexual references in the media.

Therefore, American advertising has to play a particular game: express sex without showing it. The results can end up being more sensual than if the ad actually did show something risqué.

An excellent example is a '90s shampoo commercial aimed at women. The fairly serious woman takes a shower at a public facility, such as a gym, and begins to wash her hair. This particular brand of shampoo feels *so good* that she starts shouting, "Yes!" at the top of her lungs until the neighbors stop with concern—obviously thinking something else is going on.

A sneaky, sexy advertising meme can take the back-door approach, which is more subtle than a couple frolicking in the grass and can leave us more vulnerable to having our buttons pushed.

Loneliness

Another weak point exposed in modern advertising is loneliness—not a literal loneliness, such as a person in isolation, but more of a sense of not belonging or fitting in.

There is a natural human desire to be "normal," and an advertisement pushing this button makes you question how normal you really are.

Again, drug commercials have the advertising game nearly mastered when it comes to this approach—particularly because the rules changed over the last decade. In America, the Federal Communications Commission (FCC) switched from restricting the number of pharmaceutical commercials daily to allowing companies to air as many as they can afford. As a result, recent years have seen an influx of on-air drug commercials.

HAVE YOU HEARD?

The human race is more connected than ever, with cell phones, social networks, e-mail, and dozens of ways to communicate—but recent studies show that people feel more isolated then ever. Why? Namely because the new technology we expected to be used in conjunction with traditional communication has begun to replace slower, more intimate bonding, such as hugs, walking together, sitting at a coffee shop, and simply talking face to face. The trend shows no signs of stopping, so frankly we can expect more advertising than ever to try to connect with society's loneliness.

The brilliance of these ads is that it's usually unclear what the drug actually does. One television ad may feature a woman sitting in the corner, all alone, looking like she's about to cry, while a violin plays sadly in the background. A voiceover inquires about how *you* are feeling—not the actress, but the viewer. "Do you feel like you're not fully participating in life?" The drug is mentioned, and suddenly the black-and-white scene goes color: she's out playing with her dog, literally stopping to smell the flowers, and she's happy, smiling, and free! "Ask your doctor about such-and-such," the announcer says, concluding the commercial.

It's a pretty brazen idea to keep the medicine's purpose a secret, not only because the commercial is withholding important information but also because it suggests that the company already knows your life may include isolation.

A recent report found prescription drug use was on the rise, particularly for 20- to 40-year-olds who, from 2001 to 2007, were 20 percent more likely to be taking medication for depression, Attention Deficit Disorder (ADD), or asthma. The rise was attributed to a few different factors, including more aggressive advertising by pharmaceutical companies.

Jealousy

"Keeping up with the Joneses," or wanting to have equal or better possessions than your peers, may be the most classic advertising hook. Unlike fear, ecstasy, and loneliness, jealousy has less of a chance to alienate the audience simply because it's something we freely admit or express in public.

A basic example is an ad for a fancy riding lawn mower. The commercial may open with the hero pulling out his shiny new machine, and as he cuts perfect corners and smoothly goes over his manicured grass, neighbors ogle from afar.

The jealousy route is interesting because it can go in either direction. Identifying with the main character, the viewer can be manipulated to feel two different ways:

- I must get this product because it will make me superior to my peers.

- I must get this product because I don't want to be inferior to my peers.

The latter meme is a slight nod to our first emotion on the list: fear. Both play with the viewer's ego and sense of self-worth compared to others, making the viewer more susceptible to *conspicuous consumption*.

DEFINITION

Conspicuous consumption means buying goods, services, and other related things to prove an equal or superior social status to peers. When two connected individuals or groups accept this meme, the never-ending battle can drive them to spend more than they can actually afford. It will only end when one stops believing in the meme.

Astroturfing

As the Internet opened the floodgates for memes, commercial and otherwise, many advertising messages were getting caught in the riptide and not reaching their intended audiences adequately enough. However, it didn't take long for marketers to realize that the most successful ideas seemed to evolve at a grassroots level. In other words, catchy ideas seemed to naturally evolve from the public, not from a Manhattan ad agency. Of note, marketers realized this phenomenon didn't preclude professionally tailored messages—it just couldn't *appear* that way.

Why Is It Named Astroturfing?

Named after the fake grass used in sports, *astroturfing* is when a marketer creates a viral message such that it appears to have evolved organically as a grassroots movement.

DEFINITION

Astroturfing is the act of making a professionally produced marketing campaign look like a naturally evolving grassroots movement. The assumption is that people will be more receptive to the message if it seemed to have happened organically.

A Powerful Yet Dangerous Strategy

Astroturfing is a smart, stealthy plan, but the entire marketing strategy is a virtual house of cards. One weak link in the foundation of belief—because that's what astroturfing is based on, belief in the organic nature of an idea—and all its power crumbles.

Case in Point: Twitter Astroturfing

An excellent modern example is discussing products on Twitter. The 140-character-message website took off in 2008, and in short order, celebrities were posting to more than a million people instantly. Like other Twitter users, famous people would say mundane things about their day, like what they just had for breakfast, but occasionally would mention particular goods or services they were using at the moment, as in, "I lost my phone, but [insert cell phone carrier here] hooked me up with a new one. Thanks!"

By late 2009, however, news broke that some celebrities were getting paid to mention a particular product. One news outlet, *The Daily Beast*, even went as far as showing how much celebrities were being paid for a Tweet:

- Kim Kardasian, reality TV star: $10,000 and up per sponsored Tweet, 2.7 million followers

- Soulja Boy, rapper: $10,000 and up per sponsored Tweet, 2 million followers

- Dr. Drew Pinsky, talk show therapist: $10,000 and up per sponsored Tweet, 1.8 million followers

One of the top-paid Tweeters, comedian and *The Colbert Report* host Stephen Colbert, reportedly received up to $10,000 for Tweeting about a particular product or service for his approximately 1.4 million followers. However, Colbert plays a glib, corruptible character on his television show, so people were more likely to be okay with him doing something ethically gray in real life!

PASS IT ON

People have proven time and time again that they are more likely to accept a product meme from a celebrity they feel close to rather than from a relatively generic advertisement. The only influence more powerful than a favorite celebrity endorsement is word of mouth from a friend or family member. We talk a lot more about this celebrity phenomenon, called the "cult of personality," in Chapter 8.

As for the others, the report was enough to make people consider the sincerity of their favorite celebrity. In other words, astroturfing turned into traditional marketing in one fell swoop—and lost whatever additional effectiveness it might have had.

The Least You Need to Know

- Viral marketing existed before the Internet, but the Internet enabled the memes to move faster and spread far wider.
- Most advertising before the '50s used a straightforward, nonmanipulative approach.
- Modern advertising exploits a consumer's fear, ecstasy, loneliness, and jealousy to sell products and services.
- Twitter, Facebook, and other social networking tools are used by marketers for advertising.
- Astroturfing is disguising a marketing ploy as a grassroots effort.

Memes In Action

Delivery and result of memes are two separate discussions, and while Part 2 covers the ways in which we receive ideas, Part 3 goes further—examining the ways memes influence our lives.

Almost everything of importance in our culture is affected to some extent by memes, and we examine this influence through chapters on popular culture, technology, philosophy, sex, religion, and politics. From primitive technologies such as the wheel and the arch, to social mores and rituals, memes are the way that new technologies, ideas, and beliefs spread and keep our societies evolving and developing.

Fashion and music are two obvious cultural activities that rely on memes to maintain their place in society and to find ever-larger markets, but even something as fundamental as sex evolves in meaning according to the memes that spread across the society.

In two extended examples, we consider the way that religion and politics operate memetically to keep their members, acquire new adherents, stabilize their internal structures, and inoculate themselves against outside attacks.

Popular Culture

In This Chapter

- Influences in fashion
- Music memes
- Humor and jokes
- Mimicry and homage in modern culture

One of the best ways to see memes in action is to watch popular culture. New trends weave in and out of our collective consciousness, evidenced in the clothes we wear, the music we listen to, and the jokes we tell—only to be replaced by newer trends as quickly as they arrive.

In short, pop culture is nothing if not a collection of memes. We can get a sense of these memes in action by examining three different areas:

- Fashion
- Music
- Humor

Fashion

Not unlike architecture, the clothing we wear is inspired by three things:

- Environment
- Tools
- Social norms

Of course, the environment helps us determine how much skin we reveal, what kind of shoes we wear, and so on. Ten-gallon hats are popular in Texas because they keep the burning sun out of your eyes. Scarves are worn in Paris because of the chilly wind from the river Seine.

> **INFECTION!**
>
> An artificial scarcity can also improve the acceptance rate of a fashion meme. For instance, a pair of Christian Louboutin shoes is often part of a limited run—and cost more than a thousand American dollars. They are high quality, but the real reason people are willing to pay extra money for them is because of their rarity. A fashion meme can make someone feel original and special.

Cavemen "apparel" was limited to loincloths because of the tools they had to work with—sharpened stones and sharpened sticks. Most countries have advanced to the point where literally hundreds of tools are available with which to fashion their clothing, but more remote regions still work with the limited tools that are available.

Finally, social norms play a huge part in fashion standards. The message given from the style of dress is different in various situations. For instance, an Amish woman in a knee-high skirt will look normal in a metropolitan city but virtually scandalous in her hometown, where showing ankles is controversial.

The Macro Trickle-Down Theory of Fashion

Few areas are as nondemocratic as fashion. While music has its different sects and humor can set its dial anywhere between sarcasm and slapstick, style is dictated by the major meme creators in Milan, Paris, and New York City. Trends are decided by the major fashion houses and designers, and eventually those decisions affect what is available on the rack—and therefore what we wear. Even the most *fashion-forward* consumer has only so much control over what he or she has access to.

> **DEFINITION**
>
> **Fashion-forward** describes something or someone that has a good instinct for the next couture trend and is secure enough to dress like it.

The 2006 fashion magazine movie *The Devil Wears Prada* has an insightful moment when the bookish intern gets a dress-down from the publisher for not taking her life's work—fashion—seriously, as exemplified by the lumpy blue sweater the intern has chosen to wear to work that day. The publisher informs her that her lumpy blue sweater is actually cerulean and that it is the result of several years of trickle-down fashion effect, beginning with Oscar de la Renta presenting a collection of cerulean gowns in 2002, then Yves St. Laurent showing cerulean military jackets, then cerulean showing up in the collections of eight different designers, then cerulean filtering down to the department store where the intern no doubt purchased her sweater years later. The publisher says:

> That "blue" represents millions of dollars and countless jobs, and so it's sort of comical how you think that you've made a choice that exempts you from the fashion industry when, in fact, you're wearing the sweater that was selected for you by the people in this room.

The movie argues that there is a fashion memeplex making our clothing decisions for us.

The Micro Trickle-Down Theory of Fashion

The guidelines of high couture are reflected in the local environment, too. Certain people set the pace. It has to do with meme acceptance and is based on a couple factors:

- The person's access to goods
- The person's fashion reputation

The first requirement for being a trendsetter is a person's access to goods. The individual may have awesome fashion sense, but if he or she cannot afford, steal, borrow, or find next-level clothes, the impact possible is minimal. Clothes are one of the few memes that require accessorizing to make an impact.

HAVE YOU HEARD?

Prep, private, and Catholic schools usually require all students to wear the same uniform—something kids can find surprisingly liberating. While you may think they'd all look alike, the required uniform forces students to come up with creative ways of distinguishing themselves, such as new hairstyles, earrings, socks, and so on. They are attempting to "find" themselves within the limitations of available fashion—something not too different than what people do in the outside world.

Second, a person's reputation has to be worthy of emulating. For instance, let's say you see a colleague at work tomorrow wearing a garbage-bag jumpsuit. Fear aside, there are two ways to react—both of them based on your colleague's reputation. If, in your eyes, your colleague has no discernable (or worse, tacky) taste in clothes, you will have a negative reaction. However, if your colleague is known for being fashion-forward and has a respected style, you may still have a negative reaction, but his or her reputation will probably cause you to pause and at least consider that the person is aware of what the next fashion meme will be. You may even show up in a garbage-bag parka the next day.

Music

Music is a basic part of the living experience. Animals, plants, and even beings within the underwater kingdom have been found to respond to music. The elements of a song create a distinctive collection of notes—a meme—that evokes a particular feeling or expression.

Music is as ancient as the human race. It is emotionally powerful and as readily accessible as a stick tapping on the ground, two lips controlling exhaled air, or skin slapping skin.

The Earworm

The ultimate goal of pop music creators is to create a catchy song known as an *earworm*. A memorable chorus, an impressionable rhythm, or another addictive quality will get the song "stuck" in your head and will, ideally, have you explaining the song to another person or purchasing the album.

 DEFINITION

An **earworm** is a song or a portion of a song that gets "stuck" in your head.

The Effects of Oversaturation

Turn on your radio. Ever wonder why most of the songs sound the same? There are several reasons, but a big one is the desire to imitate what happens to be selling. Eager to grab the latest hit-making trend, record execs will encourage producers to copy the latest earworm-inducing trend. When it comes to Top 10 music, modern pop music creators come in year-long chunks: boy bands 98 Degrees, N*SYNC, and The Backstreet Boys; pop rappers MC Hammer, Vanilla Ice, and Young MC; and so on.

The problem is, like other pop cultural trends, the music pendulum swings quickly. Yesterday's unique earworm—that new music idea running through your head—has become today's continuous headache. The once-pleasant idea has been passed along too much.

Backlash!

In 1979, Chicago's Comiskey Park held a Disco Demolition Night during a White Sox versus Detroit Tigers game. The local radio stations decided that the music genre, which had dominated the airwaves since the 1977 movie *Saturday Night Fever*, needed to be destroyed—literally. Encouraging attendees to bring their unwanted disco records for a cheap $0.98 admission, the event attracted an estimated 90,000 people to the 50,000-capacity stadium. After the game, the host took the records, piled them in center field, and set them on fire. The fire blazed out of control, and the fans—crammed into the stands—took to the field and started rioting. It was effectively the end of disco's popularity.

HAVE YOU HEARD?

One of the most popular videos of 2009 showed how universal music can be. The brief clip from the World Science Festival shows Bobby McFerrin of "Don't Worry, Be Happy" fame leading the audience in a musical performance. Members of the audience were not professional musicians, and they didn't have any instruments other than their voices.

McFerrin walked to a place on the stage, and by example, showed the audience what note to intone. McFerrin then moved slightly along the stage and demonstrated another note of slightly higher pitch. After defining the five notes of the pentatonic scale according to a position on the stage, he would jump from place to place with the audience singing the appropriate note, while singing a counter melody. McFerrin was even able to make the audience sing correct notes that he hadn't previously defined, but which fitted the musical schema.

In the accompanying talk, McFerrin argued that humans by nature understand the pentatonic scale—the five chords upon which all music is based. His performance at the international conference was a great testament to the memetic basis of music and became a meme in its own right. It's available online at www.youtube.com/watch?v=ne6tB2KiZuk.

Two decades later, in 2009, rapper Jay-Z released his hit "D.O.A.: Death of Autotune." Autotune was a computerized voice modifier that gave the singer an icy, robotic tone. It was used by most Top 10 pop artists in the previous years, including T-Pain, Akon, and Kanye West—the latter on Jay-Z's own record label. His no-nonsense rap was a controversial call to arms.

The ultimate irony is that the biggest artists of 2009—Lady Gaga, Katy Perry, and the Black-Eyed Peas—used fast beats per minute, cheeky lyrics, and often crazy costumes to bring people back on the dance floor. They were clearly the children of disco.

Earworms don't die, but they are often beaten into hibernation and arise like a phoenix in later generations.

The Sampling Meme

One of the ultimate music memes is *sampling*, or the practice of transforming an old song into a new one. This art form started in the early 1970s, when DJs would take the dancers' favorite part of the song—usually the bridge when the drums, guitar, or other instrument created the catchiest rhythm—and loop it live to keep them on the floor. DJs would even purchase two copies of the same vinyl album, place them on the turntables, and alternate between the two to make a continuous beat. MCs, or masters of ceremonies, would sometimes get on the microphone and rhyme over the constructed beat. This was the birth of hip-hop and sampling.

DEFINITION

Sampling is taking a portion of a song and modifying it in some way to create a new song. The process began in hip-hop music and was later picked up by pop, rock, and country artists.

Early '80s technology made it easier to sample music digitally. Hip-hop music changed from a single, repetitive loop to a layered memeplex of sounds.

One song could have the following, for example:

- Drums from a James Brown record

- Horns from a Herb Alpert song

- Piano from a Bob James recording

Some samples were immediately recognizable. One popular example, MC Hammer's '90s song "U Can't Touch This," used the guitar riff, bass, and synthesizer from Rick James's '80s hit "Superfreak." People familiar with the original had mixed feelings about MC Hammer essentially looping the instrumental break and rapping over it. In fact, MC Hammer was sued by James for writing credit, which he gave, as did Vanilla Ice to Queen and similar instances.

By the 1990s, however, some songs had distorted the samples to the point where the original songs were hardly recognizable to the untrained ear.

There were a few reasons for the shift in musical style:

- Better technology
- Copyright laws
- Subversive artists

The continually advancing technology allowed more manipulation of the original song—the principles of the original meme. A sampling machine could store, say, 64 different musical snippets at once—all of which could be rearranged and replayed to create a brand-new song.

Second, copyright laws became enforced more than before. Once an underground music style, à la punk, hip-hop was bringing in millions of dollars annually. The aforementioned "U Can't Touch This" sold 10 million copies—and Rick James's lawyers made sure their client received his piece of it. Creators were encouraged to "clear" samples; that is, get permission from the original artist before releasing the new song—but more and more artists would see dollar signs, requiring the sampling artists to give them a high percentage of the sales. In memetic terms, the older artists didn't see the new music as a new meme or even a co-meme—it was theirs, just like the original song.

HAVE YOU HEARD?

It has been about 40 years since sampling began, and artists still debate who owns the creation more—the original artist or the new artist. Part of the issue is control, because the new artist may not have taken the creative work in the direction the original artist intended. We talk a lot more about meme ownership in Chapter 13.

All these factors helped create subversive artists. They would willingly take a song, chop it into little digital pieces, and rearrange it in such a way that even the original creator would have a hard time deciphering it. The complex sampling gave artists the freedom to create without having to worry about legal issues or paying out of pocket for the original rights.

The biggest contribution complex sampling made to music was to create a language—a meme—understood only by people in the know. A man on the street wouldn't recognize the Miles Davis horn stab distorted, chopped, and changed in pitch, but a fellow sample creator would. It would be their own little way of owning hip-hop again.

Humor

Laughter is contagious—not only physically but also sociologically. You hear, see, or do something funny and want to share the idea with someone else. Laugh out loud, and the people around you will want to be infected with the meme.

Your Sense of Humor as Meme

It's easy to say, "This is funny" or "That isn't funny," but like sexual expression and fashion tastes, what we consider humorous depends on cultural norms.

Think about a current humor trend: sarcasm. Tongue-in-cheek tones can be heard throughout history, in works by Shakespeare and Voltaire, followed by eras where more direct, crude humor was considered funny. The young adults in Generation Y, born in the late '70s and early '80s, are known to go heavy on the sarcasm. For instance, heartthrob celebrities Ashton Kutcher and Justin Timberlake began capping off their tailored outfits with cheap-looking trucker hats that usually were worn by, well, professional truckers. Why would these former models put on $10 blue-colored haberdashery? They wouldn't. That's what makes it funny!

The problem occurs when folks carrying on the trucker hat humor meme actually confront someone who is genuinely wearing a trucker hat. (And the victim may wonder why strangers are laughing at him or her.) We tend to be consumed by whatever humor meme we've been bitten by and become blind to other funny (or not so funny) ideas.

Comedians vs. the Rest of Us

Jokes are meant to be shared, but professional comedians share a bittersweet relationship with the memetic nature of humor.

The comedian's goal is to make you laugh, and not unlike an earworm in music, the act will be unique enough to share with your social circle. Sharing it with others gives credibility to the comedian, adding to his or her potential fans—and, with the increasing demand, raises the comedian's potential salary.

HAVE YOU HEARD?

The 2005 movie *The Aristocrats* was a great exception to the comedians' tight ownership of jokes. The documentary shows more than 100 comedians retelling the classic joke: a producer comes into an agent's office offering an amazing circus act, and as he describes it, the act becomes more raunchy, bizarre, and offensive. When the agent finally asks the name of the act, the producer happily says, "The Aristocrats!" As with the joke, the funny part of the movie is how each comedian, from Robin Williams to Whoopi Goldberg, improvises the tale. The film producers Penn Jillette and Paul Provenza acknowledged that the origins of the joke weren't clear, but it had become a tradition for comedians to modify and share the joke among themselves. The meme had been changing and spreading throughout their culture, and with the popular movie, it had been unleashed freely into the rest of the world.

Like other creators, however, comedians need to be connected to the memetic effect they created. Professionals will spend days, weeks, or even years creating a stand-up routine and will ostracize any other comedians they suspect are stealing jokes. Unfortunately, memes don't naturally have a memory of where they came from.

The Least You Need to Know

- Fashion reflects the memes of the world.
- An earworm is the part of the song that makes it hard to forget.
- Music memes tend to return in the form of sampling or retro-popularity.
- Professional comedians want to share their memes while making sure they aren't stolen by other performers.
- Humor is a learned meme.

Technological Memes

In This Chapter

- Technology sharing
- How languages evolve
- The discovery of the wheel
- The Industrial Revolution
- The Internet and the meme

We often talk about being in the technology age, but this statement is actually delusional.

Sure, there are talking machines that tell us which direction to drive, food processors that virtually prepare our meal, and many portals to other worlds through wonderful interactive space called the Internet.

The rub is that people *always* feel like they are on the cutting edge. Imagine living six centuries ago, around the time the Gutenberg Press enabled mass print production via movable type, or millennia ago, when a caveperson figured how to create fire. You'd probably think all the secrets of the universe were suddenly unlocked—and that the people before you were now relatively ignorant! Underlying human arrogance, however, is an eternal optimism that new technology will make our world better than it is today.

In this chapter, we'll focus on:

- Architecture
- Language
- Machines

Architecture

Architecture is literally the foundation on which modern civilizations are built. The structure of an area can affect how easily memes are carried, what memes are created, and why certain memes thrive and others do not.

A simple example would be the courtyards popular in Medieval France, Spain, and England. As *The 48 Laws of Power* author Robert Greene noted in an interview, the classic courtyards made it easy for others to overhear your conversation—including the king and queen themselves. Rumors, opinions, and other cultural ideas moved quickly. Compare the open-air environment to, say, a modern-day office with long hallways, private offices, and closed doors. Spontaneously exchanging information may be harder because other people aren't in easy reach.

Besides the architecture itself, the "idea" of building has transformed our world many times over. There are two outstanding memes that forever changed human culture:

- The wheel
- The arch

Let's take a closer look at these architectural ideas.

HAVE YOU HEARD?

The saying, "It's like reinventing the wheel" means wasting time creating something new when the original is perfect as is. This axiom is not only an example of a popular meme creating another popular meme but also a testament to how important the wheel still is to modern human culture.

The Wheel

Think about how many wheels you see on an everyday basis. Even if you narrow it down to, say, the daily commute, you have the wheels that make the tires for the vehicle, the wheel that is used to steer the vehicle, the dozens of cog wheels turning to keep the vehicle in motion, the wheels on the workbag if you have a large briefcase, the wheels on the bottom of your office chair, and so on.

The wheel was invented around the fourth millennium B.C.E. The immediate benefit was the transportation of goods: an individual could now make a platform with two wheels and pull something too heavy to be carried or make a platform with three or four wheels and push the item.

Transporting heavier goods meant:

- Living farther away from resources, as building supplies could be moved more easily and therefore longer distances

- Trading more often with more villagers as reasonable distances increased

- Providing alternatives to walking for the very young, the elderly, and the sick

It's safe to say that the wheel meme was copied as soon as it was seen by new eyes. It still has not been surpassed in beauty and ease.

The Arch

It's hard to imagine in our world, but early architects dealt with a serious conundrum: How to make a structurally sound doorway. There were obviously doors in ancient times, but builders relied on large pillars or other cumbersome reinforcements to keep the ceiling from falling down and the doorway from crumbling.

The arch solved the problem. Popularized by the ancient Romans, the arch shape enabled stones to fit snugly overhead, performing seemingly magical physics. Each hanging block would be secured by the two adjacent hanging blocks.

Like the wheel, the arch could be observed and easily imitated. Rome was a capital of the world, not unlike New York City in modern times, so the many travelers from abroad saw this stunning architecture and took the influence back to their homelands.

The arch became the foundation of other innovative architectural memes, such as bridges and aqueducts. One look at the Brooklyn Bridge and you'll realize the arch is the foundation for much of our modern architecture today.

Language

Think about how you speak:

1. You form an idea—a meme, if you will.

2. You link the idea to a set of words—based on another, larger meme you've accepted called symbolic language.

3. You speak the set of words—also based on a larger meme you've accepted called auditory language.

See the pattern? The words we speak, the characters we write, and even the conscious ideas we create fall into the structure of the memes we've chosen.

How It Spreads

Traditionally, the meme of language spreads because, frankly, the recipient needs it for survival. A few reasons are as follows:

- Family
- War
- Surroundings

Family is the most common way language is learned. Early on, we are trained to associate certain sounds with our needs. In a traditional patriarchal society, "Mom" or the equivalent could be associated with food, care, comfort, and warmth, while "Dad" may be associated with safety, protection, discipline, and wisdom. "Food" is associated with not being hungry anymore. The child is taught language so that he or she may thrive in the world but also so that the child may survive within the family. Without the ability to communicate, the parents and siblings won't know what the child wants and needs. The entire family will probably not accept other language memes, so the child knows that this meme must be learned, retained, and updated as necessary if he or she is going to communicate with the family for the rest of adulthood.

War is also why language memes are accepted. Alexander the Great, Hannibal, and Genghis Khan all spread their particular language to lands unfamiliar with their words. Of course, it was often by force—either to understand what the invading enemy was saying, or worse, to survive in your newly captured country.

Surroundings play a bigger reason than ever, namely because of globalization, cheap international travel, and the Internet. Businesspeople take crash courses in languages (although this could also fit into the war category!), exchange students partner with others to gain knowledge, and travelers read books to learn words before departing.

Mutations

The beautiful thing about words is that they are constantly evolving. Memes will come in and out of vogue based on circumstances such as influence, timeliness, and use.

Language constantly evolved to get us where we are today; however, in the past, the revolutions were more sporadic and dramatic. For instance, Africans were brought to America in the 1600s and 1700s for the slave trade. Aside from the slavery itself, the biggest problem was communication: Africa literally had thousands of languages, so fellow Africans on the plantation could be from what we now call Ghana, the Côte d'Ivoire, or Nigeria. The chances of one person being able to talk to another were slim, only adding to the frustration and isolation of the situation. They needed to speak to survive, so they created a language that was a hybrid of their native tongues, English, and new words created on the spot. The influence of slavery communication can still be found today in the Caribbean, the islands off the coast of the Carolinas, in New Orleans and the surrounding Gulf Coast, and other areas in and around America—as well as in mainstream English.

Today, the language adjusts more quickly but more subtly, namely because the world is almost entirely explored—no more revolutionary shocks to the system—and our smaller world, via the Internet and other tools, allows for incremental changes.

HAVE YOU HEARD?

Around 2000, scientists noticed a sharp rise in childhood obesity in the oddest place: Japan. Traditionally healthy from a diet of fresh fish and rice, the Japanese kids were eating more heavy meals and fast foods. The new millennial influx of American brands such as Starbucks, McDonald's, and KFC were considered the culprits. In short order, the Japanese had to come up with a new term that meant, simply, "cute chubby kid." A change in diet literally required the creation of a new term—something that will probably go away if the classic diets come back into vogue for the next generation.

Dead Words

As with any memes, languages die when people don't have any personal use for them—and, as a result, stop spreading them to others. Both Latin and Sanskrit are usually cited as dead languages, but for two different reasons.

Latin is often considered a dead language simply because people learn it to read things in the past, but not new works. In other words, it's dead in that there is little to no new material of import being created for it. It is called dead because it hasn't evolved.

Sanskrit is often considered a dead language because it is rarely taught or spoken. However, like Latin, Sanskrit is the foundation for the most-used languages today, such as Hindi.

In short, the meme of a language may die, but its influence is usually felt in the next generation of words.

Machines

When we think of machines, we tend to see PCs and GPSs and other inventions with complex acronyms that run through, and occasionally actually run, our daily lives.

As was touched on at the beginning of the chapter, however, whatever the current technology offers is considered state of the art. That is, the idea of a machine-run world isn't super new.

As an example, think of the abacus. A collection of movable beads on parallel strings, the Chinese abacus was the first known device made specifically for counting. It was a precursor to the calculator, which we could call a machine. Lowering the innovative abacus to "precursor" status both belittles its impact, then, as well as its foundation for the construction of modern machines. In that train of thought, wouldn't it be the same as calling the battery-operated calculator just a precursor to the solar-powered calculator, or the desktop computer just a precursor to the laptop?

The point is, our definition of what constitutes a machine is narrow because the current generation is associated with microchips, touch-screens, and voice-activated programs. In one period of time, modern technology meant horse-driven carriages and kerosene lamps.

That said, there is one influential time in our modern history when the meme of technology was particularly innovative, fast, and groundbreaking: the Industrial Revolution.

The Industrial Revolution

Starting in eighteenth-century America and Western Europe, the Industrial Revolution was a period of time when technological progress became paramount. The factors that made it a "perfect storm" include the following:

- Colonization

- Immigration

- Inventions

Colonization gave nations a strong incentive to push technology further. Spices in India, cotton in America, diamonds in Africa, and other natural resources worldwide needed to be harvested, processed, and shipped. The faster it was manufactured, the quicker it could be sold. Cotton gins, excavation tools, and other machines enabled landowners to use locals or immigrants without educating them. For the workers, the knowledge meme was suppressed.

HAVE YOU HEARD?

The pattern of using machines to create lower-paid, low-skill jobs also became the foundation of the fast-food industry. As illustrated in Eric Schlosser's best-selling book *Fast Food Nation,* McDonald's initially began as a traditional restaurant with short-order cooks, hostesses, and other elements. Shortly after launching, however, the brothers Richard and Maurice McDonald fired most of the staff, hired low-skilled high school students, and installed the latest machines. Handmade milkshakes, for instance, were now made with the push of a button. And instead of multiple jobs, each worker had just one. The opportunity for a person to learn all the memes behind how a restaurant works was restricted to their putting ketchup on buns eight hours a day. According to Schlosser, "For the first time, the guiding principles of a factory assembly line were applied to a commercial kitchen."

Immigration also encouraged the Industrial Revolution, but for a very different reason than colonization. The millions immigrating to America, the United Kingdom, and other areas came from countries all around the globe. It gave the destination countries privileged information about the memes of the immigrant's land, almost as if it stumbled across secrets that were centuries old. For instance, Italy thrived in the tailoring industry for hundreds of years, so the influx of Italian immigrants to America in the late 1800s and early 1900s advanced the technology available within the United States. It also gave different peoples the opportunity to collaborate and solve problems, so in this example, an Italian might have connected with a German and Polish tailor in America—each holding the key to a particular blindspot within their view of couture.

As a result of these two big factors, a number of machines were invented during the Industrial Revolution. There are too many to name here, but a few are as follows:

- Cement mixer
- The cotton gin
- The reliable steam engine
- The hydroelectric engine
- The blast furnace
- The Spinning Jenny loom
- The gas lamp

Computers

The advent of computers, particularly with the emergence of the affordable PC in the late 1970s, created a new set of cultural ideas and standards.

> **HAVE YOU HEARD?**
>
> The first popular home computer was the Apple II. Released in 1977, it came with a dual floppy disk drive, a green single-colored monitor, and a thick keyboard. It ran a couple thousand American dollars. Three decades later, a smaller, much more powerful desktop computer can be purchased for less than $500.

The home personal computer was innovative for many reasons, including the following:

- Information could be written and passed along quickly.
- Cultural ideas could be backed up digitally.
- New communication formats, such as e-mail, created new meme formats.

The typewriter had sped up the ability to take down ideas in previous generations, but the personal computer had fewer physical challenges that plagued the typewriter, such as ribbon issues, jammed keys, and unrecoverable mistakes. Whereas typewritten mistakes had to be whited out and retyped, computers made it possible to carefully craft and edit an idea to near perfection, increasing the chances of it being accepted by the public. Bulletin Board Services (BBS)—essentially the online precursors to the

Internet—allowed discussions through posting, uploading pictures, and other memetic interactions.

Furthermore, the memes themselves were more "protected" on the computer. For literally ages, humans had to write on a specific material, such as a flat tablet, a piece of parchment paper, or a cavern wall. If the physical item was lost or damaged, the meme existed only in the minds of people exposed to it beforehand—assuming they remembered what it was. The digital platform allowed ideas to be printed, read onscreen, backed up in another form such as a floppy disk, and posted on a BBS. It made meme creators more confident that their meme would survive and perhaps made them more productive.

Finally, early e-mail and BBSs changed the format of the actual memes that could be created. Visual memes were easier to distribute, either through uploading photos or creating text icons—the forerunners to emoticons popular today. Text-friendly memes, such as the Nigerian Scam, could also reach more people than ever. (We discuss Web-based scams in Chapter 12.)

HAVE YOU HEARD?

Early computers weren't capable of more than a couple colors and had bad resolution, but that didn't stop complex visual memes from traveling. According to co-author Damon Brown's book *Porn & Pong: How Grand Theft Auto, Tomb Raider, and Other Sexy Games Changed Our Culture,* ambitious nerds would use text characters to recreate their favorite Playboy centerfold on the computer. The painstakingly recreated picture would be uploaded onto BBSs or simply printed out and posted on their wall like the original shot.

For all the amazing changes, the personal computer evolution seems fairly quaint compared to the meme revolution that occurred when the Internet became commonplace in the 1990s.

The Emergence of the Internet

If the computer itself changed the paradigm of communication, the World Wide Web made the new paradigm move faster. There are several reasons why the Internet was and is a game changer:

- No charge for surfing

- No separate Webs based on demographics

- No organization or board restricting content

- No facilitator required for one-on-one communication

The money aspect is important when it comes to new technology. Phones are plentiful, but most require some type of monthly plan. Letters are cheap but require access to a post office—something that some rural areas don't have—and lacks the immediacy of online communicating. The Internet requires a phone line, something that, coupled with the affordable price of computers, enables communication even in areas that aren't mail-supported.

There are no barriers to accessing information based on nationality, gender, or other demographics. A macho Nigerian male can read about Harlequin romances online as much as a suburban Detroit housewife can catch up on comic book news. And only a handful of countries restrict their citizens' access to the amount of information out there.

INFECTION!

China is one of the few superpowers that restrict what people can view online. The government restricts what can be viewed under the guise of protecting its citizens from "indecent material," although much of the blocked material includes searches and sites critical of China or its government. The practices became controversial enough for Internet search giant Google to pull its company out of China and for U.S. Secretary of State Hilary Rodham Clinton to declare, in winter 2010, that China was part of "a spike in the threats to the free flow of information." Chinese representatives called the speech "information imperialism."

There is no clearinghouse for commentary online, either, aside from the member-based websites that go through a moderator. You can upload an explicit picture (which may become a meme), type a funny joke (which may also become a meme), and post other people's ideas easily, quickly, and efficiently.

Finally, conversations aren't run through a censorship filter. E-mail and instant messaging can provide quick one-on-one communication, while a social network message can easily reach millions, if not billions, of people at once—and give you a response just as quickly.

When you look at its traits, the Internet is the ultimate meme messenger of our age.

The Least You Need to Know

- The invention of the wheel and the arch changed architecture—and as a result, human social evolution.
- Languages have to be active and evolve or they will die.
- Immigration helped different civilizations collaborate and share technological development.
- The Industrial Revolution pushed machines into all areas of our lives.
- The Internet democratized the memes available as well as the people who could access them.

Philosophy: The Memes We Live By

In This Chapter

- Paying it forward
- Social mores
- Rituals
- The pendulum swing of accepted practices
- The power of fame

"Philosophy" is such a lofty, intimidating word. We can blame the Greeks for that link, with Socrates, Plato, and other serious scholars ruminating over the meaning of a tree and whatnot.

In reality, philosophy isn't that high-minded at all. In basic terms, it is the set of rules—of ideas—that you use to make your life easier. If you think about it, we make hundreds of decisions every day, from what we eat for lunch to which pant leg to put on first. Pausing to make each and every decision would be slow and draining, not to mention a waste of time. Instead, we lean on our set of ideas—for example, you might pack your lunch the night before so you can sleep for an extra 10 minutes the next morning.

In other words, philosophy is the set of memes you live by.

However, no man being an island, our human nature inclines us to share with other people how they should live, just as people we admire or respect have an influence on the way we conduct ourselves.

In this chapter, we'll take a look at the ways we set the rules we live by, how we decide who will be an influence in our lives, and why the era we live in can determine how comfortable we are with the memes surrounding our lives.

Pay it Forward

Pay it forward became a particularly popular slogan at the turn of the new millennium. The assumption is that you probably won't be able to directly pay back a person who does something good for you, so when you get the opportunity, you do something nice for someone else.

DEFINITION

Pay it forward is the act of repaying a good deed done for you by doing a good deed for another person. One particular philosophy, popularized in the movie adaptation of the book *Pay it Forward,* is that one good deed should be repaid with three good ones.

As a simple example, a stranger holds the door as you leave a building. Paying it forward, you hold the door the next time someone is behind you. This scenario also illustrates one of the reasons for paying it forward: you don't always get a chance to pay back the person who actually did the good deed for you, so the best you can do is provide a good deed for someone else.

Benjamin Franklin and other wise individuals have discussed the merits of paying it forward, but the modern meme originated with Catherine Ryan Hyde's novel *Pay it Forward* and its movie adaptation starring Kevin Spacey and Helen Hunt. Many small organizations and universities across America started "paying it forward" clubs. In 2006, Oprah Winfrey gave her guest audience $1,000 gift cards to do good for strangers.

Practices and Mores

Memes serve as a kind of social fabric. This fabric is elastic and ever changing, however.

Our daily routines could be uprooted by major upheavals, such as a civil rights movement, or a relatively small change, such as a birth or death in a family.

Our practices and mores can be considered memes in different ways:

- Social norms
- Initiation
- Tradition

Memes as Social Norms

It's always fun to observe a social norm being broken. For instance, try watching a man order a piña colada in a biker bar. The macho guys will probably react a certain way, as if some social contract has been broken—which is essentially what has happened. Some bars even place a sign that says, "We don't serve piña coladas, cosmopolitans, or any drinks with umbrellas." In memetic language, the sign reads, "If this is your meme, we're going to reject it."

Of course, you won't find signs telling you what to do or not do most of the time. Murder, theft, and jail-worthy offenses are obviously frowned upon, but there are entire categories of social norms we are expected to observe. And they change every single day.

What is acceptable in society is based on three factors:

- Which memes are being absorbed

- Which memes are being ignored

- Which memes are being rejected

The current "rules" are rarely spoken unless there is a drastic, public shift that is discussed in the media or around the water cooler. Shortly after the shift, however, the public assumes everyone "got the memo" and will treat the new meme as if it has been around as long as the old ones—and will treat other people accordingly, whether they "got the memo" or not.

 INFECTION!

It is key to remember that social norms abroad are completely different than those at home. As an example, in Tokyo it is considered offensive to blow your nose in public. It is akin to passing gas in public. The humorous part is that, as you're reading this, the long-time stance on nose-blowing may have already changed. Social norms morph that fast.

Also, when traveling, don't even think about enforcing your social memes on natives of the area you're visiting.

A recent shift occurred in 2009 when the H1N1 virus, known as swine flu, hit the major countries. It was discovered that it passed from person to person via saliva, mucus, and other fluids. The Centers for Disease Control (CDC), as well as other international organizations, held a brief press conference to talk about H1N1. It also gave a recommendation to the public: when coughing, cover your mouth with your sleeve, not your hand, to prevent any spittle from landing on your fingers and sticking to any surfaces you touch. The following day, people could be seen coughing into their sleeves, faces covered like Dracula behind a cape. Some people coughed directly into their hands and were shot a cold, exacerbated look. The disdain for hand-coughers arose partially from anxiety over H1N1 but also from their meme not being accepted anymore. The CDC rejected the long-time hand-coughing meme, and the public co-signed the decision.

Memes as Initiation

The goal of memes is to spread as much as possible, but certain ones are meant to proliferate within a certain group. Nearly any social organization has an initiation process.

An initiation meme has two primary purposes:

- To solidify the bond between group members
- To isolate group members from nongroup members

Going through the same, often difficult initiation ritual deepens the connection between group members. You know that the "brother" or "sister" next to you understands that one particular part of your life, no matter what issues may come up in the future. The more rituals you experience together, the tighter the bond.

PASS IT ON

The initiation process for a fraternity isn't that much different than one for, say, a cult. The only change is the intention of the meme itself. In fact, intention is often what separates the different types of memes we'll discuss in Parts 4 and 5.

The beauty of initiation rituals is that, while solidifying the bond within the group, they simultaneously loosen the connection with people outside the group. There would be an obvious desire for this result in, say, a cult or a street gang, but the isolation effect can be just as important in familial, corporate, or sports situations. Let's say a basketball team always chants a particular slogan when it scores. The little, seemingly innocuous slogan is a reminder that they are all on the same team while keeping the opposing team confused as to what the slogan means—something that new team members were told during their initiation.

The initiation meme is often kept private, but if it is spoken publicly, the ritual is often misrepresented to promote confusion or fear. A deceptive meme with false information could satisfy the curious and help keep the truth hidden. A false meme that encourages fear can keep people from asking too many questions—also helping keep the truth hidden. A frightening reputation can also serve as a filtering process for the organization. Anyone scared off from the outset could be too weak to belong to the organization anyway.

Memes as Tradition

Perhaps the easiest justification for a social norm is saying, "That's the way it has always been." As we have learned thus far in this book, however, cultural ideas have a beginning, a zenith, and very often, an end. Claiming tradition in light of a positive shift is more of a passive, defensive measure than an actual decision.

HAVE YOU HEARD?

A husband is idly watching his wife prepare a pot roast when she suddenly takes out a sharp blade and cuts off the last third of the perfectly good piece of meat. "What are you doing?" he says. "This is how you prepare pot roast. I learned it from my mom," she replies. The husband looks confused. "Um, why?" The wife now looks puzzled. "Um, I don't know!" The following Sunday, the wife visits her mother and asks about the pot roast recipe. "That's just how we do it, Sweetie," the mom says, adding, "That's how my mom taught me." Now determined to get to the bottom of things, the wife calls her mom's mother, her grandmother. "Well, let me think ... oh, yes, I remember now. Your grandfather and I didn't have much money, so we had this tiny apartment and this teeny, tiny oven. Pot roasts were too big for the oven, so I would cut off part of the meat ..."

People hold on to outdated traditions because of the following reasons:

- Fear
- Inertia
- Confusion

The most common reason, fear, can keep people stubbornly clinging to an idea that has outgrown its value. Fear is often expressed in a series of questions: What if the new idea doesn't work and I have to come back to this old one anyway? If I change this one thing, will life force me to change everything else? Why can't I keep things the same?

Inertia, or the lack of momentum, can be just as paralyzing. We get comfortable in our own particular universe—our philosophy—when a radical, excellent opportunity comes our way. The challenge is that we're now not used to adapting to new circumstances—our dynamic thought process giving way to atrophy and laziness.

Finally, confusion comes from indecision over which new tradition to create or absorb. Traditions can begin from a logical place, but the need to keep the tradition comes from an emotional need.

If we do find that the tradition needs to be defended, there are several ways to protect it. Check out Chapter 20 for more information.

The Cult of Personality

Genghis Khan. Paul Revere. Martin Luther King Jr. There are certain personalities throughout history who seem to be larger than life—enough so that we continue to talk about them sometimes well after their passing. What lives on is their philosophy.

HAVE YOU HEARD?

There seem to be fewer grandiose, larger-than-life figures in today's world, perhaps because we have more access to our celebrities—making them seem more human. And we have more celebrities than ever because of reality television, YouTube, and other common formats.

The cult of personality still applies to today's celebrities, but the power is relative to why they are famous and how they access the public. A minor celebrity—ever more common these days—will have a relatively minor but persistent influence on the public.

It's important to separate them, with their human flaws, contradictions, and issues, from their image—a crystallized, often idealized image that has become a meme. The image, rather than their real selves, reverberates throughout time. For some notable personalities, they decide early on to martyr themselves—and their real selves—for pushing a particular idea or agenda. For others, they just happen to become famous.

Certain people gain a cult following for many reasons:

- A bigger cause

- An infamous event

- A first time

A Bigger Cause

Some personalities become a regular topic of discussion not because of who they are but because of what they symbolize.

One excellent example is Oprah Winfrey, who tellingly is referred to as "Oprah." A struggling television reporter from rural Mississippi, Winfrey got her big break in the early '80s on a local Chicago news program. She was popular enough to be offered her own show on the local ABC affiliate. Honest, emotional, and revealing, the homemaker audience could identify with Winfrey's empathy. Her show took off in 1986 and became the foundation of what would become a billion-dollar empire.

HAVE YOU HEARD?

Other celebrities famous enough to be known by one name are Brad, Angelina, Tom, Halle, Trump, and Denzel.

Her cult of personality, however, came from her connection to bigger causes. She personally funded The Oprah Winfrey Leadership Academy for Girls in South Africa, subsidizing the higher education of poor African students. After the Mad Cow outbreak, she said on her show she'd never eat a burger again, which precipitated a high-profile slander lawsuit by the Texas Beef Group. (She won.) Winfrey spearheaded a major fund drive for victims of Hurricane Katrina, raising an estimated $11 million.

There are hundreds of talk-show hosts, but Oprah's name stays on people's tongues because she always represents something bigger than herself. Oprah went from a hardscrabble to a billion-dollar businessperson, but so have many other Americans. She has fame because of the causes she trumpets, not because of herself.

An Infamous Event

Sometimes a person gains social significance because of an event. It's a matter of being in the right place at the right (or wrong!) time.

One recent example is Chesley Burnett Sullenberger III, known by the general public as "Sully." On January 15, 2009, the decorated pilot landed a malfunctioning U.S. Airways plane on the Hudson River. All the passengers landed safely. The media immediately called him a hero, despite Sully consistently saying he was just doing his job as a U.S. Airways pilot. Commendations, ceremonies, and more medals followed.

According to *The New York Times,* Sully eventually embraced the fame to push airline reform and other, bigger causes. As far as people keeping him and his family's name out there, he said it was like "having a fire hose pointed at us."

Most of us want to have our place in history, but we don't always have a choice as to what image of ourselves will be passed on throughout time.

A First Time

Finally, some personalities maintain their image throughout history simply because they are the first of their kind.

Barack Obama will be remembered as the first African American U.S. president, just as Amelia Earhart is remembered as the first woman to fly around the world, and so on.

The twist to being the "first" is that a person must be the first publicly *acknowledged* person to accomplish something. For instance, dozens, if not thousands, of explorers "discovered" North America, including the Native Americans, Chinese, and other people who inhabited the area before 1492. Ask any American grade-schooler, or virtually any American adult for that matter, who discovered North America, and they will say, "Christopher Columbus." They may even recite the poem that begins, "In fourteen hundred ninety-two, Columbus sailed the ocean blue." The real birth of America was a messy and confusing series of events, including Columbus's conflict with Amerigo Vespucci—the fellow Italian who America is named after.

The less detail memes have to carry, the easier they are understood and the faster they are passed on. The simpler story always seems to stick.

The Least You Need to Know

- Philosophy relates to the principles we use to live our lives.
- New social norms are accepted, ignored, or rejected every day.
- Memes can be used to embrace or alienate a person within a social circle.
- Practices and mores help society maintain social order and control.
- The cult of personality draws people to celebrities and others in the public eye.

Sex as a Meme

From a purely clinical standpoint, we know sex is both nature's way of promoting procreation as well as a bonding mechanism between people. But as humans, we know it's much more than that.

Along with death, sex is one of the few experiences that touch everyone's life. It's a subject of strong emotion and opinion. In short, sex is ripe for memes.

In this chapter, we will examine the ideas that drive physical intimacy, how traditions became gospel, and why getting the straight dope on sex is confusing—and always will be.

What Is Sex?

"What is sex?" seems like a laughable question, but "sex" is actually defined by the ideas of a particular era and social group.

In 2010, a Kinsey Institute survey found that 1 out of 5 adults did not consider anal sex "sex," and 3 out of 10 did not consider oral sex "sex"—despite sex being in both of their names! The 486 adults surveyed, between the ages of 18 and 96, show that sexuality is defined by people, not by biology.

Dr. Alfred Kinsey was one of the first people to study modern sexuality in America. He studied animal biology and applied the methods to humans—not unlike memes forefather Richard Dawkins.

He made two massive contributions to human sexual studies. First, he published two books, *Sexual Behavior of the Human Male* in 1948, and *Sexual Behavior of the Human Female* in 1953—both of which relied on years of surveys and studies to confirm or debunk stereotypes assumed of both sexes.

Second, he created the Kinsey Scale, a graph that rated sexual interest from zero to six. A zero meant the subject only had interest in people of the opposite sex—purely heterosexual. On the other hand, a six meant the subject only had interest in people of the same sex—purely homosexual. In his studies, Kinsey found that the average person was neither strictly heterosexual nor homosexual but somewhere in between.

An area of less debate is *why* we participate in sexual activities. The universally accepted memes as to why we have sex are as follows:

• Procreation

• Pleasure

• Power

Procreation

The biological reason for sexual activity is procreation. In his book *The Selfish Gene*, Richard Dawkins argues that the modus operandi of a living being is to pass on its genes, protecting the carriers (the children), cultivating more power, and in its own way, living for eternity through its ancestors.

Ironically, Dawkins, a devout atheist, is actually in agreement with one of the most memetic beings of our time: God.

Genesis 1:28 of the King James Bible says:

> And God said to them, Be fruitful and multiply and fill the earth and subdue it and have dominion over the fish of the sea and over the birds of the heavens and over every living thing that moves on the earth.

"Be fruitful and multiply" is an extremely "sticky" meme because it is simple and memorable, involves having sex, and results in adorable children—therefore becoming a desirable command to fulfill.

> **INFECTION!**
>
> Religious passages often contain a bevy of insights and wisdom, but they are almost always quoted out of context to fit the quoter's needs—and, as we have learned, meme context is as important as the meme itself.
>
> We delve into these issues a lot more in Chapter 10.

The procreation aspect of sex carries with it a potent argument against gay concepts and other ideas, including the following:

- Sex without the modern definition of commitment

- Gay or lesbian sex

- Gay marriage (because it wouldn't produce offspring)

These concepts are topics of heated, modern debate, particularly with regard to gay rights. In fact, extreme adherence to the procreation meme can lead to homophobia—a phenomenon we discuss more in Chapter 19.

Pleasure

Of course, having sex for pleasure is an accepted, if controversial, meme and is perhaps suggested in the simple meme, "Do it because it feels good."

The acceptance of having sex purely for pleasure, particularly outside the context of a committed relationship, varies widely based on social mores. Mores are usually based on outstanding circumstances—as much as we'd like to think such rationale comes from our collective inner wisdom.

For instance, early twentieth-century Germany was known as an extremely sexually accepting country, particularly with regard to alternative lifestyles, intimacy without commitment, and sex for pleasure. The 1920s, however, brought economic changes and a new, aggressive government interested in making Germany a world power, if not the dominant race. The focus shifted from sex for pleasure to sex for procreation—and therefore, sex for power. In other words, Germany traded one accepted meme for another.

America was arguably as hedonistic as turn-of-the-century Germany with its era of sexual revolution—an era also defined by outside circumstances. The birth control pill arrived in 1960, which gave women an easier way to have sex for pleasure. The meme "casual sex" came into play—a term that didn't exist before. Recreational drug use, which gained popularity in the 1960s, helped fuel the even more sexually open 1970s. The 1970s also began the modern pornography industry.

In the late '70s, scientists discovered an immunity-disabling virus that was transmitted by exchanging bodily fluids—including through sex. The discovery of HIV/AIDS affected sexual mores, because now casual sex could lead to an early and painful death. Teenage abstinence programs rose significantly as sex for pleasure took a backseat to the idea of sex for procreation.

PASS IT ON

Using condoms is a meme, although that may be hard to fathom in a post-AIDS world. The acceptance of condom usage fluctuates in popularity based on public opinion and circumstances.

Condoms date back to ancient Egypt, but their modern popularity links directly with the discovery of HIV/AIDS. According to co-author Damon Brown's *Porn & Pong: How Grand Theft Auto, Tomb Raider, and Other Sexy Games Changed Our Culture*, "… condom sales rose from 240 million in 1986 to almost 300 million in 1988, the biggest jump happening after [U.S.] Surgeon General C. Everett Koop's 1987 report on AIDS." Keep in mind that the nineteenth century had its own epidemics of herpes and other incurable sexually transmitted diseases that could have been prevented by wearing a condom, but these diseases were evidently not considered devastating enough to encourage widespread condom use.

Disturbingly, condom use has actually dropped since the late 1990s as drugs help AIDS carriers live longer and the media sensationalism around the epidemic has dissipated. It's damning proof that condom use didn't increase because of protection but because of popularity.

Like any other meme, the idea of sex for pleasure waxes and wanes based on the flavor of the times.

Power

Sex for power is another accepted meme, although it is not often discussed as such—if it is discussed at all.

There are three main themes connected with sex for power, and they often overlap:

- Romantic dominance

- Psychological dominance

- Physical dominance

Sex for romantic and physical dominance is as classic as Shakespeare and is often the root of the so-called "War of the Sexes." The problem is that men and women both fear and desire the power sex supposedly provides.

Let's take a look at one adage: "Be a lady in the street and a whore in the bed." In other words, to keep a man happy, a woman must push societal norms when being intimate but pretend not to push these norms in public.

There are multiple challenges with this accepted meme:

- What constitutes a "whore"?

- How does one learn about "advanced" sexual techniques if they aren't discussed publicly?

- Do all guys want a "whore" in their bed?

Even the first question, "What constitutes a whore?", is totally based on societal conventions. For instance, in broad biblical terms, a whore is a woman who has sex outside marriage. Based on that viewpoint, a single woman hooking up with a guy doesn't have to do anything special in bed as she already is a whore!

HAVE YOU HEARD?

Did you ever wonder where lipstick originated? It goes back to the Roman Empire. Courtesans would use herbs to color their lips red to resemble the lips of the female vulva. The reasons behind memes are indicative of the time period, obviously.

"Be a lady in the street and a whore in the bed" has another implied assumption: men always prefer sleeping with a woman who breaks social mores. This idea is both strange and false. Based on countless surveys and anecdotes, every person desires something different from a lover. One person may be interested in meek conservative women, while another would like to be ravished by aggressive experienced women. It falls quickly into stereotyping—a dangerous side effect of blindly accepting memes.

The confusion comes not from having widely accepted maxims—as we've established, this in itself helps create culture—but from people assuming everyone has the same perspective they do. One popular meme can be based on a handful of other memes, which in turn are also based on more memes. Without a deeper understanding, the meaning of the original idea can collapse like a house of cards.

Sex for physical and psychological dominance often goes hand in hand with social mores as well. As a harsh example, inmates in hardcore prison culture traditionally "break in" new inmates by having forced intercourse with them. It provides a physical release for the attackers, but it also confirms their dominance and incorporates the new guy (or gal) into the established social hierarchy. It is a widely accepted meme.

HAVE YOU HEARD?

It is also important to note that power dynamics within sex are quite natural. In fact, communities within BDSM—or bondage, dominance, submission, and masochism—explore these power dynamics within what they call a "safe environment." Sex is sometimes involved, but the focus is on examining the assumptions, stereotypes, and walls we create around sex, not the sex itself.

Accepted sexual power memes can also create an amazing double standard. In modern, straight-male culture, for instance, it is considered gay to give a man oral sex but not to *receive* it from another guy. This idea could have roots as far back as ancient Greece, when receiving fellatio from another man was considered an act of dominance by the receiver. The concept is fascinating not only because the supposedly subservient person has more physical power—the receiver is in a much more vulnerable position—but that the subservient person is considered homosexual, and the receiver is not. This memetic discourse assumes other factors, namely that being perceived as gay is something to be loathed and feared. Imagine if homophobia weren't a constant throughout our history? This established power meme wouldn't be as strong as it is today.

All these examples prove that power, especially when it comes to sex, is a truly subjective idea.

Pornography

Pornography is one of the most loaded expressions in our modern age, and believe it or not, it also is memetic in nature.

> **DEFINITION**
>
> **Pornography** is the depiction of something or someone performing an act a viewer could interpret as sexual. It is subjective in nature.

Pornography is complicated for quite a few reasons:

- It is irrepressible.
- It is hard to define.
- By nature, it challenges accepted memes.

Irrepressible

Porn is anything but new. Watercolor scrolls depicting nude women date back to early Japan. Explicit drawings were discovered under the ashes and rubble of Pompeii—most describing services available at the local brothels. Egyptian hieroglyphics arguably contained sexual depictions. And, in perhaps the most-known example, ancient Greek and Roman urns graphically show acts between numerous combinations of people—and other beings. Its continual presence confirms something: we have a need to observe our own sexuality.

Hard to Define

Pornography is controversial not just because of its inherently sexual nature but because we still have a hard time defining it. To paraphrase one cultural critic, if you see a woman in a bikini and it says *Sports Illustrated* on it, it can be on the newsstand—but if the same magazine cover says *Hustler*, it is pornographic and must be covered up. Essentially, the established meme, or concept, surrounding the medium is as important as the expression itself.

HAVE YOU HEARD?

The United States Supreme Court has struggled for decades to define what constitutes pornography (and, more importantly, what is considered obscene). The modern challenges began in 1873, when U.S. Postal Inspector Anthony Comstock made it illegal to ship any item that was "obscene, lewd, and/or lascivious." The measurement, of course, was determined by Comstock himself. The Supreme Court followed suit.

Almost a century later, Associate Justice of the Supreme Court Potter Stewart made his famous statement that he couldn't define obscenity, "but I know it when I see it." Again, the focus was on using subjective—that is, personal— views of sexuality to determine what was and wasn't fit for everyone else.

The loosening of obscenity laws during the open decade of the '70s, the crack-down on pornography during the Reagan-era '80s, and the explosive growth of the porn industry in the '90s and the new millennium reveals the confusing relationship between Americans and pornography.

Furthermore, as we touched on earlier in the chapter, sexuality is personal, subjective, and fluid. The definition of pornography changes literally every day. For instance, you may find women with large feet attractive. Is a video of a woman trying on size 13 high heels pornography? It may be to you—and to others who have created or accepted the meme that large feet are sexy.

Challenging Accepted Memes

Pornography reflects our desires. Because it is often produced by a business, it must appeal to what the customer needs. In turn, these customer needs are influenced by the most accepted memes. For instance, the average modern porn star is short, rail thin, blonde (dyed or natural), large breasted (fake or natural), and looks younger than 30. The current, albeit stereotypical, standard of beauty is reinforced by pornography, and the cycle continues.

However, there is a twist: unlike other products, mainstream pornography must differentiate itself from the competition. Therefore, pornography is more apt to threaten, if not destroy, the status quo—that is, the widely accepted memes—to make a profit, or at the very least, create notoriety. In this way, pornography pushes what is socially acceptable.

An excellent example is the movie *Deep Throat*. Released in 1972, it was the first modern porn film. The main actress was noted for her oral sex techniques. Prior to the film, however, oral sex was still considered a taboo topic both in and out of the bedroom. However, the massively popular *Deep Throat* brought fellatio and cunnilingus into public discussion, and according to some studies, oral sex has been on the rise ever since.

PASS IT ON

Movies are one of the best ways to examine which memes are popular within a culture. For instance, the 1977 John Travolta film *Saturday Night Fever* introduced middle America to the popular disco trend happening in New York, Los Angeles, and other urban areas.

The Internet pushed this meme-creator/meme-destroyer phenomenon into overdrive by:

- Creating more sexual memes
- Replacing more sexual memes
- Destroying more sexual memes

As a creator, Internet pornography pushes niche interests. For instance, the concept of a cougar, or an attractive older woman interested in dating younger men, was pushed into our collective consciousness partially because of porn websites dedicated to the concept. Before the cougar concept became popular, men were thought to be only interested in younger women. Now, it is accepted, if not encouraged, to pursue an older woman of interest. The Internet is literally an infinite space, so the number of niches that can come from the ether is enormous.

As a replacer, Internet pornography can quickly switch out content based on consumer feedback. If a site gets less traffic, the owner can choose from the myriad of other sexual ideas to create an experience. Memes are short-lived on the Internet.

HAVE YOU HEARD?

The *Kama Sutra* is one of the most powerful pre-Internet sexual memes, although for a different reason than you may think. Created around the second century, the *Kama Sutra* is an Indian book describing the different ways two committed lovers can bond. It is a six-section book, but the most remembered portion is the extensive list of sexual positions—particularly because some editions contained pictures.

The *Kama Sutra* is important for two reasons. First, it introduced India and other lands to what was possible between two people. It's hard to picture it in our post-Internet age, but there wasn't a Dr. Ruth or a *Playboy* magazine as a sexual reference.

Second, the name of the book became more of a meme than the book itself. A modern-day Lothario or Lolita may say, "We went through the whole *Kama Sutra* in bed," but he or she isn't literally talking about going page by page through the classic text. Instead, *"Kama Sutra"* became shorthand for either a bevy of sexual positions or a person with an encyclopedic knowledge about sex. The number of people alive today who actually read the *Kama Sutra* is probably quite small—especially now that we have a living, current version of the *Kama Sutra* called the Internet.

As a destroyer, Internet pornography automatically goes after the next big thing: crushing most memetic half-lives into nothing. A user may enjoy watching, say, two people kissing, but the nature of Internet porn, via the infinite nature of the Internet, proves that there is always something more erotic, more interesting, and more fulfilling available. The user is always enticed by the next meme.

The Least You Need to Know

- Procreation, pleasure, and power are universally accepted memes behind why we have sex.
- The major sexual memes are based on a series of assumptions that are also memes.
- What is and isn't pornography is in the eye of the beholder.
- Pornography creates, promotes, and destroys memes.
- The Internet has expanded the number of sexual memes.

Religion

Chapter 10

In This Chapter

- Religion as a meme
- Axioms and principles
- False memes based on faith
- Religion as a weapon
- Social power via belief systems

Do you go to a place of worship once a week? Or do you wake up and meditate daily? Alternatively, do you regularly read a text sitting on your nightstand? Despite our advanced technology, high-speed lives, and relatively cynical media, most of us observe some type of religious ritual.

In fact, according to Gallup International, 87 percent of the world's population considers itself religious.

Think for a second: What exactly is religion? Personal feelings aside, it is a set of actions meant to give praise to a higher power or powers, to outwardly express one's spiritual beliefs, and/or to bond with others of similar ideas. It is something passed on from generation to generation, master to student, and colleague to colleague. It is an idea, or better yet, a set of ideas that can be practiced by one individual or by billions of people. Sound familiar? A religion is a meme.

In this chapter, we'll look at how religion is created, ways rituals are spread, and why the meme can be a formidable weapon.

Religion and Spirituality

The center of most religions, of course, is faith, but the ritual—the routine performed to establish, confirm, or prove faith to oneself or others—is often created as a disciplined way to express that faith. The faith is spirituality, while the practice is religion.

Religion as a Meme

Religious rituals are routines originally created by an individual because of logic, necessity, or faith. The process is championed by a particularly influential person or group, and in turn, it develops into the opportunity to become a meme that spreads.

Religion as Routine

Think of making the sign of the cross—a long-standing Christian tradition. For Western Christians, the routine goes as such:

- Touch the index and middle finger to the thumb to represent the Father, the Son, and the Holy Spirit.
- Motion toward the forehead.
- Motion toward the heart.
- Motion toward the left shoulder.
- Motion toward the right shoulder.

The routine of Orthodox Christians goes as such:

- Touch the index and middle finger to the thumb to represent the Father, the Son, and the Holy Spirit.
- Motion toward the head.
- Motion toward the heart.
- Motion toward the *right* shoulder.
- Motion toward the *left* shoulder.

There are many theories behind the preferences, including the Western Christian left-to-right motion symbolizing Jesus Christ going from misery to glory, but the now-ancient origins are unclear. What matters is how the subtle difference is extremely important within the individual communities.

Scholars say the cross gesture starts at the head and proceeds to the heart to symbolize Christ's resurrection. But does it *have* to be performed that way to connect with God? To many Christians, it does, just as prayer five times a day is necessary in the eyes of most Muslims. It is a philosophical routine—a meme—that was agreed upon at a certain, ancient point.

A Renewed Idea

The view of religion as a meme isn't new, but it definitely has had a renaissance of late. *The Selfish Gene* author Richard Dawkins published several titles after his landmark meme book, but the most popular one was 2006's *The God Delusion*. As you can imagine, the title went over very well with the general public!

INFECTION!

Social critic Christopher Hitchens released the controversial book *God Is Not Great: How Religion Poisons Everything* in 2007, about a year after *The God Delusion* from fellow atheist Richard Dawkins. The two best-sellers ushered in a renewed discussion on atheism. Remember that the nonbelief in a higher power can be as powerful a meme as belief in one!

An atheist himself, Dawkins has argued that religion, at least with regard to believing in higher beings, was a coping mechanism for people. He believes this is religion's sole purpose.

Championed by an Individual

The blueprint for the major religions today can be traced back to a particular individual and the devotees who passed along the information. For example:

- Jesus Christ for Christianity
- The prophet Muhammad for Islam

Their ideas, of course, usually come from a higher source, but the message—and most important, the rituals—are delivered by these enlightened individuals.

Interestingly, when it comes to religion, the higher power can be considered the memetic engineer, and the religious figure is the host who spreads the meme to others.

Breaking Down a Religious Meme

Let's break down a well-known example: the King James Bible story of Moses and the Ten Commandments.

Referenced in both Exodus and Deuteronomy, books of the Bible, Moses climbs Mount Sinai to receive a message from God—a set of 10 commandments for the faithful to live by. They are written on two stone tablets and carried down by Moses to the people.

For Moses and the Ten Commandments:

- God is the memetic engineer—the creator of the meme itself.

- The hook, or what makes the meme enticing, is God's credibility. This isn't a random list. God has a lot of street cred!

- The bait, or reward for accepting the meme, is that following these rules will give the believer guaranteed salvation; more cynically, not following these rules will earn you guaranteed damnation.

- The vector, or the impartial medium used to transport the meme, is the tablets themselves. The slabs of stone didn't care whether there were 50 commandments or 5 listed.

- The host, or the deliverer of the meme, is Moses himself.

- The memotype, or request of the meme, are the Ten Commandments.

- The sociotype, or actual expression of the meme, are people treating themselves and others differently in accordance with the Ten Commandments.

Religious Memes vs. Spiritual Feelings

To fully understand the religious meme, consider the difference between spirituality and religion. Spirituality is a personal belief system, usually faith-based, concerned with why our world operates the way it does. Religion is a particular set of practices, also usually faith-based, used to observe one's spirituality.

Spirituality Is Not a Meme

Spirituality is not a meme, but religion is. Now, this doesn't mean that your belief system is based on what's cool right now—although that may be the case for some people—but that the practices themselves are learned.

Consider the following example: three brothers grow up in a religious household. Each brother respectfully goes to a place of worship every Sunday. Each brother also performs the rituals associated with the religion, including reading texts and observing laws. However, the brothers can have totally different perspectives on their spirituality. The youngest brother, for instance, considers one particular verse the guidepost in his life, while the middle brother feels closest to a higher power when at his place of worship and slightly lost during the remainder of the week. The three brothers have received a set of routines from their family, their friends, or their community, but their inner belief system—their spirituality—cannot be duplicated. It is too personal and simply too complex to be boiled down into a meme.

HAVE YOU HEARD?

Certain sects of monks wear a rope belt to tie their robes. According to some historians, this tradition comes from ancient times. Monks could be considered the original "Ghostbusters"—if an area was thought to be filled with dark spirits, they were the ones to cleanse the place and evacuate the ghosts. Before entering, the monk would tie a long rope around his waist and hand the other end to a set of townspeople. The rope served as a safety valve: if the situation got too hairy, the townspeople could pull the monk back out. The frayed rope belt is a reminder of the monk's heritage, although like many memes, the habit of wearing the belt is more remembered than its actual original meaning.

The Dangers of Outside Justification

The memetic quality of religion is one of the reasons it can be as enlightening as it can be dangerous. It is a wonderful tool to remind someone of his or her spiritual beliefs and to create a sense of community among fellow worshipers, believers, and supporters.

The trouble arises when the routine—the religion—is separated from the faith—the spirituality. The rituals can provide a sense of rhythm throughout life, but without a deeper, individual spiritual connection to what the habits represent, a person can cling to the dogma and fight others who don't perform the same actions. To a spiritually insecure person, the religious meme must be spread and accepted by others for him or her to justify it internally.

Religion as Axioms

As we discussed in earlier chapters, the more complex the meme, the more difficult it is to pass on to the masses. As humans, we usually have fewer than 100 years to learn, absorb, and accept or deny literally millions of concepts, beliefs, and values that come our way—which, when you think about it, isn't very long! As a result, we have to make judgments quickly using shorthand based on other people's opinions, news summaries, or excerpts of bigger texts.

The Gist, but Not the Entire Idea

If we mention the video game *Pac-Man*, a ton of images and ideas probably come to mind: arcades, quarters, youth, the '80s, and wasting time. The twist is that you may not have played *Pac-Man* for decades and can barely remember it, or you may have never played before, but you likely still have a strong idea of what the game is and what it represents. You understand the idea of *Pac-Man* based on pieces of information and opinion. Personal experience makes it richer, but it isn't mandatory to your forming an opinion. The same could be said for our view of most religions.

PASS IT ON

A meme is the main idea behind something, but it can also represent a lot of associated connotations. Some opponents of memetics have claimed that this association sounds a lot like a doctrine of the famous philosopher Plato, who first said that ideas and objects in the world were merely imperfect representations of some metaphysical ideal. Need more detail? We talk about it much more in Chapter 23.

Knowing Enough to Judge

The perception of a particular religion can easily fall into this realm of popular idea, or meme, as opposed to a personal experience. Within certain sects, a monk will give up his worldly possessions, go to a remote area, and live in solitude to contemplate his or her religion of choice. Rabbis, priests, and other religious leaders spend their entire lives trying to better understand their faith and their higher purpose in this lifetime.

The average person in the world, however, does not dedicate himself or herself to religion day in and day out. Instead, spirituality is squeezed in between taking care of oneself and family, maintaining food and shelter via physical or mental work, and just surviving. No wonder other religions are often misunderstood and misrepresented—most people do not or will not make the time to completely understand other belief systems, much less their own.

Simple Memes Are Easy

The simplifying of religious "understanding" is further compounded by the heavy text usually involved, whether it's the King James Bible, the Quran, or the Torah. How does one parse the meaning of a religious faith, often the result of centuries of tradition, by reading a single book? Reading, of course, must be supplemented by practice, just as you can only begin to understand a language by actually using it with other people.

Because of time, commitment, and perhaps laziness, complex spiritual ideas are often compressed into memes tiny enough to fit in your pocket. It is an overarching idea of, say, Buddhism to envision someone sitting quietly, legs folded, and thinking about the sayings of a portly man versus the delicate thoughts, layered narratives, and rigorous willpower emphasized within the particular faith. Shorthand is often more easily remembered.

Memes as Dogmatic Weapons

Memes favor simplicity. In a religious context, the simplicity that makes it memorable can also make it one-dimensional and exploitable for malicious use.

Out of Context

For example, the phrase, "An eye for an eye" is mentioned several times in the King James Bible. In one example, Deuteronomy 19:21, "Show no pity: life for life, eye for eye, tooth for tooth, hand for hand, foot for foot." Oh, boy. You can imagine how much pillaging, pain, and death has been justified by a bastardization of this verse.

Interpreted to Fit the Situation

However, negative ideas aren't the fault of a particular religious text, nor are they the fault of the original writers. People often create a meme *inspired* by the verse, perhaps to fit their own agenda, and others see fit to use the meme for their purposes as well. In other words, one particular interpretation of a text can catch on and be taken at face value, as is the case with "An eye for an eye."

HAVE YOU HEARD?

One of the most recent egregious uses of religious text was the idea that the Quran justified the September 11, 2001, attacks on America. A popular meme claimed that chapter 9, verse 11 of the Muslim text said, "For it is written that a son of Arabia would awaken a fearsome Eagle. The wrath of the Eagle would be felt throughout the lands of Allah and lo, while some of the people trembled in despair still more rejoiced; for the wrath of the Eagle cleansed the lands of Allah; and there was peace."

If people read a translation of the Quran, 9:11 reads roughly, "But if they repent, perform prayer and give charity, then they are your brethren in religion. We explain the revelations further for people who are aware."

Even an awful translator couldn't botch up Arabic-to-English that badly! It was a strong urban myth in the year following the 2001 attacks, more than likely started to help Americans point blame and more than likely perpetuated by both American ignorance of Islam and the citizens' reluctance to read the Quran itself.

The Big Picture

The meme, "An eye for an eye," not the literal text, is usually the limit of understanding for two reasons. First, people rarely quote any of the entire verse, just the small portion they have heard from others (in other words, the meme). Second, several versions of "An eye for an eye" are located within the King James Bible, some of which would serve as much more complex memes. Leviticus 24:19–24:21, for instance, says:

> Anyone who maims another shall suffer the same injury in return: fracture for fracture, eye for eye, tooth for tooth. The injury inflicted is the injury to be suffered. One who kills an animal shall make restitution for it, but one who kills a human being shall be put to death.

This particular quote could be interpreted as a call for having a fair court system with impartial laws, or it could encourage a vegetarian society, or it could literally mean you have the right to attack someone, physically or otherwise, who has attacked you. We certainly don't know *exactly* what it means. But that's the point: full religious text can be debated, discussed, and deliberated, but memetic religious sound bites often cannot. Short, pithy religious memes are easy to remember but often have a judgment built within simply because they are excerpts—and such excerpts, by their very nature, must be judged to be created.

Seeing Religion

Most major religions do not claim that God interacts with followers directly. Instead, He usually interacts through a mediator, such as a priest, or through a text, such as the King James Bible.

However, we sometimes feel as if we are in the presence of God because of an unusual act or a symbolic gesture. For example, a plane crash kills all passengers except for one baby girl onboard. Based on media spin, the child will probably become a symbol of hope and peace. In other words, her survival has created a meme.

Odds of surviving a devastating plane crash may be one in a million, but as humans we tend to forget that there will eventually *be* one million plane crashes and someone, based on these statistics, will eventually survive the disaster. The odds are one in a million, not zero.

We suspect this is where Dawkins, Hitchens, and other atheists hold their argument—people always believe what they want to believe, even if it means putting logic aside.

The Shroud of Turin

The Shroud of Turin is perhaps the biggest physical religious meme of all time. Discovered a century ago in the Italian city of Turin, the cloth seems to have the imprinted face of Jesus Christ.

Scientists have been experimenting on the cloth, particularly over the last three decades, as post-dating technology has drastically improved—but there is still an intense debate over whether it actually is the face of Christ or even whether the cloth was around when he was.

One thing we know about memes, however, is that the "truth" doesn't matter. This cloth is revered as one of the few artifacts of Christ and is considered a focus of faith.

Christ on Croissants

There are also some amazing—and we mean *amazing*—other items with memetic qualities.

HAVE YOU HEARD?

According to MSN.com, the Virgin Mary grilled cheese sandwich sold on eBay for $28,000. Let's hope the cook paid her tithes—for her sake.

Here are a few notables:

- Jesus Christ's crucifixion on a tie-dye T-shirt (2010)
- Jesus Christ's face on toast (2009)
- Jesus Christ's face on a cider drink wrapper (2008)
- Jesus Christ's face on a half-eaten prawn (2006)
- Mother Teresa's cameo on a sticky bun (2006)
- The Virgin Mary on grilled cheese (2004)
- Jesus Christ's face and torso on a tree (2002)

The Least You Need to Know

- Spirituality cannot be passed on, but religion is by nature a meme.
- Religious memes usually are simplified and removed from their original context.
- Religious memes can be used to justify nearly any action.
- Most major religions have a leader who serves as the host for the religious meme.
- People usually learn of new religions through sound bites, not from studying the material.

Politics

In This Chapter

- Slogans that stick
- Platforms of memes
- Lies and compromises
- Meme overload
- Promoting conflicting memes

Did you hear that Senator James had an affair? Is it true or a rumor? I wouldn't want to vote for an adulterer.

A hardy combination of intended lies, unintended consequences, and perception over truth, politics are a great microcosm for understanding how memes are created, perpetuated, and spread.

We're going to talk about the races for public office, political slogans, and deceptive practices. The brilliant part is that, as shown with the Senator James example earlier, traditional politics reflect the everyday politics we deal with in our social circles, our jobs, and our families—ideally in a less-dramatic fashion!

Slogans, Soapboxes, and Partisan Memes

From ancient Egypt and Greece to modern Japan and America, politics have played a continuous role in human societies.

The people, technology, and traditions may have updated, but the political methods have changed very little. In that sense, we can also say the strategies, ideas, and tools used to become the prime minister of the United Kingdom aren't much different than those to be elected president of the local Parent-Teacher Organization.

There are three major meme-based tools in a politician's arsenal:

- Slogans
- Soapboxes
- Partisan memes

Slogans

Perhaps the ultimate political example of a meme, the slogan, is a simple idea expressed in a sound bite. A successful slogan is catchy, memorable, and expresses a desirable outcome. Also, it doesn't have to be true. Let's break down this phenomenon.

Catchy

A successful political slogan has to have a hook—which, not coincidently, means the same to both a researcher of memes and a political campaign manager. A hook, you may remember, is the part that makes the meme enticing.

For instance, U.S. President Dwight D. Eisenhower became America's thirty-fourth leader based on a simple slogan: "I Like Ike." It rhymes. Looking back 60 years, what did it mean? Who knows, but it was easy for people to remember at the ballot box. It's unclear what would have happened if his nickname had been "Pete."

HAVE YOU HEARD?

Sayings can be just as important after the victory. At a press conference following his win, newly elected U.S. President Harry S. Truman triumphantly held up the day's *Chicago Tribune* newspaper, which bore the huge headline, "Dewey Defeats Truman." Daily newspapers have to go to press the evening before distribution, so publishers have to make an estimated guess at the outcome of late-night events, such as tallied elections. It was more than that, though: the conservative paper's editorials had aggressively attacked the liberal candidate during the campaign. "Dewey Defeats Truman" became a meme associated with Truman's presidency and remains an iconic moment. In winter 2010, one visual artist modified the classic press picture with "Apple Announces Tablet," showing the anticipation for the company's iPad device. As mentioned earlier, parodies are only as powerful as the memes they are based on, because the observer must know the reference to understand the relevance.

Memorable

Like all memes, there must be a certain memorable quality that makes a slogan stick. Brevity helps.

With the Eisenhower example, a less-effective campaign may have pushed for, "I Like Ike Because He's Right." The more complex the meme, the more difficult it is to pass on—and the more difficult it is for the infected to pass it on to their social circles. As many a failed politician has learned, heavy narratives and layered resolutions are best saved for after getting into office.

Desirable

Aside from being catchy and memorable, a successful slogan has to contain an outcome that the general public desires. In both meme and political campaign terms, this would be the bait, or the reward for accepting the meme and passing it on to your social circle.

Having a slogan that expresses a desirable outcome seems obvious, but it's not so easy when politics often put candidates between a rock and a hard place. Let's say the public is sick of underfunded schools and would like the next official to turn around their run-down teaching facilities. The public, through the government, funds the schools, so the money will actually have to come from the people themselves. Think about an appropriate slogan to reflect the public's concerns and interest. "Pay Taxes for Your Future!" doesn't sound desirable at all, even if it is exactly what the public says it wants. "Save Our Schools!" is desirable, however, surely because it leaves out the details.

Expresses Intent but Does Not Guarantee

If a car doesn't achieve the distance per gallon promised in its slogan, it won't be long before word gets around and sales of the vehicle go down. Ditto for diet supplements, toothpaste, and most any other product.

Political slogans are unique in that they don't have to tell the complete truth, due to a few reasons:

- Political terms
- Compromise
- Meme overload

From the local Kiwanis to the United Nations, each political organization gives its leaders set terms of office. Once elected, the official must perform an egregious violation to be kicked out before the term ends. The number one reason deceptive politicians aren't held accountable to their promises is that we can't immediately get rid of them!

HAVE YOU HEARD?

Politicians benefit from our low expectations. In some ways, we don't expect them to keep all their campaign promises! In America, the cynical view of politics wasn't always commonplace.

Historians attribute the change in public attitude to one event: Watergate. The conspiracy that led to President Richard Nixon's impeachment made the general public lose faith that the government had its best interests in mind.

A more practical reason for political slogans not always being taken seriously is compromise. The saying, "You scratch my back, I'll scratch yours" describes the political game in which favors have to be traded, bargaining "chips" issued for past help, and general flexibility required to get things done. A promise of no new taxes becomes no new taxes for small business owners, pet owners, and people between 25 and 45—and a jacked-up tax hike for everyone else.

Finally, politicians aren't always held accountable to their political slogans simply because the onslaught of memes leaves the citizens tired, confused, and forgetful. The winner of a small election may be watched like a hawk, but a major political race can have dozens of candidates each with his or her own batch of slogans, promises, and perspectives. It often takes a reminder, such as an astute piece of media or an historical book, to repaint the picture of the candidate we saw pre-election.

Soapboxes

Candidates are often said to stand for something, such as breaking down "big business," unifying a society, or helping the environment. This big idea, or collection of ideas, is the candidate's *soapbox*.

DEFINITION

A **soapbox** is the collection of ideas a politician stands for during a particular campaign. The most successful soapboxes have memes that create a particular overarching theme.

Where Did the Soapbox Come From?

Why the funny name? It comes from the late nineteenth century, back before politicians debated on television and elected officials had Twitter accounts. Speaking on the street corner was an excellent way to send the campaign messages out to the public, not to mention a very effective way to get feedback on the issues. The talking would happen on the sidewalk rather than on an elevated platform or in an official theater, so candidates would grab a soapbox or another available platform to stand above the crowd. The practice changed, but the name stuck, and the soapbox became the platform the candidate *figuratively* stood on.

Many Memes Creating One Big Idea

The soapbox isn't just one idea but a cornucopia of goals and promises the candidate is offering to the public. The candidate is essentially painting a socioplex for the future: the world that will be created if the public officer is able to implement his or her memes. It is literally the ideal.

Consistency Is Key

The memes within the soapbox have to be consistent. For instance, a candidate may champion ending an unpopular war but support an increase in military spending that can only be justified by more war. At best, conflicting memes are ineffective and cancel each other out. At worst, contradictory memes reflect badly on the candidate and make him or her seem indecisive or duplicitous.

Partisan Memes

So far, we've discussed memes being used to create a political campaign, but a carefully targeted idea can also destroy one.

The most basic level of negative criticism is creating an epitaph for a particular group and associating the candidate with it. Here are some common ones:

- Bleeding-heart liberal
- Ultra-conservative
- Socialist
- Pork-belly politician

The impact of a derisive meme, or any meme for that matter, is mostly based on context. Socialism may be looked at as a threatening label, particularly within modern capitalist societies—but the "barb" wouldn't make any sense in China, a socialist country. Like having a duplicitous soapbox message, a poorly executed attack can make the deliverer seem confused—and at worst, impotent.

Spreading Messages

Well beyond the soapboxing of yesteryear, political memes are spread in a variety of ways, including the following:

- Paraphernalia

- Media ads

- Internet campaigning

INFECTION!

Candidates can easily be associated with memes created by others, particularly because of the Internet. During the heated 2008 U.S. presidential campaign, model Amber Lee Ettinger released an online video called, "I Got a Crush … on Obama." Plastered with images of Ettinger singing to the camera and media pics of Senator Barack Obama shirtless at the beach, the video quickly went viral. The media had a field day with the playfully sexy video, and luckily for Obama it didn't hurt his image. Regardless, it's doubtful his team would have suppressed the video even if they could have.

Let's take a look at each of these ideas.

Political Paraphernalia

Paraphernalia may seem relatively old school, but it's arguably more popular than ever because it has become cheaper to mass-produce stickers, buttons, and other takeaway items. The idea is simple: give out a pen, and every time the person uses the pen to write, he or she will get the meme message. Of course, with our current technology, there's no reason to really measure their effectiveness. Why do candidates continue to pass them out? Ironically, the belief that passing out paraphernalia gets people into office by spreading their meme is an accepted meme in itself. Wrap your brain around that one.

That said, passing out political paraphernalia may be a dying meme. In our increasingly green world, paraphernalia isn't the most environmentally friendly approach to campaigning—something that could reflect badly on the candidates themselves.

Media Ads

Media ads are a great way to hit "common folk" because, regardless of the hundreds of millions who have Internet access, there are definite billions watching television at this very moment.

In fact, according to a recent Pew Institute study, approximately half of America does not have a broadband/high-speed Internet connection. The average American can't easily access the fancy Flash-based websites, image-intensive e-mails, or YouTube videos. Traditional advertising is still necessary to penetrate as many minds as possible.

The challenge here is that the message is one-way. Unlike traditional soapboxing via a town hall meeting or a street corner, the candidate receives no feedback until the polling results come in.

Internet Campaigning

Internet campaigning is obviously the newest method of establishing campaign messages. Major candidates are expected to have a website, a video stream, a social network page or account, and an active e-mail address. It can facilitate a great amount of conversation between the candidate and his or her potential constituents—at least the illusion of such—and may be the modern-day equivalent of street-corner soapboxing.

PASS IT ON

Image control is nearly impossible on the Internet. Search for images of any major political candidate, and chances are the most popular are graffitied or Photoshopped pictures (devil horns seem to be a favorite accessory).

If you missed it, check out our discussion on the "blank slate" nature of online pictures in Chapter 4.

The big issue with Internet campaigning is that rivals and dissenters use the Internet, too. Here's a simple example: a YouTube video may be watched by a million voters, but the comments below it could poke holes in the argument or provide links to websites with contradictory or embarrassing information. Worse, YouTube allows users to create response videos, and for a candidate the responses could be from political adversaries, aggressive dissenters, and others interested in sinking the campaign.

The Least You Need to Know

- Slogan memes are best when they are brief and memorable.
- Soapboxing occurs when a politician publicly defends his or her socioplex for the future.
- Successful politics requires compromising idealized memes.
- Simple memes are better used for getting into office; then, complex memes can be shared.
- The Internet has become a major tool for giving and receiving political messages.

Complex Memes

From toxic memes to memeplexes, from retromemes to dormant memes, there are dozens of different types of meme classifications that affect our everyday lives. Part 4 explores the more prominent types of memes, and helps us understand the complex ways that they can interact, combine, and sometimes form large structures of meaning.

Some memes are also dangerous, and chapters in Part 4 discuss malicious memes ranging from annoying hoaxes and scams, like chain letters and urban legends, to deadly memes that can influence their hosts to kill others or even themselves in the name of a memetically transmitted ideology. Along the way we look at end-of-the-world scenarios that spread like wildfire because the memes carry the idea of urgency and a desire to rescue as many people as possible.

Chapter 16 in Part 4 looks at how memes die, and whether they can ever be resurrected.

The Mischievous, Malicious Memes

In This Chapter

- Scams and schemes
- Hoaxes
- Origins of urban legends
- Dangerous memes

Before we get into complex types of memes, let's get one thing straight: memes don't have personalities. They're cultural ideas, and their only mission is to propagate and multiply.

That said, some memes have a more adverse effect on their environment than others. As an example, the '60s meme, "Give peace a chance" promoted a particular type of thought, while the classic King James Bible verse, "An eye for an eye," promotes a different set of ideas.

Here, we dive into what could be called mischievous, malicious memes.

Defining Malicious Memes

Mischievous, malicious memes are cultural ideas that can create chaos, loss, and even death to people who believe in them. Certain memes, such as "RickRolling," at worst cause a loss of productivity—but others, such as a money scam, can have serious consequences. In any malicious meme, the messenger wants something specific from the *mark*, or victim.

DEFINITION

The term **mark** comes from hucksters on turn-of-the-century boardwalks and midways. If a grifter spotted a guy or gal who seemed dumb enough to part with their money, he would come close and discretely mark the person's back with chalk. The other cons would then know that the person passing by was an easy mark.

We're going to look at four different types of mischievous, malicious memes:

- Scams
- Hoaxes
- Urban legends
- Conspiracy theories

Scams

There are plenty of schemes, traps, and grifts that people play, but a few characteristics make scams unique:

- They are always executed for money.
- They are done under anonymity.
- They are usually focused on one individual.

Scams always try to illicit cash from the mark, or victim, of the crime. Second, scams are usually done so the victim doesn't know the person. How is it possible to scam someone and not have them figure out who you are? In-person scammers wear disguises, make fake IDs, or fully flesh out a separate identity while doing the grift—and the temporary identity is tossed once the job is done.

Perhaps the most important distinction between scams and other malicious memes is that, despite the anonymity, the attack is personal. By personal, we don't mean that the con has a vendetta against the victim but that the con must get to know the person quickly to determine how likely it is he or she will fall for the scam.

In this sense, scams are deeply psychological. Experienced grifters can almost instantly know which memes to which a person is most vulnerable. When done in person, the grifter can read clothes, facial expressions, and demeanor. When over mail or e-mail, the con can read between the lines of a person's reply.

The Nigerian Scam

Scams are usually carried out in person, but certain ones, such as the Nigerian Scam, thrive in a text-only format. In fact, it works best this way, which is why the Internet blew up this long-running grift.

INFECTION!

Many a con has said that scams only work on greedy people. It may be some twisted Robin Hood justification for them doing dubious deeds, but the axiom is absolutely true. The best defense against a scam meme is to not be greedy.

The letter setup is simple:

- Offer a large sum of money.

- Ask for money to get the large sum of money.

- Receive the mark's money.

- Never give the promised money.

- Spend the received money as desired.

For instance, the letter or e-mail may go as follows:

"Dear Sir or Madam, I am sorry to trouble you as a stranger, but a colleague suggested that I reach out, and from your references, you seem trustworthy with my information and understanding of my dilemma. I am the new 15th Magistrate of Sunoki Town in Nigeria, and as part of my new role, I have access to my share of the city's wealth—about $15,000,000 U.S.D. The problem is that the money is currently locked into a Swiss bank account overseas, and to release the money immediately, it will require a small investment. I do not have much money, as what I am worth is tied into this account, but I would be most grateful to have your investment to access this money and give you 25 percent of the money. Is that enough? I would hate to insult you. I'm told the money can only be accessed this way within a 14-day period, so time is of the essence. Let me know when you'd like to proceed."

A well-crafted letter would take care to mention the total amount locked away but *not* to ask for a certain amount of money upfront. An aggressive play may scare off wiser individuals, and constantly interested in getting as much as possible, the scammer would want to wait for your reaction to gauge how much he or she could bilk you for.

The Nigerian Scam and others like it are called *advance-fee scams* because they get the mark to pay up front.

> **DEFINITION**
>
> An **advance-fee scam** requires the potential victim, or mark, to give the con money on the promise of getting more money back. Like a true scam meme, the grifter is lying about the money available and disappears after receiving the victim's cash. If the con suspects a particularly greedy victim, he or she will likely up the ante and suggest a bigger investment to get more money out of the mark.

The Internet provides a cloak of anonymity, so the Nigerian Scam seems tailored for the Web—but its history goes back much earlier. According to an excellent 2006 *New Yorker* article, the Nigerian Scam dates as far as the sixteenth century, when it was called the Spanish Prisoner Letter. Instead of e-mailing unsuspecting people about an African fortune, the scammers would write the English upper-crust about a rich official needing to be bailed out of Spanish jail.

The scam never went away, but mass e-mailing definitely brought the practice back into vogue: instead of writing one potential chump, a con could contact thousands at once. The Nigerian Scam seems more successful than ever, simply because of the odds.

To quote a Nigerian scammer interviewed in the media, "Now I have three cars, I have two houses, and I'm not looking for a job anymore."

Ponzi Schemes

As classic as the Nigerian Scam, Ponzi schemes are a slightly more complex way to use greed to bilk people out of their money.

The Ponzi scheme goes as follows:

- Offer an investment opportunity.
- Take the mark's money.
- Successfully offer an investment opportunity to two other marks.
- Take the two new marks' money.

- Give the two new marks' money to the original mark.

- Convince the original mark to invest *much* more money.

- Continue the cycle or disappear.

HAVE YOU HEARD?

The Ponzi scheme is named after Charles Ponzi, an Italian immigrant who successfully brought the technique to America around the turn of the twentieth century. It is unclear how old the scam actually is, but historians know Ponzi didn't invent the technique—he just happens to be the first famous case in modern times.

If you're sharp at math, you might have noticed the problem with the Ponzi scheme: it will eventually fail. The con must regularly recruit more individuals to accept the meme, but the more people involved, the more new marks he must find. Mathematically, it would never end. In fact, you could call the Ponzi scheme both a malicious meme—and, if it isn't stopped in time—a self-destructing meme! (Auto-toxic memes, which eventually destroy the host, are discussed in Chapter 17.) The best a scammer can hope for is to gain enough cash to disappear permanently between the cycles.

The most well-known Ponzi scheme of our time was carried out by New Yorker Bernie Madoff. The well-to-do stock broker used his investment firm to create a gigantic Ponzi scheme. When he was caught in 2008, an estimated $65 billion was missing from his clients. After a trial during which he was placed in protective custody because of death threats, Madoff was sentenced to 150 years in prison.

Hoaxes

If scams are committed for tangible goods such as money or property, hoaxes are memes that bring notoriety, power, or another intangible.

Hoaxes are usually committed for three reasons:

- Attention

- Power

- Curiosity

Attention

Attention is one of the main reasons people create hoaxes. Creating an awe-inspiring meme in our current age can give a person the admiration of the entire planet—if only for a few hours.

One of the bigger hoaxes in recent memory is the so-called Balloon Boy. In October 2009, a Colorado dad watched helplessly as his homemade spherical balloon floated up into the air. The twist was that his young son, ironically named Falcon, was inside the balloon. America tuned into the major TV networks to watch the Armed Forces try to contain the free-floating object without harming the child within it. The "Balloon Boy" took over conversations on Twitter as thousands provided play-by-play commentary as more news came in. The balloon finally crash landed at day's end—with no little boy inside. A few hours later, authorities found Falcon hiding under a box in his family's attic.

PASS IT ON

One of the best indicators of U.S. pop culture is Halloween, a virtual cornucopia of the biggest memes. On Halloween 2009, the most popular costume by far was Balloon Boy, often with a helium balloon tied to the back—or, perhaps more appropriately—a cardboard box on the head. In this sense, the hoax family got what it wanted: immortality.

It took a few days for authorities to confirm the intended hoax, especially after it was discovered that the father had been vying to get his family a reality television show. The father was given 90 days in jail for the Balloon Boy hoax and a $42,000 fine.

Power

Imagine getting people to believe exactly what you want them to believe. There is a certain intoxicating power when a person, or a group of people, is willing to believe anything you say to them—simply because they trust you.

It's one of the reasons why hucksters, grifters, and cons have a hard time leaving the profession. When asked why they kept breaking people's trusts—even when they didn't need to—many say it's the adrenaline rush from the hustle and knowing they have power over someone else.

Curiosity

The 48 Laws of Power author Robert Greene once wrote that our modern society has a veneer of niceties and rituals, but underneath it all we still have the same ruthless instincts and barely controllable desires as cave people. Things are more complicated now, because unlike previous societies, we have to keep these desires hidden.

An elaborate hoax can bring people's unfiltered feelings to light—something that, consciously or not, the meme messenger may desire to see.

> **INFECTION!**
>
> No offense to the Harry Houdinis and David Blaines of the world, but being a magician is the perfect profession for a hoax messenger. There is a great deal of attention on the performer—a sense of power because he or she is usually doing what others wouldn't dare—and great opportunities to explore human nature through the reaction of the audience. There is immediate feedback as to whether a meme is being accepted by the group.
>
> Of course, the entire goal is to fool the audience into seeing one thing when they are actually experiencing something quite different.

In October 1994, American Susan Smith called the police and reported that her car had been stolen—with her toddler and her baby in the back seat. She identified the suspect as a young African American man. Because it occurred shortly after the Rodney King–inspired Los Angeles riots and other minority-based acts of violence and theft, people in her small South Carolina town believed the young Caucasian woman and shared disparaging ideas about African Americans.

After nine days of making pleas on morning news shows and inciting a nationwide manhunt, Smith confessed that she wasn't carjacked at all. She drove her kids to a local lake, and while driving toward the water, jumped out of the vehicle. The children drowned.

Smith engineered the gruesome hoax to literally get away with murder, but the fact that she claimed an African American man was the culprit played into the stereotypes, fears, and issues people still have in America in general (and in the deep South in particular). The confession had many people eating their words, embarrassed by the racist things they said—and, perhaps, curious as to whether they would have caught on to her hoax sooner if race had not been a factor.

Urban Legends

Urban legends are myths that play on people's fears of the moment. The term "urban legend" could stem from the scary myths countryside folks heard about the big cities in the late 1800s. As Erik Larson emphasized in his nonfiction book *The Devil in the White City: A Saga of Magic and Murder at the Fair that Changed America*, upwardly mobile women would leave home to work in the big city—in this case, Chicago—and never be heard from again because of a malicious crime or a travel mishap. Unlike now, the suburbs didn't exist at the time and most people still lived in the country, so urban cities seemed like the most dangerous part of America.

INFECTION!

When it comes to urban legends, remember that they are not only caused by the creators and the people who pass them on. Not demystifying an urban legend gives it just as much power as sharing it with others, as it gives it the opportunity to keep "living"!

There can be many reasons to create an urban legend:

- To protect
- To imagine
- To believe

Urban legends are created for reasons much more complex than just fear.

Created to Protect

In the eyes of a concerned individual, an urban legend can help protect people they care about from harm—even if it means lying to them.

For example, a myth told by parents to young teenagers is that you can get pregnant from kissing. It makes absolutely no sense (biologically or otherwise!), but the goal isn't to help the child learn anatomy. The intention is to prevent the child from being physically intimate at all, which can circumvent major issues such as pregnancy, sexually transmitted diseases, clouded judgment, and so on.

The problem, of course, is that a warning not based on fact actually blindsides people from real trouble. In the same example, a "smart" teenager might take the myth to heart and do everything *but* kiss! There are sheltered teens and young adults who have gotten into serious situations because of a myth passed on by their partner, their friends, or their parents.

Unfortunately, urban legends can create an inordinate amount of damage, despite coming from a place of love and protection.

Created to Imagine

Life can be pretty boring, so urban legends can be created to, well, liven things up.

One urban legend is Bloody Mary, a long-time tradition at teenage girl slumber parties. The legend goes as such: light a candle, turn all the lights out, stare in a mirror, and say "Bloody Mary" 13 times. Say it passionately enough, and "Bloody Mary" will jump out of the mirror and take off your face. Ouch!

Urban legends are like lies in that there is a kernel of truth from which they grow, and believe it or not, Bloody Mary is no exception. Historians say Bloody Mary could be based on Mary I of England, the icy queen who used to bathe in the blood of virgins to stay young. There are a lot of Marys throughout history, however, and a lot of adult women who still have their faces.

Created to Believe

People can be moved by ideology, but they are more often called by a symbol or a martyr who represents the ideology. Urban legends can be created for inspiration and belief.

PASS IT ON

Craving more urban legends and myth debunking? Visit Snopes: Rumor Has It, a website dedicated to dubious history. It offers more than 40 categories, including Horror, Luck, Racial Rumors, and Science. Each rumor, labeled true or false, is followed by a description of the meme, its possible origin, and reasons why it is or isn't factual. The website is located at www.snopes.com.

The world was caught off guard by Haiti's 7.0 earthquake on January 12, 2010. The poor island nation lost its fragile infrastructure, and tens of thousands of citizens were dead, injured, or trying to escape. The world seemed eager to help, and within the first day, two companies were portrayed as leaders. American Airlines would fly doctors and volunteers to Haiti for free, and the United Parcel Service (UPS) would deliver supplies for free. The problem was that neither was true. It took days of damage control—not to mention a front-page CNN article—for the rumors to stop.

This urban legend may have inspired people to give, but it also created chaos and confusion by both delaying any real efforts being carried out by the two companies and giving false hope to suffering family members, eager volunteers, and caregivers interested in getting involved.

Conspiracy Theories

Another meme that tends to cause problems is the one that persuades people to cling doggedly to a belief even after it has been disproved. Some scientists, for instance, continue to try and prove an old theory even after most of their colleagues have moved on to new ideas. We tend to think of the Copernican revolution—the cosmological theory that placed the sun at the center of the universe, rather than Earth—as a sudden enlightenment, but it actually took more than 150 years before a majority of astronomers had accepted the theory.

This conservatism in the face of new ideas is not necessarily a bad thing. In Chapter 20, we will see how conservatism can be a defense against malicious memes.

But sometimes, this conservatism goes beyond simple caution or skepticism—and then is in danger of becoming a *conspiracy theory*.

DEFINITION

A **conspiracy theory** is the usually far-fetched idea that an organization or group is manipulating weaker individuals. From a memetic perspective, it is usually a meme-complex or memeplex (see Chapter 14) that carries within itself auto-immune memes that attempt to protect the memeplex from infection by other memes.

One of the most effective ways of protecting itself is to cause the host to believe that any criticism of the memeplex is itself part of the conspiracy. Evidence against the theory is merely held up as proof of how wide-ranging the conspiracy is.

Conspiracy theories range from relatively contained ones, such as the belief that the moon landings were faked on an Arizona soundstage, to widespread theories that have some potentially dangerous implications for security, such as the theories that the U.S. government was responsible for the September 11, 2001, terrorist attacks.

Other conspiracy theories simply boggle the mind. In Chapter 16, we look at flat Earth theories, which require their adherents to believe that a round Earth is a vast conspiracy involving astronomers, cosmologists, rocket scientists, entire government agencies, the designers and builders of both publicly and privately funded satellites and rockets, all agencies who use satellite photography, and all pilots and passengers of very high-flying aircraft, from which the curvature of the earth is readily apparent.

How Conspiracy Theories Develop

Over the next couple chapters, we will look at ways in which memes can work together to support each other, eventually resulting in vast structures or memeplexes. A religion is a commonly used example of a memeplex.

Memes that ask a host to believe something outrageous are unlikely to survive very long, so most conspiracy theories start their lives as small, believable snippets—the sorts of things you talk about over the water cooler or in the bar after work. Perhaps someone has doubts about some official explanation for a crime or other events and seeks clarification.

INFECTION!

"Just because you're paranoid, that doesn't mean they're not after you."

—Author Joseph Heller in *Catch-22*

In a democracy, many people have a healthy skepticism for the explanations of elected officials, who we think always have one eye on the next election. This is a pretty widely spread meme, and if our friend with the question doesn't get a satisfactory answer about the crime, the two memes might join up to form something like an "official cover-up" co-meme.

As the cover-up meme starts to spread, other memes get involved. There may be other "cover-up" memes going around, and if two are similar, they might join and turn the cover-up into a major piece of official corruption. Note that at this point, our suspicious friend might be absolutely right, but that doesn't matter to the memes—whose purpose is to replicate, regardless of the truth or otherwise of their content.

Self-Defense

Another common meme that we find in many situations might be called the "You're either with me or against me" meme. If this meme is somehow co-opted by the growing memeplex, we are close to a fully fledged conspiracy theory. Explanations or excuses that don't accept the growing memeplex are seen as part of the corruption, and as the conspiracy seems to become wider and wider, the hosts are compelled to warn more and more people about it.

PASS IT ON

Part of the "bait" that a meme uses to get itself passed on is that good feeling someone gets when they do a good deed—warning a friend about a coming storm or recommending a good book, for example. Political ideologies and religions reward evangelism by giving hosts the feeling that they are making the world a better place. Warning your friends about a hidden conspiracy does the same thing and encourages the host to spread the meme.

In Chapter 13, we look at the conspiracy theories surrounding the assassination of President John F. Kennedy. One interesting thing to note about this phenomenon is the speed with which conspiracy theories grow. It took barely three years to turn from a vague belief in the cover-up of a bungled investigation to the belief that the assassination was a vast conspiracy from within the government itself.

In time, the conspiracy theory will have a wide range of defensive memes for protecting itself against infection. The host might believe that he or she has special insights that the dupes can't see or that critics are actually agents of the conspiracy itself. The memeplex might have ways of expelling memes that are diverging from orthodoxy, such as the ways in which cults and narrow sects often have purges of members who have lost the faith.

Back to our suspicious friend at the water cooler: he wasn't necessarily buying into a conspiracy theory when he started thinking that he wasn't getting the full story, but slowly the memes formed around the idea, dragging him along with them. It's not hard to fall for things when they happen this way, and probably most of us have woken up at some stage thinking, "How did I believe that?"

But don't worry. In Chapter 20, we'll show you some ways you can protect yourself against malicious memes.

The Least You Need to Know

- Scams are carried out for money while hoaxes are usually committed for attention.
- The popular Nigerian Scam goes back at least to the sixteenth century.
- Ponzi schemes take from one victim to pay the previous victim.
- Urban legends blossomed as more people moved from the country to the city.
- Conspiracy theories are created when people believe a memeplex is suppressing the truth—usually about dastardly deeds.

The Marching Retromemes

In This Chapter

- Understanding retromemes
- Memes infecting other memes
- Memes joining together
- Neutralizing memes
- Ineffective retromemes

"Retromemes" is an odd word, and there's a bit of confusion about what it means. *Retro*, of course, is the Latin prefix meaning "back," and it gives us words such as retrospective, retrograde, and retro-rocket. Things that are old-fashioned are often described as "retro." (Sometimes, even the latest, up-to-the-minute fashion is retro!)

A lot of people on the Web and elsewhere talk about retromemes as memes that have been around for a long time or are based on an old idea. One example is the phrase, "Move along. Nothing to see here," which has become the clichéd police crowd-control statement—but it's so old that no one knows when it was first used. It has been used in contexts from feature films to songs and in episodes of *The Simpsons* and *South Park*.

But there is a more technical meaning for retromeme, and that is the one we explore in this chapter. In this second case, retromeme is analogous to retrovirus, a type of virus that is composed of RNA rather than DNA and has the unique property of being able to copy its RNA into the DNA of the host cell, thus changing the cell's makeup and potentially leading to mutations such as cancers. HIV is a retrovirus.

Defining the Retromeme

Like a retrovirus, a retromeme transcribes a bit of itself into an existing meme, attempting to commandeer the original meme for its own purposes.

PASS IT ON

What's retro about a virus? The "retro" prefix is a reference to the way in which the virus transcribes its code into the nucleus of the host cell. Normally, DNA transcribes (the term for the way in which chromosomes are copied) an RNA copy. A retrovirus involves a reverse transcription—from RNA to DNA.

We will explain more about genetics and how it relates to memes in Chapter 21.

Retromemes produce results that are strange, unexpected, and often aren't of interest to the original creators.

Co-Opting Another Meme

The title track of the 1984 album *Born in the U.S.A.* by singer Bruce Springsteen is an up-tempo but sobering description of life in small-town America, with references to unemployment, hopelessness, crime, imprisonment, and ultimately the destruction and futility of the Vietnam War. Despite these downer lyrics, the anthemlike qualities of the song and the prominence of the Stars and Stripes on the album cover led to displays of flag waving and patriotism at Springsteen's concerts at the time, and the song started to gather a reputation as a patriotic anthem.

In September 1984, President Ronald Reagan, in his re-election campaign, referred to the song approvingly, saying it was a message of hope to young Americans (he presumably had never read the words!). Reagan's campaign even briefly used the song as its campaign anthem until Springsteen—a lifelong Democrat—asked them to stop.

The Republican campaign was a retromeme, infecting Springsteen's song with a meaning almost the opposite of its original intention. In the process, the campaign not only altered the memetic content of the song but also piggybacked off the popularity of Springsteen and this song in particular. We don't know whether the song was instrumental in getting Reagan re-elected in 1984, but it must have helped.

The Internet has exploded the number of these types of retromemes. Check out Chapters 4 and 6 to get a refresher course on how art is co-opted, remixed, and used for purposes unintended by the original creator.

Divide and Conquer

A variation of the retromeme occurs when a meme that carries some political or other significance is neutralized and made to seem ordinary. An example of this retromeme is the Guy Fawkes meme.

Guy Fawkes was a British Catholic and member of the Gunpowder Plot that planned to blow up the British parliament in November 1605, killing King James I and most of the Lords. The plot was partly in protest of the way in which English Catholics were treated during the reign of James I and partly as the first strike in a rebellion that planned to place a Catholic monarch on the throne (James's daughter, Princess Elizabeth).

Fawkes was to detonate the 1,800 pounds of gunpowder placed in an undercroft beneath the Palace of Westminster, but the plot was discovered and the conspirators were executed. To mark his escape from assassination, the King decreed that November 5 should be a day of celebration, and very quickly the lighting of bonfires became an annual tradition. Even today, Guy Fawkes Night is celebrated in Britain and other parts of the Commonwealth with bonfires and fireworks.

HAVE YOU HEARD?

Periodically, someone will try to reinvigorate and repoliticize the Guy Fawkes story. During the 1970s, Fawkes's name was associated with various anarchist movements, and he was described as "the only man to enter Parliament with honest intentions."

The 2005 film *V for Vendetta* makes the character of Fawkes a freedom fighter in a totalitarian future, where he inspires the population to throw off their oppression.

No doubt for Catholics in Britain in the years following the plot, this celebration would have surreptitiously been a commemoration of Fawkes and the plot and a gesture of political defiance. However, over the years, this political aspect has faded, and Bonfire Night—as it is also called—has become a quaint tradition with little political significance (a retromeme with all its dangerous DNA removed).

Fawkes is no exception, as history shows us that the most complex and feared memes are often neutered when they return. Malcolm X was an intense, polemic leader within the African American and Islamic communities—killed in a hail of gunfire in 1965, likely because of his inspiring oration and controversial views. Three decades later, young, hip Americans wore his likeness, his letter "X," and his quotes (such as

"By all means necessary") on T-shirts, jackets, and medallions. To some of the later generations, the cultural warrior was a nice fashion statement. The same could be said for Fidel Castro, Che Guevera, and other figures of yesteryear.

Examples of Retromemes

The concept of the retromeme is sometimes hard to wrap your head around, so let's look at a few more examples.

Crazy for Light Foods

In recent years, there has been an increase in concern about health and fitness. In fact, as the average waistline has grown, so have the diet and health food industries. Take a wander down any supermarket aisle and you will see plenty of items marked "low-fat," "zero sugar," or "light" as manufacturers jump on the bandwagon and develop products that sound like they are better for us than the high-fat or high-sugar versions. The low-fat meme is particularly potent in these health-conscious times.

But here's an interesting thing: if you go to the olive oil section, you will probably find a variety of oil marketed as "light." Now, people who know their cooking oils will realize that the "light" refers to the color—light olive oil is paler and slightly milder in flavor. But many people will associate "light" with "low-fat" and buy that product because they think it contains less fat than other brands. In fact, cooking oils—apart from containing some food acids—are pretty much 100 percent fat!

INFECTION!

If you do any regular grocery shopping, you're probably aware that the olive oil meme is just one of literally hundreds of ideas pushed by corporations. Over the years, cholesterol, eggs, hard alcohol, wine, cigarettes, and red meat have all been trumpeted or trounced by public opinion—usually the result of a study, mishap, or diet trend.

The major shifts just over the past decade show one thing: there is no absolute truth.

Here, the olive oil meme (and all the health and authenticity issues associated with it) has infected the low-fat meme, trying to get itself replicated—along with the product it represents—by incorporating the implied benefits of the healthy product into a product that might appear to be unhealthy.

Killing for Religion

Here's another example. Many countries around the Middle East, western Asia, and northern Africa tend to be relatively underdeveloped because of the harshness of the environment and for a variety of historical and political reasons. These regions are often politically unstable as their citizens, frustrated with the levels of poverty, jump from one political or religious leader to another, seeking someone who can solve the intractable problems of the region. In these situations, memes of intolerance often lead to periods of political unrest or even civil war.

In recent years and in some places, these intolerance memes have become retromemes, infecting existing religious memes and altering that meme's DNA from "this religion is a good way to find God" to "this religion is the *only* way to find God, and anyone who disagrees should be killed." Thus, out of poverty and despair comes a virulent new strain of intolerant religious fundamentalism, and the world has to contend with suicide bombers.

A good example would be the effect of the events of September 11, 2001, on Islamic culture. Islamic extremists took credit for these attacks on the World Trade Center, the Pentagon, and the crash of four different major airline flights. The attackers represented only a tiny fraction of worshippers—hence the term "extremists"—but their extreme views were retrofitted onto the rest of Islamic culture. Islamic hate crimes jumped significantly in America and in countries with close American ties, although those attacked had absolutely no connection to acts of terrorism. A decade later, extreme prejudice toward Muslims is still a serious problem.

INFECTION!

Political groups regularly use retromemes to get their point across. For instance, People for the Ethical Treatment of Animals (PETA) illegally used the image of U.S. First Lady Michelle Obama in an advertisement. She was quoted as saying that she doesn't wear fur—which was enough for PETA to include her in its campaign. The White House was not pleased.

That's the subtext of retromemes—people automatically assume the original meme creator agrees with the new context. By including her in the ad, PETA implies that Michelle Obama approves of all of PETA's controversial actions.

For a better understanding of why religious extremism occurs, refresh yourself with Chapter 10. Chapters 17 and 19 go even deeper into the cultural idea.

Using a Children's Show for Political Means

Periodically, people with political agendas will try to hijack a meme and use it for their own purposes. But memes are impossible to control, and the attempt can make the person who tries it look foolish.

In 1999, televangelist Jerry Falwell tried to convince people that Tinky Winky—one of the four characters in the British preschool television show *Teletubbies*—was gay and that the show was spreading pro-gay propaganda. Falwell's evidence was that Tinky Winky was purple, had a triangle on his head, and carried a handbag.

HAVE YOU HEARD?

Most everyone is familiar with the popular *Sesame Street* characters Bert and Ernie. They were created by Jim Henson for the Children's Television Workshop (now Sesame Workshop) in order to show two roommates who were quite different in personality, interests, and appearance but who could still get along and remain friends.

The fact that the puppets are portrayed as sleeping in the same room, albeit in separate beds, has led to some speculation that they might represent gay lovers. Despite repeated denials from the creators, some gay activists have tried to hijack the pair—the gay tolerance retromeme infecting the acceptance meme and associating the familiar characters with the gay rights movement.

This attempted retromeme takeover probably played well to Falwell's constituency but more broadly was less successful, reflecting worse on Falwell than on the fictional character.

Co-Memes

One final type of retromeme is the co-meme, also known as a symmeme. In this situation, two memes have co-evolved, forming a *symbiotic* relationship that benefits both memes.

The assassination of President John F. Kennedy in 1963 was a dramatic, shocking event. The assassination of any world leader is rare, and the compelling film footage by Abraham Zupruder, coupled with the outpouring of national grief in the days that followed, ensured that the event would quickly become a potent meme. In fact, it led to the common phrase, "Where were you when J. F. K. was shot?"—which has since spread to other major events, such as the Apollo 11 moon landing, the death of

Princess Diana, and the toppling of the Berlin Wall. In years to come, people will probably ask where you were when Michael Jackson died.

 DEFINITION

Symbiotic means the relationship between two things (usually beneficial). In memes, the term describes the co-meme or symmeme relationship, when two ideas build and feed off each other.

In the days immediately after Kennedy's assassination, questions were asked about whether Lee Harvey Oswald acted alone, as the investigation claimed, or whether he was part of a conspiracy. There are sufficient doubts about elements of the case, including the following:

- The number of bullets fired

- The direction of the shots

- Oswald's required marksmanship

- How many people were involved

- Whether Kennedy's own government had him killed

Movies, books, and even clubs are dedicated to that one autumn afternoon in Texas. It has become a fertile area for conspiracy theories.

As we discussed in Chapter 12, a conspiracy theory is a particular type of meme-complex, or memeplex, in which different memes work together to protect and help replicate the meme. We'll look at the memeplex in more detail in Chapter 14, but for now it's enough to know that they co-opt memes for rewarding transmission, memes for punishing nonconformity, and even auto-immune memes that protect the memeplex from external attack.

It didn't take long for the conspiracy theory meme to join with the potent J. F. K. assassination meme to form a particularly virulent "J. F. K. assassination conspiracy" co-meme. A survey as recently as 2003 suggested that 70 percent of Americans believe that Oswald acted as part of a conspiracy, while the themes and structures of the co-meme have provided the template for other conspiracy theories, such as the moon landing hoax meme and the growing number of September 11 conspiracy theory memes, right up to the theories of anti-Obama "Birthers" (people who suspect that President Barack Obama isn't an American citizen).

The advantages of co-meme evolution are clear: when already successful memes combine, the new meme is usually assured of a good chance of replicating. In the next chapter, we'll look at complexes of many memes that form large structures of meaning.

The Least You Need to Know

- Memes can infect other memes, changing their original meanings or purposes, as when a protest song is used to promote war or a peaceful religion inspires an unforgiving belief system.
- A meme change can be effected deliberately or through the natural selection of the meme.
- Memes can evolve together, forming more virulent strains that are even harder to resist.
- Sometimes parts of a meme can be neutralized so that what once was a powerful political message can become merely an empty tradition.
- Connected retromemes are called co-memes or symmemes.

The Layered Memeplex

In This Chapter

- Defining memeplexes
- Evolving memeplexes
- Memes referring to other memes
- Understanding corporate memes

In Chapter 13, we touched on the idea of co-memes, or symmemes, wherein two memes form a symbiotic relationship that benefits both parties. If the coevolution of two memes can create a more virulent strain with a better chance of survival, think how much more successful memes would be if they teamed up into big groups—all building on and reinforcing each other.

In this chapter, we consider the ways in which memes can grow into large, articulated structures, or memeplexes.

Defining the Memeplex

A meme-complex or memeplex is an association of similar memes that work together to assist in the survival of the participating memes. This idea was proposed by Richard Dawkins at the birth of memetics. He drew it as an analogy to the gene complex, which describes the ways in which mutually suitable characteristics evolve together in different species. For example, the teeth, claws, and digestive systems of carnivores are different from those of herbivores and contribute to the survival of the species. A lion with hooves wouldn't last very long!

As we saw in Chapter 13, conspiracy theories can build up very elaborate memeplexes in which different memes support belief in the underlying theory. In these cases, almost anything can be incorporated into the memeplex; even criticism of, or opposition to, the theory becomes just more evidence of how widespread the conspiracy is!

Building a Memeplex

Remember that memes are hard to control. Once they have left the original host, they can develop in different ways. A meme might be co-opted by a retromeme (see Chapter 13) and made into something else entirely; it might join with another meme that makes it evolve in other ways.

A Collaborative Effort (Sort of)

With a memeplex, we might say that there are many memes working collaboratively to ensure the survival of the complex, but this description makes it sound a bit too much like the memes are consciously cooperating with each other. Of course, nothing of the sort is happening. Memes are blind pieces of information that live in the minds of their hosts. They replicate because that is what they do. A memeplex is not a consciously built structure such as an ant colony; instead, it's a randomly built conceptual structure—and the memes that create it are there because they fit. Memes that don't fit with the structure soon die out. The meme for accepting authority simply wouldn't get picked up in the conspiracy theory memeplex because it is incompatible with all the other memes.

Removing Useless Memes and Unconsciously Preserving Others

In highly structured memeplexes, those in control need to be constantly vigilant in weeding out aberrant or contradictory memes. The history of the Christian church is full of controversies about doctrine, and the great councils of the early church—such as the Council of Nicaea in 325 C.E. and the Council of Ephesus in 431 C.E.—were called to codify which memes were allowed and which were not. The foundational creeds of the church date from this time.

INFECTION!

Some people may be uncomfortable with the example of religion as a memeplex and may be inclined to dismiss the entire theory because of it. But remember, memetics is about the replication of ideas, not about truth. That we consider the Christian faith a memeplex doesn't make it less real or less truthful. One of the most successful memeplexes of modern times is the science of memetics, and this book is merely one vector in its replication.

Richard Dawkins is a renowned atheist who writes and lectures on atheism and religion as well as biology. Dawkins's prime example of the memeplex is religion. Inevitably, he draws many of his examples of pernicious memes from religion, which he typifies as using a variety of threats and promises to trick people into following the rules of the priests. He sees the architecture, rituals, laws, music, art, and written traditions of religions as forming a set of mutually assisting memes. For instance, many nonreligious people still love and reproduce the art and music of different religions—Handel's *Messiah* or the intricate patterns of Islamic geometric art—and in the process continue to unconsciously support the memeplex as a whole.

The Corporation as a Memeplex

Let's consider a common memeplex. A large corporation might employ hundreds or even thousands of people; have associates in the form of customers, clients, partners, and suppliers numbering even more; and maintain links to a variety of industry, government, and public-sector institutions. It will have a carefully managed set of practices, covering its internal and external financial dealings, its human resources obligations, its service provision, and other matters dealing with running the corporation. It will also have, implicitly or explicitly, a company credo, a mission statement, a series of assumptions about the goals of the corporation, and a company history that may or may not share details with what actually happened.

All this activity is governed by a series of practices that are based in the corporate culture of the company, and that corporate culture is maintained by a complex interaction of memes.

The sets of memes fall into four broad areas:

- Fundamental memes

- Public-relations memes

- Rules memes

- Unspoken memes

Each area has a different, but equally necessary part in helping the memeplex function.

Fundamental Memes

At the base of the memeplex are fundamental memes such as service, profitability, loyalty, and duty. They, in turn, mobilize other memes such as respect for authority, reward through hard work, and conformity over individuality.

INFECTION!

In his book *Outliers,* author Malcolm Gladwell argues that fundamental ideas, often based on stereotypes, can be self-fulfilling. For example, if a particular race is thought to be good with numbers, their families and social networks will be more apt to encourage mathematic careers early. As a result, they are more likely to become accountants—which ends up confirming the theory! It is a cycle that often reinforces stereotypes.

Other well-established memes might get co-opted into the memeplex. The Protestant work ethic is a powerful meme that for centuries has been convincing people that hard work is its own reward. This is a very convenient meme to have on hand if you employ hundreds of people! Many businesses have dress codes, which is a memetic way of controlling employees.

Public-Relations Memes

The company might work hard to develop a corporate image that shows consistent branding across all its departments—marketing, finance, public relations, and so on. This image is also the result of memes.

The company logo will try to evoke particular ideas in its iconography, and this will be influenced by memes that code for, say, simplicity, elegance, or sophistication. The IBM logo—bold capital letters behind horizontal stripes—stands for solid dependence and reliability. The meme that suggests a casual playfulness—the eBay logo, for instance—would be out of place in IBM's culture and cut out of the memeplex.

The same memes will also influence the architecture of the building. The memes for ostentatious and conspicuous consumption might lead to the large, marble-paved foyers you often see in banks and finance institutions (money allowing, of course), while other companies might prefer a smaller, less-confrontational entrance with wooden floors and natural lighting (but which is nevertheless in keeping with the corporate culture). Again, all are governed by the memes that support the entire complex.

Rules Memes

There will also be meme conflicts to manage. If the company has a retail arm, it is quite likely that there will be a place for the "customer is always right" meme. But most corporate memeplexes will also contain memes having to do with professionalism, product knowledge, and respect. As the corporation has grown, it will have found ways to manage the tension between staff owning their product knowledge and allowing customers to dictate the terms of the encounter. These meme-controlling structures are the policy manuals and how-to guides that every corporation generates.

These manuals will also mandate against the potential for random breakouts of memes, such as the *Casual Friday* meme, which encourages people in some organizations to show up for work in relaxed dress, such as jeans and T-shirts.

DEFINITION

Casual Friday is a tradition in many U.S. and Canadian businesses that is slowly spreading to other countries. Also called dress-down Friday, it's the day of the week when the company's dress code is relaxed. Casual Friday is seen as a morale-building exercise for workers in carefully managed situations.

Casual Friday is an interesting meme because psychologists tell us that happy workers are more productive, so it really works for the benefit of the company.

Every organization, institution, or other grouping of human practices conceals a memeplex that maintains, but also influences, the institutional structure. In some instances, the memeplex might get out of control completely, leading to industrial action, sabotage, or a takeover by staff. A company that cannot change its memeplex quickly enough in new circumstances runs the risk of becoming irrelevant and going out of business.

Unspoken Memes

Finally, there is a set of ideas that are never addressed directly—at least, until they are violated. For instance, when in a meeting, it may be corporate tradition to wait for the CEO to sit down before sitting yourself. It is part of protocol—a meme that is woven into the company's culture as much as the logo, the mission statement, and the dress code. Not following this virtually hidden meme can be terribly offensive to believers, but in a corporate structure, the newcomer isn't likely to be pulled aside. Instead, the believers will think the individual "doesn't fit within the company" or "just doesn't get it."

Going to Harvard Law School, being a Kappa, or doing a Marine tour is noteworthy—but for different reasons than you may think. Corporations and the people within bond over such experiences not only because of the knowledge gained but also because individuals raised in the "right" culture do not need to be taught much to become part of the memeplex. They already know most of the unspoken memes. These unspoken memes are what create challenges for outsiders trying to become part of the memeplex. In corporate-speak, it is the *glass ceiling*.

DEFINITION

The **glass ceiling** is the idea that a person can climb the corporate ladder only so far because of demographic or cultural differences. It is usually used in reference to women in a male-dominated environment.

Originally used to describe the limits of women in the workplace, the glass ceiling has spawned quite a few different phrases:

- "Reverse racism"—limited growth opportunities at a minority-run organization for a person in the majority population

- "Old boys' club"—limited growth opportunities at an older male–run organization for a female or racial minority

- "Obsessed with youth"—limited growth opportunities at a young adult–run organization for a person older than a certain age

What is interesting is that although these instances can stem from flat-out racism, sexism, or ageism, they are just as likely to be about the *fear* of someone not understanding the culture. As an example, an all-male law firm may assume that a female lawyer will crumble under its intense cases. The assumption is based on the collective perception of women; that is, the view of women decided within the corporate memeplex. It may take an extraordinary amount of work for a woman to get into the organization, much less to thrive in it, for she not only must prove her own worth but also shift the actual memeplex with her ideas.

In short, corporate glass ceilings aren't necessarily about blind discrimination but about the stereotypical assumption that a particular type of person can understand the culture of the memeplex only to a certain point.

The Role of Bait in a Memeplex

One very effective way in which memes survive is by combining replication behavior with reward behavior—using bait to spread the meme. This process is probably how memeplexes start to evolve. To survive in this manner, the meme must offer an appetizing reward and fulfill a primitive need.

An Appetizing Reward

The simplest meme is the one that says, "Copy me." The problem, however, is that it isn't a very good meme. Sure, if the cost isn't too high you might pass on the meme, but it's unlikely unless there is some additional reason for you to make the effort. So a joke is a meme that says, "Copy me, and you'll get a laugh." That's better but still unlikely to result in a high level of replication.

What if the "Copy me" meme joined forces with the fear meme—"Copy me or you'll have bad luck"—or better, the greed meme—"Copy me and Bill Gates will send you $1,000"? Now, there is a reason to obey the meme's instructions! The chain letters and hoaxes we looked at in Chapter 12 all follow this formula. Of course, there are other co-memes than fear and greed. Some memes appeal to our better natures— "Copy me and make the dying child happy" or "Copy me to warn your friends."

Memeticists from Dawkins to Susan Blackmore (a post-Dawkins researcher we'll talk about in Chapter 22) have claimed that evangelism is little more than "Copy me or you'll be punished in the afterlife," but others might see it as "Copy me and save your friends from damnation."

PASS IT ON

Memeticists often refer to rewards such as promises of wealth or punishments such as bad luck as the bait that memes use to influence hosts to spread them. But maybe there's more to it. Psychologists talk about internal feelings of well-being that are associated with the satisfaction of doing a job well or achieving a goal.

Could it be that memes and genes evolving together have created the perfect scenario? No longer requiring an external reward, certain memes become their own reward. For example, I don't have to be rewarded for donating to the charity, because the feeling of well-being is enough to encourage the behavior.

Large and complex memeplexes still use this simple model to ensure replication. The rewards that religion offers are payable in abstract, feel-good ways and in the afterlife; the rewards offered by a corporation memeplex involve the promise of advancement, wealth, or power.

Fulfillment of Primitive Needs

As we will examine in Chapter 21, underlying most memes are primitive human drives left over from our prehistoric development—the most powerful involving food, sex, and fear. The memes that can tap into these primordial urges are better able to influence behavior and get passed on. A meme might no longer be able to bait a potential host with the promise of food, but the promise of security is still a powerful drive—and we have seen how effective the appeal to greed is.

It's not that memeplexes discovered that they needed to bait potential hosts in order to get themselves replicated; it's more likely that the ones that didn't use bait simply ceased to exist.

Understanding Meta-Memes

One final version of the memeplex is a rather specific example. A meta-meme is simply a meme about memes. In many ways, the science of memetics is a meta-meme—an idea that spread slowly at first, but as it infected more and more people, it became better known and was replicated more often until there was even a *Complete Idiot's Guide* to the concept!

At a slightly more abstract level, there are memes that implicitly refer to other memes and can therefore be considered meta-memes. One such meme is tolerance. The tolerance meme influences its host to accept other memes on merit, without dismissing them until they can be critically examined. The flip side of the tolerance meme is the intolerance meme, which influences its host to reject other memes immediately.

Some memeplexes contain within themselves memes that are intended to limit the influences of other memes. As we will see in Chapter 19, most religions carry a meme that insists the religion is the only true path to God. Similarly, as we saw, conspiracy theories have autoimmune systems so that every potential counter-meme is immediately dismissed as part of the conspiracy and therefore is unable to infect the memeplex.

These meta-memes are an important part of the memeplex, forming its defenses against infection and co-option. Without them, the memeplex would be less stable.

The Least You Need to Know

- Two or more memes can work together to support each other.
- Large groups of memes are called a memeplex.
- Some memeplexes use bait, such as an appetizing reward and the fulfillment of a primitive need, to snare a host willing to spread the meme.
- Meta-memes are memes that refer to other memes.
- Memeplexes reject or eliminate conflicting memes to survive.

The Doomsday Millennial Memes

In This Chapter

- A history of Chicken Little
- The year 2012
- Millennial memebots
- The psychology of fear
- False prophets

Doomsday. Apocalypse. Judgment Day. Each of these sayings conveys a series of ideas, visions, and stereotypes humans have feared throughout time. You can almost picture the old man walking down the street with a slightly crazed look in his eye, wearing a sandwich board that says, "THE END IS NIGH!"

From early B.C.E. to the year 1999, people have predicted that humans are in their last days. But why? Why would we *want* to think we're going to die?

In this chapter, we'll take a look at the doomsday memes and figure out why they're popular, where they come from, and what people gain from being the bearer of bad news.

Defining Doomsday Memes

A doomsday meme is the idea that most, if not all, of the human race will die from a particular event at a specific time.

There are quite a few ways it can be disseminated:

- Passed from person to person like an urban legend

- Described in a religious text or sermon

- Declared by a leader

As you can gather from the name, doomsday memes are usually extreme prophecies, such as multiheaded demons coming down from the sky, a thousand-year nuclear winter, or Earth imploding. And you usually can't do anything to prevent it from happening, unless it is part of a cult's mythology and a specific ritual must be performed to survive the apocalypse.

Like all life and death–related cultural ideas, doomsday memes, once accepted, have a high chance of creating *memebots*—people consumed by an idea.

 DEFINITION

A **memebot** is a person completely controlled by a meme. It is an obsession with a particular cultural idea.

A History of Chicken Little

Some of us growing up heard the story of Chicken Little and his chaotic situation. More of us may never have heard the story but know the basic meme and are familiar with the concept. (You need not have read the Dracula books to know he bit people on the neck.)

You might know the gist, but the Chicken Little story (also known as *The Sky Is Falling*), is worth breaking down because of its awesome millennial meme relevance.

A Children's Story

Dating back to B.C.E., "Chicken Little" is usually attributed to the classic writer Aesop.

HAVE YOU HEARD?

Most children are familiar with Aesop's fables, including "The Boy Who Cried Wolf," "The Tortoise and the Hare," and the aforementioned "Chicken Little," but not much is known about the prolific writer. Aesop was allegedly a Greek slave in the sixth century B.C.E., but even that has been questioned because some historians believe he was an African slave in Greece.

We actually don't know much more than that, but in many ways the mystery makes his memes feel more pure. Like the equally mysterious Homer—who historians now believe might have been a group of people—the lack of personal information on Aesop leaves his work the only thing being judged. The undecorated narrator keeps the memes within the story clear and easy to understand.

In the parable and its variants, Chicken Little is quietly resting below a tree on his farm. A strong wind blows, shaking an acorn out of the tree and onto his head. Suddenly startled, Chicken Little jumps up and thinks the sky is falling.

"The sky is falling! The sky is falling! The end is near!" he begins shouting to other folks on the farm. He runs to the cow, who in turn runs to the rooster and tells him. The rooster tells the mouse as the cow runs to the cat, and Chicken Little himself talks to the pig. Then, the rooster … well, you get the idea.

Not among Chicken Little's friends is the sly fox. He's not welcome on the farm, but he is carefully watching the chaos. Like a horror movie, the fox waits until the moment each animal is alone and carefully picks it off. After running in circles, panicking and shouting for minutes, the tired animals are no match for the energetic fox.

The most common ending has Chicken Little quietly realizing that the sky isn't falling. He finds his remaining friends and apologizes for overreacting—just in time to see the real danger, the sly fox. Now that they aren't panicking, the animals are able to be present, work together, and kick the fox off the farm for good.

The simple tale has many doomsday memetic lessons:

- Avoiding the most logical conclusion
- Unquestioning absorption of a meme
- Premature passing of a meme
- Missing the big picture

Let's look at each piece.

Avoiding the Most Logical Conclusion

Feeling a little bump on his head, Chicken Little ignored the fact that he was under a tree, which presumably shed a loose acorn. Instead, he went straight for the most dramatic conclusion.

We won't even hypothesize why people (or chickens) look for emotional drama: you'll want to pick up Joni E. Johnson's *The Complete Idiot's Guide to Psychology* for that. However, we will say that it isn't unusual for humans to be attracted to the more dramatic conclusion just because it's more interesting.

One meme in this regard is using Earth's climate changes as a doomsday indicator. Looking at the evidence:

- The major ice caps are melting, making the sea levels rise and pushing both humans and animals out of their usual habitats.

- Water storms are becoming more prevalent and seemingly larger, as was the case with 2005's Hurricane Katrina on the Gulf Coast.

- Traditionally warm areas now experience colder winters, while colder areas have warmer summers.

- The earth's overall temperature has increased over the last three decades.

Depending on what meme is absorbed, these facts are proof of global warming—or, more obliquely—proof that the apocalypse is starting. Or, in more cynical terms, would you rather feel responsible for the earth and have to make sacrifices in your lifestyle or bear witness to the end of human kind, not unlike some awesome disaster movie? We're the same human race that, during the height of the enlightened Roman era, thought feeding people to lions was cool. We've done odder things for entertainment.

INFECTION!

While we authors have our personal opinions, it's important to recognize that the global warming idea is a meme, too! A significant contingent of scientists firmly believes that the temperature changes are natural and our part in them is minimal, if nonexistent. To keep a fairly independent mind, it's important to consider popular memes carefully—even if they're from a bunch of scientists.

Unquestioning Absorption of a Meme

In the next part of the story, Chicken Little ran around the farm warning everyone of the clear and present danger. Notice, however, that there weren't any other objects that hit his head. Was there further evidence that the sky was falling? No. The apocalyptic meme was already in motion, though, so contradictory ideas didn't matter. Observation becomes a selective process.

The world is a big place, and as a result of our tight communication systems, information travels fast. Natural disasters great and small occur regularly, whether it's a mudslide in Fresno or an earthquake in Japan (in fact, minor earthquakes happen across Japan nearly every single day!). The earth is a living thing that jiggles, tosses, and turns.

Set yourself in a doomsday frame of mind, however, and the daily newspaper reads as further proof of man's finality. The human mind is excellent at seeing what it wants to see and ignoring the rest.

Premature Passing of a Meme

Chicken Little had literally an acorn of evidence (sorry, we couldn't help ourselves) to go on when he decided to spread the meme to all his friends. It sounds altruistic, because Chicken Little cares about his buddies and wants them to be safe. Chicken Little gets something out of the deal, too: power.

For instance, in the mid-1970s, television evangelist Pat Robertson had a prediction he needed to share with the world: in 1982, the final judgment would happen as predicted in the King James Bible. It got *The 700 Club* host plenty of national, if not international, attention and certainly helped him increase his flock. When the time came, the most dramatic thing to happen in 1982 was Michael Jackson's *Thriller*. Robertson would also predict a 2006 U.S. tsunami—a weather phenomenon that doesn't happen around America—and a 2007 U.S. terrorist attack—which also didn't happen—and several other visions he said he received from God.

The point isn't whether Robertson actually received these false alarms from his God—that's his issue. The point is that there is a strong human temptation to be the messenger. Despite the dangers pointed out by the famous axiom, "Don't kill the messenger," there are several things to be gained from being the deliverer of news both good and bad:

- Power

- Respect

- Attention

The power comes from knowing something other people don't know yet—and, by telling them, you're making sure that they know this fact, too! Furthermore, what if you decided not to tell them, as if Chicken Little kept his "secret" and ran off to save himself? Either subconsciously or explicitly, other people understand this power you have over their well-being.

The respect comes from you being privy to a knowledge resource, whether it's your high intellect or your direct link to a higher power.

As a result, attention comes from people being curious about what you're going to say next. It may change their life.

> **PASS IT ON**
>
> Did you ever notice how some prophetic cult leaders will destroy themselves and their flock as a way to "save" the community? It can be gruesome and delusional, but the ritual also saves the leader from perhaps a worse aftermath: being proven wrong.

With every misfire, Robertson seems to lose credibility within the general public, not unlike Chicken Little. It's no coincidence that Aesop also wrote "The Boy Who Cried Wolf."

Missing the Big Picture

In the final act, Chicken Little finally calms down and accepts that his meme is incorrect but is horrified that, while he was focused on a nonexistent problem, a real terror—the sly fox—was gobbling up his friends.

The biggest danger to accepting a doomsday meme is the weakened state of mind. Notice how none of Chicken Little's friends pulled him aside and said something like, "Hey, I appreciate the warning, but … I'm looking up and the sky isn't falling. Maybe you should calm down." In short, no one stopped to think about the big picture.

By accepting a doomsday scenario, we go into survival mode and are more susceptible to doing things out of desperation. We are also less likely to question those who seem like they can save us.

It's no coincidence that doomsday ideas are often tied to cults—a subject we touch on more in Chapter 17. Members are focused on the gloom-and-doom scenario told by the leader but fail to notice details such as fellow members disappearing without notice, their family crying every time they get a chance to see them, or the slightly acidic smell coming from a glass of Kool-Aid (à la Jonestown). While indulging in an unlikely doomsday fantasy, a very real danger is in front of them.

Prophets

Whether through God, the devil, or a higher power, soothsayers have been a tradition throughout recorded human history. Greek heroes would visit the Oracle of Delphi to be told their future; touched churchgoers speak in tongues that can only be deciphered by the spiritual leader; and gifted tarot readers tell their subjects what they themselves can't see.

Extrasensory Perception (ESP) has been studied by major universities over the last century. However, here we're talking about people saying they have a unique spiritual connection that provides a specific vision of an important future.

HAVE YOU HEARD?

Co-author Damon Brown actually studied the beyond for his 2009 book *The Complete Idiot's Guide to Communicating with Your Angels* with spiritual teacher Cecily Channer. Neither he nor Cecily received any doomsday memes along the way.

How to Be a Good Doomsday Leader

When it comes to doomsday memes, there are certain rules to being a good leader:

1. The prophet is special and has the connection to the spiritual source.

2. The doomsday meme is dramatic and scary.

3. The prophet is telling people because he or she wants them to survive the onslaught.

4. The chances of actually surviving the onslaught are slim, so followers had *better* pay attention closely.

Without accepting the first idea—or meme within the meme, if you will—then the doomsday meme will fail. The carrier must convince others that he or she is the only gateway to this privy doomsday information. Otherwise, why would anyone listen, much less follow?

The more intense and vivid the vision, the more it will trigger the survival instinct within potential followers. Briefly going back to Chicken Little, imagine what it would be like if the sky really were falling! There would be nowhere to hide. Everyone would probably be crushed to death. Survivors wouldn't be able to live long because the sky would be gone. Ironically, the scariness of the doomsday meme makes people cling to it even more.

Third, the best doomsday messengers express a strong love for humanity. They say their only desire is to save as many people as possible. The outward nobility usually masks the power, respect, and attention the messenger desires from the flock.

Finally, the messenger makes it clear that everyone won't make it—even if they do everything he or she says. There will be casualties and loss. Therefore, it's doubly important that you do what he or she says exactly as told.

All four rules create the same message: "Follow me to live."

Why People Follow

You still may ask, "Why do people follow?" As any armchair psychologist would say, anyone who stays in a relationship, no matter how good or bad, must be getting something out of it.

Not coincidently, what the follower gets isn't that much different than what the leader gets:

- Power
- Respect
- Attention
- Security

As we discussed earlier, the power comes from knowing a secret, the respect from possibly knowing other secrets, and the attention from supposedly having direct access to privileged information.

Security, however, is important to the follower. The follower has a family of believers, whether they are fellow theorists across the Internet or roommates on a commune.

The follower has a leader that has promised to protect them. Most importantly, unlike the average person, the follower knows how this game will end.

The real twist, however, is that even if the follower has doubts about the validity of the vision or the honesty of the leader, he or she is still getting security from the meme as long as it continues to give him or her power, respect, and attention from the general public.

Either way, the follower has little to no social incentive to quit, which is why so many people have willfully put their lives in the hands of a doomsday leader.

Y2K

Starting in the mid-'90s, the impending turn of the century brought with it a creeping paranoia. What would happen in the new millennium? Would it be the end of days? The Y2K bug, which was thought to be able to paralyze computers on 1/1/2000, was the perfect tangible event to justify any fears of sudden eternal darkness, rivers of blood, or *Mad Max*–style anarchy. You may remember that there was even a term for the fear: pre-millennial tension.

On January 1, 2000, nothing special occurred. The Y2K bug was more hype than reality. What was very real, however, were the shortages of bottled water, flashlights, and other emergency supplies, because healthy people were hoarding as many goods as possible for their own benefit—and limiting the ability of those in need to receive access to critical items. The paranoia over the new millennium created a real crisis. The general public realized how much it overreacted to the situation, and normalcy soon returned.

2012

A few years ago, the nightly media, Internet sites, and the people around the water cooler started talking about an ancient Mayan prophecy. Our highly advanced civilization was discussing the world ending in 2012.

There isn't a term for our new fear yet.

You might have heard about the action movie *2012*. A big-budget action movie from Roland Emerrich, the director of *Independence Day, 2012* shows all these natural disasters happening around the world in Hollywood glory. Unlike many prophecies, the catastrophes are actually based on man's actions—a neutron-based laser is shot in a mine, triggering an extreme change in climate. Also, no other prophecies have actor John Cusack as a limo driver.

The 2009 movie was critically panned for wooden acting and following too closely in the footsteps of another Emerrich climate movie, 2004's *The Day After Tomorrow*. The CGI-laden apocalypse resonated with audiences worldwide, however, bringing in more than $750 million. The poster only said three words: "We Were Warned."

Why 2012?

According to the thorough *The Complete Idiot's Guide to 2012* by Synthia and Colin Andrews, the year corresponds to the Mayan time cycle. The Mayan people prophesied that 2012 would mark the return of Kukulkan—a god often called the creator of Mayan culture—and the end of this particular age.

To quote:

> In the Mayan creation stories, three previous worlds, or ages, have been destroyed. According to current interpretations of the Mayan calendars, 2012 is the end of the present age. The calendars say this age will be destroyed by fire. However, the end of each age is the birth of the next age, and there is never complete destruction of the old … This makes the ending of the old age a time of purification, not destruction of the earth, and the beginning of the next age is a time of transformation.

A great synopsis with reasonable perspective, especially for a doomsday meme—but as we discussed back in Chapter 10 on religion, people often don't take the time to study text-heavy memes. Instead, the bottom line is often assumed: "My world is going to be destroyed."

Expected Events

The Mayan calendar may have started the discussion, but it has created an opportunity for others to chime in with events that could be slated for 2012.

The triggers include the following:

- A shift in sun spots

- A magnetic pole reversal

- Cracks in the magnetic field

Sunspots are occurring on our sun, which is a precursor to its beginning a new solar cycle. That means a change in sun temperature, which technically means a higher chance of extreme weather.

Simultaneously, Earth is going through its own cycle, undergoing its regular magnetic pole reversal. We always think of the North Pole as, well, the north, but it moves slightly every year. The pole will soon be in the opposite position it was halfway through the cycle. What's going to happen? Nobody has a clue—the last reversal happened about 780,000 years ago.

Finally, NASA noticed a few cracks in the magnetic field that protects Earth from the rest of the universe. NASA isn't sweating it—according to Andrews and Andrews, the organization says it's a result of the magnetic pole shift—but it is observing the cracks carefully. A big crack could blow some nasty, very extreme weather our way.

There are literally dozens of other 2012 theories, many of which are explored in the Andrews and Andrews book.

A Grain of Salt

As we mentioned earlier, we traditionally "freak out" before entering a new age. The anxiety feeds the meme to the point where the timing is just an excuse to express negative emotions.

For instance, 1000 C.E. brought as much drama as the Y2K—with the changes caused by scared people and not the imagined force expected to descend on the population. France was in the middle of a four-decade food shortage which many blamed on the end of days, while the rest of Europe pointed to meteor showers, bad weather, and other normal activity as signs of the apocalypse. Rioting and wars occurred, but so did a resurrection of spiritual devotion through church, cults, and organized faiths.

The Mayan 2012 philosophy is technically based on math—something these people were great innovators of—but other doomsday memes have curious timing.

Number one, there is no clear reason why, say, the sun would suddenly heat up in 2012, unless it happens to be on a specific, oddly coincidental schedule that we're not aware of.

Number two, Earth is constantly under "attack" by space objects, adjusting to climate changes, and spinning to and fro through vast territory. It has been around for relatively countless millennia, from the time of amoeba, through dinosaurs, and now us. Why would it suddenly implode now?

Fascinating ideas, but if the earth wanted to have a meltdown, it probably wouldn't fit neatly into our homemade Julian or Mayan calendar.

The Least You Need to Know

- The Aesop fable "Chicken Little" illustrates the doomsday meme perfectly.
- Doomsday memes can give leaders power through the fear they create.
- The 2012 doomsday meme originated from a Mayan calendar prophecy.
- Doomsday meme followers get security from supposedly knowing how human life will end.
- Some scientists have connected planetary events to 2012, but there is scant evidence that any major event will happen that year.

The Passive Dormant Memes

In This Chapter

- When memes die
- The journey to death
- Resurrecting memes
- Memes living through other memes
- How passive memes survive

Most of what we've talked about to this point is how memes replicate and the things they do to ensure that they get copied.

But what happens to those memes that don't manage to get copied? Can a meme die? In this chapter, we'll look at what happens when people stop spreading memes.

Defining the Dormant Meme

Memes are kind of like Peter Pan—they need to be believed in to actively exist. *Dormant memes* are ideas that aren't actively in people's minds. In other words, a dormant meme is a meme that has no human hosts. As memes can only exist in a human mind, this means that they are dead.

DEFINITION

A **dormant meme** is a meme left with no host because the last carrier either died or stopped believing in the idea. It can be resurrected, however, usually through another active meme.

Of course, it's not quite as simple as that. Genes have only one vector for replication— genetic reproduction—and once that line is broken, that is the end of the species. But as we have seen, memes have a number of different vectors for transmission, and some of those are persistent; that is, they leave a record. Memes that currently have no human hosts may still be inscribed in books or in some sort of archaeological record and therefore have the potential to be revitalized if someone should read and understand them.

Therefore, we tend to talk about memes being dormant rather than completely dead. On the other hand, if a meme doesn't leave any permanent trace, there is no chance of it being restored.

Of course, it is possible that a meme with the same properties could evolve independently—in the same way that Gottfried Wilhelm Leibniz and Sir Isaac Newton independently invented calculus only a few years apart from each other. However, in a case such as this one, it wouldn't really be the same meme.

How a Meme Dies

There are several ways in which a meme can die. The two most common ways are the following:

- Its host, or host community, dies.

- Hosts stop believing the meme.

In other words, death is caused by either the spokespeople disappearing or the faith of the spokespeople disappearing. This interesting subject is worth breaking down more.

Death by Proxy

Quite simply, a meme dies when it stops spreading. Because a meme continues to live in the mind of its host, it is active to that person provided that he or she doesn't forget it—but unless the host spreads the meme to others, it will only last until the host's death. Thus, if a particular meme is closely related to a small community, with little traction outside that community, its survival is dependent on the longevity of that community.

For instance, in many parts of the world, small native communities of very few members have their own customs, heritage, and even languages. If those communities die or are assimilated into the larger surrounding communities, all the memes that are dependent on that culture will die.

HAVE YOU HEARD?

According to the Living Tongues Institute for Endangered Languages, nearly half the world's languages will disappear in the next 100 years. Most of these are the languages of small, indigenous communities—some with only hundreds or even dozens of speakers. Many indigenous dialects are oral languages, so when their final speakers die, there will be no trace of the language or much of the culture left.

Organizations such as the Living Tongues Institute, as well as many universities' linguistics schools, are developing programs to document, preserve, and if possible, revitalize endangered languages.

Even if a dead culture leaves a permanent record through inscriptions, it may be insufficient to revitalize the dormant memes. Fragments of text exist for a pre-Greek Minoan language that scientists refer to as "Linear A," but no one has been able to decipher the language.

More progress has been made on the later "Linear B" script, and linguists have identified the semantic values of about 200 ideograms—mainly a catalog of trade goods—leading researchers to suggest that it formed the records of a professional trade guide. It is doubtful, however, that any memes originally embedded in the language will survive.

Death by Disproving

Another common way in which a meme dies is when it can no longer find hosts who believe it as new facts are discovered. For instance, until the mid-eighteenth century, scientists believed that the reason why some substances were combustible was because they contained a colorless, odorless, and massless element called phlogiston, which was liberated during burning. This meme remained active until the true composition of air was discovered, which accounted for the results of burning better than the phlogiston theory.

Just to complicate things a little, the phlogiston meme didn't completely die; rather, it just changed its meaning. If it were dormant, we wouldn't be able to talk about it at all. Now, however, the meme carries the meaning of "a defunct scientific theory" and is frequently used as an example in books (such as, well, this one).

We'll talk more about the resurrection of memes a little later in this chapter.

Why Do Some Die and Others Don't?

Sometimes memes die without a fuss when the available evidence causes people to stop spreading what has become known as incorrect. We saw this situation with the phlogiston theory, and the same thing happened with the Steady State theory of cosmology, popular in the 1950s and 1960s, which claimed that the universe was expanding but that new matter was being continually created in order to maintain its average density. The theory was largely abandoned in the 1960s after discoveries including that of cosmic background radiation tipped the balance in favor of the Big Bang Theory.

Other times, however, a meme is much harder to kill, which is especially so if it:

- Is a memeplex, or a meme composed of multiple memes

- Has co-memes as a reward

- Has auto-immune memes to protect against attack

It Is a Memeplex

Let's take a mainstream example: picture an iconic '80s rock band (à la Poison, Mötley Crüe, or Whitesnake) with its big hair, leather pants, and suggestive lyrics. The band may have been extremely successful, selling millions of records, but its strong brand is tied to a dying meme—specifically, the '80s decade. The people who purchased its music have grown into other, more sophisticated styles, and the young people alive now consider it a relic of the past (if they know who it is at all). Hair rock was replaced by boy bands, then grunge, then materialistic rap and … well, its time was several memes ago. In a sense, new "facts" were discovered: big hair isn't sexy, leather pants should only be worn by beautiful women, and most suggestive rock lyrics sound hilarious once you grow up. This is the new meme.

As pop culture shows, however, a disproved meme can be resurrected, even in irony. See one of the extremely popular *I Love the '80s* shows on cable, the Def Leppard tour, and so on.

The old hair bands actually have an army behind them. Think about all the nostalgic ideas tied to the '80s:

- The Rubik's Cube
- Pac-Man
- Cabbage Patch Kids
- Jazzercise
- Michael Jackson

Talk about a massive memeplex! No wonder they never seem to go away. A trigger, such as Michael Jackson's death, the 30th anniversary of Pac-Man, or the return of the TV show *Alf* could automatically bring '80s hair bands back into fashion.

As we discussed in Chapter 6, seemingly dead ideas can come back to the mainstream in weird, unpredictable ways.

Co-Memes and Auto-Immune Memes

Another example is the old wedding-tradition rhyme:

Something old,
something new,
something borrowed,
something blue.

Probably dating from Victorian times in England, these were items that the bride was supposed to wear to the wedding to give her good luck. The rhyme is still familiar, kept alive in the names of songs and films, and quite a few couples still adhere to the ritual—even if it is a superstition meme.

Why still follow it? The reward is a good marriage, but it also ties into dozens of other ideas, including throwing rice, the groom not seeing the bride before the wedding, carrying the bride over the threshold, and so on. The reward seems multiplied if you do everything right.

More importantly, the auto-immune memes say that *everything* must be done right to have a prosperous marriage. With the major countries facing a high divorce rate, we're surprised there aren't more wedding memes than before!

The Flat Earth Meme

One very significant reoccurring meme is the Flat Earth Theory. This memeplex has one strong advantage: it seems common sense. If you look out the window, you don't see a sphere—you see a disk spreading out in all directions to the horizon. This commonsense approach is easily disproved, however, and Greek astronomers had established the spherical Earth as fact by the third century B.C.E. The Spherical Earth Theory was sufficiently widespread in the fifteenth century so that Christopher Columbus was prepared to risk his voyage of discovery (and Queen Isabella was prepared to fund it).

PASS IT ON

The 1828 novel by Washington Irving, *The Life and Voyages of Christopher Columbus,* introduced to modern audiences the idea that the Flat Earth Theory was widely accepted in the Middle Ages and that Columbus had to contend with the near-mutiny of his crews, who believed that they were about to fall off the edge of the world. In fact, this was far from the truth—and the Spherical Earth Theory was widely believed at that time. Sailors in particular would have firsthand experience in seeing mountains and islands disappearing over the horizon, due to the curvature of the earth. Columbus did have to contend with his crew's attempted mutiny—but because they nearly ran out of food and water, not because of belief in a flat Earth.

Nevertheless, the Flat Earth Theory has persisted in various places right up to the twenty-first century. The main reason for this persistence is that it is actually a memeplex with some powerful co-memes supporting the main concept.

Powerful Co-Memes

One of the main co-memes is religion—itself a memeplex of stunning complexity. English writer Samuel Rowbotham published *Earth Not a Globe* in 1881 to prove that the earth was flat. Among his various "proofs" are many biblical references, and the implication is clear: if you accept the Bible as the Word of God, you cannot believe that the earth is round. The religion meme continues in modern versions of the Flat

Earth Theory. The last president of the International Flat Earth Research Society, Charles K. Johnson, grounded his beliefs firmly in a literalist interpretation of the Bible.

Another prominent co-meme is an anti-science meme that contrasts scientific theory with common sense. This meme contends that people are fooled into believing nonsense by the assumed authority of political elites who have their own agendas. As we have seen, conspiracy theory memes are hard to displace, because any objection to them simply becomes incorporated as part of the conspiracy.

Flat Earth in Modern Times

The Flat Earth Society was dealt what was probably its death blow in the early 1960s, when satellite photographs started being published—although a small group of stalwarts continued to maintain that the photos were fake and that the space program was a vast government conspiracy.

When Johnson died in 2001, the society effectively ceased to exist as an organization, and one of the main vectors for transmitting the meme—the society's newsletter, as well as other publications—disappeared. There are still people who claim to believe in a flat Earth, but it is difficult to distinguish their writings from the parodies and jokes that litter the Internet and other places.

Like the phlogiston example earlier, the flat Earth meme has changed its meaning to now refer metaphorically to someone who willfully holds outdated and disproved beliefs. Proponents of the manmade global warming theory often refer to their opponents as "flat-Earthers."

Resurrecting Dead Memes

If the dormant meme has left a written trace, it may be possible to resurrect it. The flourishing of classical Greek culture between the sixth and fourth centuries B.C.E. brought many advances in diverse areas such as politics, philosophy, art, and science. These ideas survived the fall of Greece and the rise of Roman dominance in the region, but with the fall of the Roman Empire between the third and fifth centuries C.E., most of this learning was lost to Western scholars, ushering in what we call the Dark Ages.

Most of these memes would have been lost were it not for Islamic scholars who had translated the works of Plato, Aristotle, and others into Arabic and eventually re-introduced them to European intellectuals, thus giving rise to the Renaissance.

Think about the names mentioned here: Plato and Aristotle. The importance of the text itself cannot be denied, and the philosophies made an indelible impact on society at large—but there is also a value here in their names (their reputations). Plato's reputation as a wise man pushed scholars to translate the text into other modern languages. Here, it would be wise to remember that translation was undertaken painstakingly by hand, with most texts transcribed by monks who dedicated their lives to it. Translating a single text could take months, if not years. Why take the time to translate a text from a dead language to a new one? There would have to be some kind of selection process—and there is a reason why not every Greek or Roman text has survived to this day. Plato and Aristotle have high cultural currency, a concept we discussed in Chapter 3.

Hieroglyphics

Probably the most famous example of the resurrection of a dormant meme is the case of Egyptian hieroglyphics.

Originally the writing of the priest class, hieroglyphs probably evolved from the scripts of Sumerian and Mesopotamian traders (a very successful meme!). In time, the language divided into two separate scripts: the original sacred script and a simpler, common script used for everyday life (called Demotic).

In time, Demotic evolved further and further away from the sacred hieroglyphs, and by the fourth century C.E., not even Egyptians could read the priestly script. The hieroglyph meme was dead.

It might have remained that way but for the habit of the ancient priests of carving writing on every available surface, leaving a huge number of examples for archaeologists and linguists to study.

Resurrection!

Many people attempted to decipher hieroglyphs over the centuries, some meeting with minor successes, but most failing completely.

When it seemed that the meme would remain dormant forever, a discovery changed everything. During his 1799 military campaign in Egypt, Napoleon's soldiers discovered a stone engraved with three different languages: Greek, Demotic, and hieroglyphics. It was the famous Rosetta Stone.

> **INFECTION!**
>
> Remember that some languages are solely dependent on other memes. For instance, *The Hobbit* author J. R. R. Tolkien spent years creating dozens of original languages for his characters. Luckily, *The Lord of the Rings* series was a massive hit, as were the big-budget movies released decades after. Hardcore fans actually speak his languages. If the book series had faltered, however, then little to no one would be speaking Sindarin, Quenya, or any other language he created.
>
> An original language was made for James Cameron's *Avatar* movie as well, but time will tell whether devotees will be speaking Na'vi after 2009.

Linguists quickly determined that the three passages were translations of the same statement, and this provided the key to unlock the meaning behind the hieroglyphs. Within 20 years, the entire language had been deciphered, and the statements covering the walls of tombs and temples were once again carried in human minds.

A Question

The return of hieroglyphics and the memes carried within that language raises an interesting question—one that this book isn't able to answer. We'll leave it to you to think about …

In 1820, memes that had lain dormant for more than a millennia were again active—memes such as "Ra the sun god is the ruler of all" and "Akhnaten is a heretic." But while we may now understand the words, are the memes the same? Presumably, few people still worship the ancient Egyptian pantheon, so the words must carry a slightly different meaning. Could it be that, like phlogiston, these memes are merely the memotype carrying the meaning "ancient language"?

The Least You Need to Know

- Memes die when the last host dies or forgets the meme.
- Memes also die if people simply stop believing them and stop spreading them.
- Some memeplexes carry strong defenses against death by disbelief and can survive long after most people cease to believe in them.
- If a meme leaves a written trace, it is possible that it can be resurrected.
- Memes can sometimes be resurrected by another thriving meme.

The Deadly Toxic Memes

Chapter
17

In This Chapter

- Memes that make people suicidal
- The memetic basis of terrorism
- Memes that lower intelligence
- Cults
- Killer memes

We've looked at some negative memes, such as scams and hoaxes (Chapter 12) and doomsday memes (Chapter 15). These memes can inflict significant damage to people by fooling them into doing silly things or making bad choices.

But can a meme actually kill? At first, this scenario seems unlikely—after all, if a meme only lives in the mind of its host, a meme for suicide (for instance) would surely soon die out.

In this chapter, we look at those memes that can prove fatal to the host or to other people.

Killer Memes

There are two types of killer memes:

- Auto-toxic
- Exo-toxic

These are memes that are, respectively, dangerous to the host and dangerous to other people.

Auto-Toxic Memes

An *auto-toxic meme* pushes the carrier to engage in risky and perhaps deadly behaviors. The meme obviously doesn't put survival first, as it only lives as long as the host itself—and in some ways, self-destruction is the actual goal. Sometimes, the act of destroying the host actually spreads the auto-toxic meme to others.

> **DEFINITION**
>
> An **auto-toxic meme** is one that encourages behavior that is dangerous or even fatal to its host.

There are two signs of a potential auto-toxic meme:

- It encourages suicide.
- It encourages reckless behavior.

Obviously, neither one is good for the meme host or for the affiliated. It may be hard to imagine how a thought could hurt or kill someone and others, so let's look at some examples.

Suicide

How can a meme that kills its host survive? Remember that even if we carry a meme, we don't necessarily have to follow its instructions. The range of police procedural shows on television at the moment—shows such as *CSI* and *Law and Order*, as well as many others—mean that many of us know a lot about murder. We carry some sort of murder meme. But that doesn't mean we are going to put the instructions of that meme to use.

Also, there are far more people who *attempt* suicide than *commit* suicide, so the suicide meme isn't perfectly able to control behavior.

But there's another reason why the suicide meme exists and is perpetuated. Suicide, especially if it is sensational or makes a political statement, as in prisoners who starve themselves to death in protest of their conditions, is highly publicized. From the meme's point of view, if ten people are infected because of the death of one host, it is still winning. Provided that the rate of infection remains higher than the mortality rate, the meme will continue to spread.

The examples aren't necessarily always negative. The media is fond of stories about people who selflessly give their lives so that others might live—soldiers throwing themselves on live grenades to contain the blast, for example, or bodyguards stepping in front of bullets to protect their charges.

HAVE YOU HEARD?

Probably the most infamous example of an auto-toxic meme was the Jonestown mass suicide in 1978, when more than 900 members of the People's Temple cult drank cyanide-laced soft drinks on the instructions of cult-leader Jim Jones. That so many people would kill their children and themselves at the command of their leader shows how powerfully the auto-toxic meme had taken control of their minds. See the section "Memeoids" later in this chapter.

Of course, in these cases the hosts are not necessarily responding to the suicide meme but to another meme that causes them to value the lives of their friends over their own—something like, "The needs of the many outweigh the needs of the few."

Recklessness

We probably all know people who act like they are invincible. They might drive recklessly or dangerously, follow extreme sports without taking due precautions, or fail to plan for unexpected events.

You might have heard about the Darwin Awards, the light-hearted website (and now book) about people who commit the most outrageous acts of stupidity—who, according to the website's tag line, "improve the gene-pool by accidentally removing themselves from it."

While we shouldn't make fun of tragic situations, some of the examples on the website show clear signs of infection by an auto-toxic meme. In one example, a Russian man somehow came to believe that he had the psychic power to stop vehicles in their tracks. He made the mistake of testing his theory on a freight train. (No need to explain what happened next.)

All these examples show that an auto-toxic meme can be dangerous indeed.

Exo-Toxic Memes

An exo-toxic meme is one that is dangerous or fatal to other people. As we will examine in Chapter 20, these sorts of memes are common in particular versions of religious and political ideologies.

Probably the most infamous exo-toxic meme of modern times is the political doctrine of Nazism. Growing out of the political and economic devastation of World War I in Germany, the doctrine originally worked at restoring lost pride to a disillusioned community.

But as the philosophy took hold, more sinister memes joined the memeplex: first, ideas of racial purity, and then a meme that sought someone to blame for the country's economic difficulties: Jews.

It took only a few years before the growing memeplex turned exo-toxic, and blame for economic depression turned into a murderous hatred for the Jews. Hitler's "final solution" was to "cleanse" Germany of impure races—Jews, gypsies, and others who didn't conform to the Aryan ideal. Some 6 million people were executed under the influence of this meme, while possibly 70 million more were killed in the world war that it sparked.

INFECTION!

It may seem unlikely that people would fall for memes such as these, but we only look at them retrospectively and in terms of their ultimate effect. Frequently, at the start of their spread, the memeplexes seem reasonable. Hitler was elected chancellor by a German people who supported his position on national pride. The members of the People's Temple didn't think they were joining a cult. They thought they were supporting the views of Jim Jones, who in his early years was a respected community organizer who worked hard to bring about social inclusion and respect for the African American community.

We don't know when a meme might turn bad, so we need to stay alert and not accept an idea because it sounds nice (more about this topic in Chapter 20).

World history is littered with these sorts of conflicts, from the Spanish Inquisition of the fifteenth and sixteenth centuries, to the English repression of Roman Catholicism in the sixteenth and seventeenth centuries, to the murderous regimes of Stalin in the U. S. S. R., Pol Pot in Cambodia, and Idi Amin in Uganda in the last century.

Memeoids

Memetics has a word for people who are completely influenced by a toxic meme: memeoid. Unlike a memebot, who is obsessed with a particular meme, a memeoid is connected to a meme in a way that can definitely harm him or her.

These are people for whom the meme is so important, their own survival is irrelevant. The members of Jim Jones's People's Temple were memeoids. Although the cult had armed guards, there is no evidence of anyone attempting to flee the compound, or—with the exception of one lone voice that did not comply, at least initially—resist Jones's instructions.

Suicide bombers and World War II Japanese kamikaze pilots are people who put the instructions of the meme above their own survival. This doesn't mean that they were like madmen obeying the "voices in their heads" but that memeplexes carry memes about "the greater good" and "serving the cause." To the hosts of these memes, these ideas are as respectable as the intentions of the soldier who is killed protecting his comrades.

Cults

Cults such as the Jonestown People's Temple are classic examples of out-of-control toxic memes. This particular meme turned out to be auto-toxic, but cults can also be exo-toxic, such as the Japanese Aum Shinrikyo cult, which was responsible for the saris gas attack on the Tokyo subway in 1995.

Like other negative memes, cults often start as good ideas about justice, love, or inclusion. Jones had worked hard to fight injustice and segregation in his hometown, and the People's Temple was an attempt to build a socialist paradise on Earth, where people of all colors and beliefs were safe and welcome.

No one knows how Jones changed from a genuine reformer to the paranoid who murdered government officials and ordered the deaths of his followers because he thought the cult was about to be attacked by government agents. In the same way, it is hard to understand how the memeplex evolved from something that attracted people with its philosophy of inclusiveness to something that ordered their deaths, but the change was gradual and not noticed by most people.

There is a thin line between passionate leadership and obsessive fanaticism—something we touched on in Chapter 10.

Meme Self-Defense Against Cults

Most toxic memeplexes associated with cults contain sophisticated defenses to protect themselves from the disillusionment of hosts or takeover by other memes.

Many cult leaders have the status of truth-givers or lawmakers. Memes adhere to the leader, influencing members to see them as having powerful knowledge not available to ordinary people or even having a godlike status. At the same time, other memes influence people to dismiss opposing voices, even moving them to violence against people who disagree with the leader's teaching.

HAVE YOU HEARD?

The Heaven's Gate UFO cult in California was another cult that committed mass suicide. The teachings of their leader, Marshall Applewhite, convinced members that Earth was about to be cleansed and the only way for members to save themselves was to "leave it." In 1997, 39 members of the cult poisoned themselves with vodka laced with cyanide or arsenic. Apparently, they expected that after physical death their souls would be picked up by UFOs and taken to a higher plane of existence.

Other memes help protect the complex by making the cult highly insular: members are usually not allowed to leave, and relatives are not allowed to visit. The activities of the cult become increasingly secretive, as memes convince members that they are in possession of privileged knowledge that must be protected.

There are memes common in conspiracy theories that convince people that anyone who disagrees with them is part of the conspiracy. These sorts of memes commonly get co-opted into cult memeplexes.

Part 5, "Defenses Against Memes," goes much more in depth on what you can do to protect yourself from unwanted memes.

A Dramatic End

Not all cult memeplexes turn toxic, but those that do often do so with spectacular, and usually tragic, results. When the memes that give the leader an aura of truth or mystique combine with those that lead to a secretive and introverted organization, the stage is set for a tragedy. All that is needed, then, is a meme for belief in some sort of afterlife reward—and as we have seen, all religions have those beliefs.

As with everything, the best defense against a toxic meme cult is an open mind and a solid dose of common sense.

Terrorism

As with cults, the memes behind terrorism can be either auto-toxic or exo-toxic.

PASS IT ON

The exo-toxic terrorism memes control their hosts in the same way as the memes that influence soldiers fighting for legitimate causes. In these cases, the soldiers are still operating under the influence of an auto-toxic meme in which they are prepared to risk their lives in the service of their country. We call this "patriotism" and think of it approvingly. But remember, memes don't have morals: the meme that causes a soldier to die for his or her country is not much different from the meme that asks a terrorist to die for his or her religion or ideology.

We, of course, might draw a distinction between a terrorist and a freedom fighter, but memes aren't that fussy.

Exo-toxic terrorist memes require less control because they don't have to overcome the normal self-preservation memes of the terrorist. But they still need to be powerful enough to influence the host to break the law and endanger or kill innocent people in the name of their cause.

Conscious Self-Sacrifice

Auto-toxic terrorism memes often lead to suicide bombings or other acts in which the terrorist is unconcerned about his or her own survival. The terrorist may even welcome his or her impending death as a path to an eternal reward.

Terrorism is often closely linked to religious or political memeplexes, which are already highly influential. So the toxic meme may appear to be service to a higher spiritual power or a broader ideology, and the terrorist act is justified by its religious or political end—protection of the faith, or social revolution.

Immune to Argument

Terrorist acts such as the ones that have become increasingly common over the last decade are very difficult to control. A memeoid is notoriously immune to logic or argument, so he or she usually cannot be reasoned with—and any attempt to do so is seen as part of the evil the host is fighting against.

In the same way, any attempt to stop the terrorists by military force simply reinforces the memes that encourage defense of the country or religion and spawns more terrorists. Where all the memes are in place, it can take very little encouragement to tip a believer over the edge into being a memeoid.

Copycat Crimes

The memes that influence copycat crimes are exo-toxic memes that tend to use the mass media as a vector. Police are often reluctant to reveal too many details about a highly publicized crime for fear of copycats who will reenact the crime for their own purposes.

Copycat crimes are usually carried out for one of two reasons:

- A person is driven to repeat something shocking or infamous because he or she wants to be part of something bigger.
- A criminal is attempting to create confusion and cover the traces of his or her own crime.

These two reasons are simple, but they make for a fascinating study on the power of memes.

To Cover Tracks

Based on countless examples, criminals usually leave some type of calling card, called a *signature*. Like a handwritten name, the signature is a unique mental or physical mark left at the crime scene. For instance, one American bank robber became infamous for being extremely nice to his victims. In this case, his, ahem, gentlemanly demeanor was the signature. We as humans have a need to be recognized in some capacity, and for some, it's the very reason they partake in dastardly deeds. In many ways, we're not too different from the memes.

DEFINITION

A **signature** is a distinct action a criminal creates at a crime scene. It comes from a need to be recognized for his or her work. Criminal psychologists claim that nearly every "bad guy" has one. In fact, a copycat crime is defined by the signature of an act—the duplication of the original meme.

Of course, when you think about it, the desire to leave a signature is totally counter to not getting caught! Therefore, a criminal may encourage a "colleague" to perform a copycat crime—say, when the criminal has several witnesses seeing him at another location. It enables the original criminal to get away with the crime while still releasing his or her meme—his particular signature—into the collective consciousness.

To Be Part of Something Bigger

There are millions of murders and perhaps billions of robberies per year. How does a devious individual make a mark on the world? For every Son of Sam, Al Capone, or Charles Manson, there are an uncomfortable number of murderers, gang leaders, and cult leaders who are forgotten—if they were ever known in the first place.

Accepting the meme of an infamous individual not only allows a follower to pay homage but also raises the profile of the follower. It is a fast-track toward fame.

It's akin to a third-tier actor becoming a professional imitator; the meme notoriety of Bill Clinton, Madonna, or Clint Eastwood automatically makes him or her a star. What are the chances of an actor making it to that level on his or her own?

The Least You Need to Know

- Auto-toxic memes are dangerous or fatal to the host.
- Exo-toxic memes harm people other than the host.
- Much of the behavior of religious cults can be considered memetically.
- Terrorism has many causes, but memes play a considerable role.
- A memeoid is someone who is connected to a meme that can definitely harm him or her.

Defenses Against Memes

Memes, by definition, are cultural ideas passed on to others, but that doesn't mean all memes find a home in our collective cultural consciousness. In fact, because of your personality, you may be naturally protected against some of them. Part 5 shows our different defenses against taking in an idea.

We consider memes as contagion—a virus that wants to infect the carrier for its own purposes—and look at ways that we can protect ourselves against infection. Part of this inoculation is to be aware of situations where we might be more susceptible to infection by memes. We also look at ways in which governments and other bodies might try to censor particular memes.

One damaging consequence of certain memes is they can produce extreme reactions such as hate crimes against people of different races, religions, or sexuality.

Finally for this part, we suggest that the best defense against malicious memes is a good general knowledge and a healthy skepticism.

Memes as Infection

In This Chapter

- Why memes are contagious
- Susceptibility varies
- Protecting yourself against memes
- Examining carriers
- Observing sneaky memes

As we discussed in Chapter 2, memes are analogous to genes, and this analogy forms the defining metaphor. Actually, it's a bit more complicated than that. Dawkins and other proponents of meme theory say that memes don't just act like genes, they are also replicators in their own right. We'll discuss this idea in more detail in Part 6, but for now, let's stick to the metaphor theory.

One of the early researchers whose work led to the development of memetics, Ted Cloak (you'll find out more about him in Chapter 21), once pointed out that the influenza virus had evolved a side effect that caused its host to sneeze, thus spreading copies of the virus to different hosts. This observation introduces the idea of memes as infection. In later chapters, we'll look at books titled *Thought Contagion* and *Virus of the Mind*, which develop the infection metaphor even further. If our minds can be infected by memes in the same way that our bodies can be infected by the flu virus, what are the similarities? And can we immunize ourselves against memes?

The Vector, or Carrier

In medicine, a vector is the carrier of a disease or parasite. So the vector for the parasite that causes malaria is the mosquito, and the vector for the Black Death in Medieval Europe was the flea carried by rats.

Delivers in Countless Ways

As we said in Chapter 2, the vector for a meme can be a book, a television show, an e-mail message, or any other way of transmitting an idea. With the development of fast communication infrastructure such as the Internet, vectors can spread information fast. Periodically, the unofficial news of a celebrity's death will pop up on blogs, in e-mails, or on social networking sites such as Facebook or Twitter.

HAVE YOU HEARD?

As bizarre as it seems, websites exist that allow you to tailor a fake news report of a celebrity death and embed it in a realistic-looking online newspaper, which can then be forwarded to friends via e-mail. This is apparently how rumors started about the "death" of Jeff Goldblum in 2009—a report that was carried without checking by some mainstream media outlets, still reeling from the (real) death of Michael Jackson.

As in medicine, the vector of a meme is a neutral medium that has little control over the infections it carries, so all those people who complain about what the Internet is doing to society have rather misplaced their anger.

Surprise Delivery

One important way that a vector can deliver its parasitic passenger is through a "Trojan horse." You've probably heard about computer Trojans, in which an innocuous vector—a joke e-mailed by a friend, for example, or a funny video on YouTube—slips a hidden virus into a computer to wreak havoc at a later time. Biological infections and memes can travel the same way.

An effective example of a biological Trojan horse is the bubonic plague, a pandemic in Europe that peaked around 1350 and was estimated to have killed 100 million people. The plague was caused by a bacterial infection carried by fleas, which were spread across the world by rats hitching rides on merchant ships. The ships were welcome for carrying goods from foreign parts; the rats were tolerated because no one could get rid of them. But no one knew that the rats were carrying deadly invaders.

Sometimes Delivers More Than Intended

Daniel Dennett (you'll hear about him in Chapter 21 as well) once said that a wagon with spoked wheels delivering grain to early settlements didn't just deliver grain—it also delivered the great idea of spoked wheels. Here, the wagon becomes the vector for a new form of infection—a radical new design of wheel that was cheaper, lighter, and more effective.

The Host, or the Infected

In medicine, the host is the organism that is infected by a parasite and supplies the parasite's nutrients.

Because a meme is a mental entity, it needs a human mind in which to "live." A sketch on the old British television comedy *Monty Python's Flying Circus* took the form of a mockumentary about a joke that was so funny that it would instantly kill anyone who heard it. The sketch told how the military had the joke translated so that it could be used as an offensive weapon in the war. An amusing premise, but impossible— because if a meme doesn't have a host to live in, it can't exist. We saw earlier how memes die when they stop spreading and stop being believed.

Because a meme wants to replicate, it will cause the host to spread it. Just as the flu virus causes its host to sneeze, the joke provides certain benefits to its host to encourage him or her to spread it. The host gets the positive feedback of having other people laugh at the joke told, which makes him or her feel good and encourages the telling of more jokes. The people who hear the joke see the reactions of the group and want to get that same feeling of happiness, so they later tell the same joke, hoping for the same reaction. And the meme continues to spread.

Immuno-Depressant

So if a meme can be compared to an infection, are there times when we might be more or less susceptible to its effects? In Chapter 20, we'll talk about ways of protecting yourself against memes, but here we want to mention immuno-depressants.

Suppresses Resistance

Medically, an immuno-depressant (also called an immunosuppressant) is an agent that suppresses the body's immune response. Doctors administer immuno-depressant drugs following organ transplants to prevent the host's body from trying to destroy the new part, and they are also used to treat autoimmune diseases. Certain conditions can also naturally depress the immune system. Tragically, the HIV/AIDS virus attacks the host's immune system, leaving him or her susceptible to other infections. But even conditions as common as stress can leave a person run-down and likely to catch the first bug that comes along.

INFECTION!

If the stress and disorientation of travel leaves many people susceptible to memes, think how much more susceptible they might be if they are subjected to the stress, worry, and anger of unemployment or poverty. People in these situations often fall prey to the pernicious memes of racism, homophobia, or intolerance, and it is no accident that many of the adherents of racist organizations come from disadvantaged groups or from low socio-economic areas.

Unlike the physical and mental weakness associated with travel, constant socio-economic pressure can be released if there is a target to blame. The uneven spread of wealth is an extremely complex issue, which is why it is easier to blame a particular race, sex, or orientation for the undesirable—and unfair—situation.

We discuss the complexities of homophobia, racism, and sexism in Chapter 19.

In the same way, a person's resistance to memes can become run-down and disoriented. Parents will recognize that there are times when the incessant begging of a child will eventually break down all their defenses and logic, and they will give in to the request—for more toys, candy, or something they know is not really appropriate. There are times when the same thing happens, not because of a child's whining but because the person is tired, stressed, or distracted—and he or she agrees to things that he or she would never consider at other times: giving in to the high-pressure salesperson or agreeing to try some product that's not really needed.

Weakness During Travel

It is argued that the stress and disorientation that often accompanies long-distance travel—along with the associated emotional and physical fatigue, isolation, and insecurity—can suppress a person's immunity against invading memes. Could this be the reason religious cults often target airports and bus stations in search of converts?

Meme Censorship

One very effective way of treating bacterial infection is with the use of antibiotics such as penicillin. The only problem with antibiotics (apart from their overuse, which leads to resistance to certain strains of bacteria) is that they generally don't target particular infections but kill *all* bacteria they come in contact with—including the beneficial bacteria that aid in digestion.

Government Censorship

As we discussed in Chapter 7, some repressive governments try to stop the spread of memes that they consider dangerous by controlling the vectors that the memes use—by censoring newspapers and electronic media or placing filters on the Internet. These actions might prevent the spread of inappropriate ideas, but they can also stop the spread of good ideas or neutral ideas that might prove beneficial if they were allowed to develop. Because, as we have seen, memes cannot be controlled, we cannot know where a particular meme might end up or what sort of advances or discoveries it might make if it were allowed to run free.

This sort of blanket censorship might provide short-term advantage to a government, but only by risking long-term progress. Imagine if the Catholic church had succeeded in repressing Galileo's discoveries.

As Ineffective as Pest Control

Another consequence of blanket censorship has its analogy with pest control. Frequently, a problem with spraying an insecticide is that it kills only the milder, weaker insects, leaving the hardier and often more dangerous insects untouched. Further, the hardier insects now have less competition for resources and become even more prevalent. With meme censorship, the innocuous ideas may be easily controlled, but when it comes to the big, powerful memes—such as freedom and democracy— people will die for those.

The author Aaron Lynch posits seven modes in which memes spread—one of which is the "adversative" mode. This term refers to movements that attempt to protect their memes by aggressively sabotaging the opposition, as with the various religious crusades that offered the enemy the choice of conversion or death (something we touched on in Chapter 10).

PASS IT ON

A mathematician by trade, Aaron Lynch is best known for his book *Thought Contagion: How Belief Spreads Through Society: The New Science of Memes.* Lynch determined seven different ways we transmit memes: quantity parental, efficiency parental, proselytic, preservational, adversative, cognitive advantage, and motivational. In short, family, religious leaders, and society at large have specific methods to entice you to believe in their ideas.

Are you eager to learn more about these theories? Go to Chapter 22 to hear more about Lynch's innovative ideas.

This is an extreme form of censorship—and historically, one that has had limited success (at least, in the long term). As Victor Hugo said, "You can resist an invading army; you cannot resist an idea whose time has come."

Ultimately, censoring memes will prove to be counter-productive. The better option is to find ways to resist memes or disinfect ourselves from those negative memes that cause us problems.

Three Steps to Disinfection ... Maybe

Some time ago, hospitals discovered that their increasing use of powerful disinfectants was having the opposite effect on the infections they were trying to control. Instead of killing them, the chemicals were making the bacteria stronger as more and more strains developed that were resistant to them. Eventually, it was discovered that the best disinfectant was simple soap and water and an intelligent approach to hygiene.

There is no magic bullet for protecting yourself against memes. And anyway, not all memes are negative, just as not all ideas are bad. "Love your neighbor" is a meme. So is "From each according to his ability, to each according to his need." The secret is to be aware of memes, to understand how they replicate, and to realize that our behavior is often a result of memes that influence us without our knowing. The first step in disinfecting yourself is becoming aware of the issue: if you've read this far into the book, you've just about completed step one.

Richard Brodie, another author we'll meet in Chapter 22, believes that the way to achieve happiness and fulfillment in life is to be in control of your memes—to accept the ones that lead to fulfillment and to discard the ones that become an impediment.

There are three potential steps:

- Be aware of memes.

- Find appropriate memes to replace the undesirable ones.

- Spread memes that you support.

You've almost completed the first step: becoming aware of memes and what they can do to you. The second step is to reprogram yourself with those memes that support your own values in life, rather than the ones that support the meme's own agendas. The third step is to reinforce those values by consciously spreading the memes you think are important.

Be Aware

Completing this book will make you less susceptible to undesirable memes! This is one of the reasons we decided to write this book and help educate others in a post-Internet world.

It's possible to go through life without considering where ideas come from—what made your definition of personal success, why you've always had your hair cut a particular way, or how you decided on your religion (if you decided at all).

Find Appropriate Memes

In the new millennium, there is a continuous dialog about "information overload." This is a misnomer. The term makes it sound like we're drowning in a sea of spreadsheets. The problem isn't the bevy of information, per se, but the number of competing ideas with which we must grapple.

There is no one trusted source anymore. As recently as the previous generation, we had newscaster Walter Cronkite, historian Studs Terkel, *The New York Times*, and other primary sources. The classic journalists and mediums—the meme deliverers and in some ways creators—are dead, figuratively and/or literally. Bloggers are as resourceful and as trusted as the traditional outlets, if not more so. We have the same amount of facts, but the opinions and perspectives with regard to the facts are exponentially higher than at any other time in human history.

PASS IT ON

As we discussed earlier in this book, the Internet increased the number of virtually all memetic multimedia, including those set to pictures, videos, and sound.

You might want to hop back and check out Chapter 4. With all your new-found memes knowledge, you may understand things on an entirely new level.

So defending yourself requires more than it did in the past because you need a more stringent filter. You need to actively participate in finding appropriate memes rather than blindly trusting everything that is read, said, and shown.

Spread Positive Ideas

The final step to achieving happiness and fulfillment in life (according to Brodie) would be to become a cheerleader of what you decide to believe. In a modern example, you may create a Facebook group advocating a particular idea. Notices would automatically go to your circle of Facebook friends—your group of influence—and, because they are already affiliated with you, they are more likely to support (if not advocate) your position.

Sometimes it becomes a zero-sum game: defending and suppressing an undesirable meme requires taking attention away from it.

After chapter after chapter of talking about the power of memes, it's easy to feel overwhelmed. Remember, what you do is up to you. Realize that *you* are the master of your life, not those pesky memes. Within some limitations, you can choose to do anything you think is worthwhile—sponsor an orphaned child, join a reading group, become a vegetarian, or buy that motorcycle you've always wanted. The choices are endless, and they are yours—provided you can disinfect the tyranny of the meme.

The Least You Need to Know

- Memes can act like infections.
- At certain times, we are more susceptible to meme infection.

- There are ways to treat meme infection, but sometimes treatment only makes it worse.
- The best defense against memes is understanding how different ones work.
- A meme sometimes hides within a more desirable meme, à la the Trojan horse.

Meme Allergies

In This Chapter

- Defining meme allergies
- The extreme results of meme allergies
- Hate crime memes
- Memes as a genetic necessity
- Memetic inertia

Why do we hate? Not in an "I hate my job" way, but in an "I hate her because her people are ignorant" way, or, "I hate him because he's a man" way.

It may be because of a bad personal experience, but the isolated experience usually is compounded and solidified by cultural stereotypes. The bad personal experience becomes Exhibit A in the case for believing a particularly nasty meme, and we can take our fear, our ignorance, or our insecurity and justify them within one or more tidy memes. These are meme allergies.

We're going to dive into meme allergies, discussing the major ones, determining further why they are so popular, and showing how seemingly altruistic ideas can be some of the most dangerous meme allergies.

Hate Crimes

> I was asleep on the front porch and a Molotov cocktail was lobbed up onto the second-story front porch where I was at … And it immediately ignited the porch. I was asleep in that porch. As the building was burning I could hear the windows being broken out of the cars. And the people doing it laughing and screaming "[a sexual orientation slur]" at the top of their lungs … There was a note attached to the windshield of my car: "The [slur] that lives here will be dead within a week."

This is a description of a hate crime as described to researchers at the University of California, who had been funded by the National Institute of Mental Health to investigate the victimization of sexual minorities. The FBI reports that in 2008 alone, there were almost 10,000 instances of hate crimes—that is, crimes that are motivated by hatred toward persons of a particular race or ethnicity, religion, sexual orientation, or disability. That's the number of *reported* incidents; 12 states in the United States don't bother to gather data on hate crimes, and the researchers mentioned above point out that many cases go unreported, because the victims fear the consequences of going to the police.

Most people would regard attacks such as this one as abhorrent and hard to understand. What could possibly cause so much hatred in a person that he or she would act in this way?

PASS IT ON

The research project mentioned in this chapter was led by Gregory Herek, professor of psychology at the University of California at Davis, and a well-known campaigner for the rights of sexual minorities. Researchers interviewed 450 volunteers from the gay and lesbian community around Sacramento, California in 1994 and 1995, and in the course of face-to-face interviews, found that some 94 percent of respondents had experienced at least one instance of hate crime, with many reporting multiple instances.

No Simple Answers

There are no simple answers to this question, and law-enforcement officers, judges, and academics struggle daily to understand and deal with the pain and destruction that these crimes cause.

We are not going to suggest that all hate crimes stem from memes, but you'll remember in Chapter 18 when we pointed out that certain situations—such as poverty and hopelessness—can make people more susceptible to infection by memes, and that it is often the more pernicious memes that find willing hosts in these situations. Evidence suggests that the perpetrators of hate crimes are often economically disadvantaged, poorly educated, and alcohol abusers.

Homophobia, Racism, and Sexism

A large number of *meme allergens* exist, but we're going to focus on three major ones:

- Homophobia
- Racism
- Sexism

DEFINITION

A **meme allergen** relates to the medical term "allergen," which is any foreign substance that causes an extreme reaction in the body's immune system. A meme allergen may cause surprising and excessive responses that seem completely out of proportion to the stimulus.

Homophobia

In Chapter 17, we looked at toxic memes that motivate some people to extreme reactions in the presence—or perceived presence—of a hated stimulus. As the earlier quotation indicated, homosexuality can be a potent meme allergen.

Many religions teach that homosexuality is wrong and that people practicing homosexuality should be "corrected," so it is inevitable that members of those religions would disapprove of homosexuality. Most religions also teach that adultery is wrong and that adulterers should be "corrected," and yet adultery doesn't produce the same sorts of extreme and violent acts such as the one we mentioned at the start of this chapter. So there is obviously something more going on than a religious injunction. Memetics can help us here.

A Scientific and Religious Conflict

Genetically, homosexuality is an interesting case. According to geneticists, a form of sexuality that precludes offspring should die out within a couple of generations. Obviously it didn't, so we need to look beyond simple genetics to understand sexual orientation. As we will consider in Chapter 21, geneticists point out that genes are not the simple "atoms" of inheritance that they were originally thought to be, and it is possible that the gene that influences sexual orientation is associated with other characteristics as well.

Because of the religious injunctions mentioned earlier, historically there have been strong taboos against homosexuality. These taboos are likely to have pressured gay men and women to hide their orientation or to deny it altogether. Ironically, this self-repression might have actually increased the instance of homosexuality by spreading the genes that favor the orientation. As the number of homosexuals in a community rises, the chances of "closet gays" finding each other increases—and slowly, the "homosexuality is legitimate" meme begins to spread. The meme encourages some gays to "out" themselves, and their action encourages others to do the same. When there are sufficient numbers of openly gay people spreading the tolerance meme, it tips over into a political rights issue.

A Scientific Mystery

Of course, the "homosexuality is legitimate" meme doesn't only infect gays—heterosexual people can also become pro-gay and help spread the meme through political action and displays of tolerance.

This can cause a problem—young heterosexual men without partners may be suspected of being homosexual, thus reducing their access to potential mates. In response, a new meme was created, causing young men to loudly proclaim their heterosexual orientation or to deny or even disparage homosexuality as a way of proving their heterosexual credentials. This may be especially so if the young man is concerned or confused about his own sexuality.

INFECTION!

Research suggests that people who have friends who are gay, lesbian, or bisexual are more likely to be supportive of gay rights issues such as the marriage equality movements in various countries. They also tend to be less prejudiced against people of different orientation to their own. It seems reasonable to extrapolate this acceptance to people of different race, religion, or political views. So if you make friends only with people who are like yourself, you may be making yourself more susceptible to those malicious memes of homophobia and racism.

Paranoia Turns into Violence

How the "I'm not gay" meme turns into fear, hatred, and violence is a complex process and not fully understood by psychologists, but it is recognized that instances of homophobia are more common in places where people living in openly gay relationships are rare than in places with vibrant gay communities. You'll remember that people living with the stress of unemployment, poverty, and hopelessness are more susceptible to memes than they would be at other times. We often find that in places where economic depression is common, there is a high allegiance to particularly fundamentalist forms of religion—such as the form of Christianity practiced in the American South or the form of Islam common in countries such as Afghanistan. The combination of the "I'm not gay" meme, the fundamentalist religion meme (with its strong anti-homosexual injunction), and the violence that is common in desperate and hopeless places means that the instance of anti-gay actions is higher than in other places.

This intolerance for gays is itself a meme, and in small, closed communities it can spread easily—leading to a full-blown epidemic of homophobia and related violence.

Racism

Racism, or racial discrimination, is the belief that racial heritage is the defining characteristic of a person and that people can be classified as superior or inferior on this basis.

Effects of a Memeplex

Versions of racism are the ugly side of a memeplex that nature equipped us with to help with the propagation of the gene. Most religions and societies approve of altruism—the motivation to help others without the expectation of a reward.

Altruism is often associated with two dominant memes that appear in most societies and that are so deeply programmed that they are often thought of as instinctual. They are "helping children" and "birds of a feather." The first is about selflessly providing for those who are too young to help themselves, and the second is about our feelings of concern and responsibility to family and close friends.

HAVE YOU HEARD?

During the nineteenth century, a number of scientific theories—most based on a misunderstanding of Darwin's Theory of Evolution—tried to show that certain races and ethnic groups were intellectually inferior to white European races. Some entrepreneurs went as far as exhibiting members of colored races in "human zoos."

These theories eventually led to the science of eugenics—the study of selective breeding in humans in order to raise the intelligence of the race. Eugenics is now largely dismissed because of its association with Nazi Germany.

It may seem unfeeling to reduce these noble human sentiments to mere memes, infecting us for no better reason than to propagate themselves—but it is obvious that these two versions of altruism are important to the survival of the gene. If a person dies in childhood before he or she is able to pass on his or her genes, all those genes (from the genes' point of view) are wasted. Similarly, geneticists point out that families and small kin groups share many genes, and it is not unreasonable to suggest that nature evolved a way to influence humans to privilege the care and protection of kin over strangers, who carry less closely related genes.

Selfish Altruism

But there is a darker side to this altruism. A meme that encourages someone to care for people who are like them obviously also encourages them to ignore, or even harm, people who are not like them. A meme that says we should spend precious resources on our children because they are our future is also saying that we should withhold resources from those who are not important to our future, including the children of other racial or ethnic groups.

Of course, we don't think about it in such blatant terms, but buried deep within our memetic makeup is a program that encourages altruism toward people who are like us and hostility toward those who are not like us.

When these memes intersect with the sorts of anger and desperation that we spoke about earlier in the chapter, the scene is set for the hostility that some people feel toward immigrants—especially when they are accused of taking resources that could go to *my* family and children.

The "Burden"

Another hidden form of racism is the concept of one race being a burden to the others. Often called *white man's burden*, the idea is that one particular group is disenfranchised, so the group in power must make concessions to make sure it can thrive. It can come off as exceedingly responsible and altruistic, especially when a colonized group of individuals is given a helping hand.

DEFINITION

White man's burden is the belief that the race in power must help the "less-sophisticated" race with the socio-economic and/or intellectual disadvantage. The term comes from an 1899 Rudyard Kipling poem of the same name. The poem pushed for colonization of lesser cultures, and it's still unclear whether the English author of *The Jungle Book* meant it as satire or truth. But, like most popular memes, it doesn't really matter—the idea has taken on a life of its own, and believers apply it as they see fit.

However, the issue here is that forced assistance could reinforce the very power dynamic the offender originally created. For instance, the U.S. Affirmative Action program, initially instilled to push corporations to bring more women into the workforce, has shifted to create opportunities for the African American community. Proponents within the community say the law is a form of restitution for American slavery—the violent removal of millions of Africans from their homeland to servitude in pre-Colonial and Colonial America—an event that set African Americans back for generations. Opponents within the community say the law continues the same power dynamic created four centuries ago—the white majority controlling the advancement of black minorities—and that true growth can only happen from inside the African American community.

Obviously, there is no easy answer to these conflicts of race, racism, and power.

Sexism

Evolutionary psychologists are fond of pointing out genetic and developmental reasons for the different gender roles of men and women. They explain that because the female body must invest a lot of time and energy into producing eggs, gestating a fetus, and nursing a baby, women have developed a patient nature that looks for stability and protection—while the flighty male, who need not invest more than a minimum amount of energy into producing and disseminating his tiny sperm—looks for instant gratification and hunts down new and different sexual conquests as opportunity allows, thus spreading his DNA as broadly as possible.

Maybe. What is clear is that the stereotypes that see women as passive and men as active are deeply programmed and must be the result of memes that were embedded in prehistoric times.

Ghosts from the Past

Based on these deep-seated memes are the memetic assumptions that feminists and others have started questioning only in the last 100 or so years. These are the memes that convince us that women are better suited to domestic and child-rearing tasks than to professional work outside the home. They tell us that women are too precious and vulnerable to survive without the protection of a man—that it is the woman's duty to subsume all her ambitions and desires in order to support and nurture her husband and her children.

HAVE YOU HEARD?

One of the more famous sayings associated with feminism is the catch phrase, "A woman needs a man like a fish needs a bicycle." This phrase is usually attributed to American journalist and political activist Gloria Steinem, although she says that she first heard the phrase from Australian writer and politician Irina Dunn. Dunn, in turn, claims that she was merely paraphrasing a statement from a philosophy text she had read at university. The line even appears in "Tryin' to Throw Your Arms around the World," a song on *Achtung Baby*, the 1991 album by Irish rock band U2. The saying has gone on to be repeated endlessly in different contexts, inspiring songs, books, and websites.

This is a particularly good meme. It is easy to remember and funny, so it is likely to be passed on. But embedded in the humor is a little political message that confronts the expectations of many of its hearers. So it is also a Trojan horse meme.

These memes are so entrenched that they have become "naturalized"; people think that they are merely statements of some external truth. They think they are true because that's the way it has "always" been or that is the way that God ordained it.

Memetic Inertia

It is difficult to unseat memes as powerful as these, which is why after nearly 200 years of feminism, the struggle to ensure equal rights for women continues. There can also be a lot of resistance to giving up these sorts of memes. Men, and even women, who are accustomed to gender roles can become confused and disoriented when ideas they have always believed are shown to be wrong, resulting in hostility and denial.

One of the more interesting phenomena is watching the modern feminist movement. Starting in the 1960s, as women fought for equal pay and treatment in the workplace, the movement shifted into different causes as the times changed. A big splinter within the movement, however, was deciding whether it was more beneficial for a woman to be a homemaker or a professional. Some felt that it was ultimately a woman's choice to do what she liked, even if her choice was to be a stay-at-home mom, while others felt like not being in the workforce was a waste of potential.

The modern feminist movement is just one example of the complex roles facing both men and women. And remember from Chapter 18, people who are disoriented and vulnerable are easy prey for other memes, and just as there are white pride groups and violent anti-gay gangs, there are organizations that pander to some men's sense of loss when facing a new set of values for which they are unprepared.

The Least You Need to Know

- A meme allergen is a situation that causes an extreme reaction in someone.
- Cultural factors, such as wealth and education, can affect how people will react to meme allergens.
- In extreme cases, reactions to memes can lead to hatred and violence.
- Deep-seated memes can make it seem that certain situations are natural, rather than the result of memes.
- Altruistic actions toward one's own kind can turn into racist behavior.

Immuno-Memes: The Meme Blockers

In This Chapter

- How immunization works
- Totalizing systems that lock out alternative views
- General knowledge as the ultimate immuno-meme
- A taxonomy of immuno-memes

If all this talk of hate crimes, intolerance, and bigotry is too much—relax! There are solutions to the meme allergies that lead to these conditions, and in this chapter we are going to look at some of the ways you can protect yourself against pernicious memes.

Continuing with the medical metaphors, we will talk about immuno-memes—the memes that act to immunize us against other memes. Some people have also referred to them as "vaccimes" or "histamemes."

The idea of using memes to protect yourself against memes may seem strange, but that's how immunization generally works. In most cases, the immunological vaccine contains microbes, or parts of microbes, associated with the disease being treated. These produce an immune response in the body, boosting the body's natural defenses and enabling it to respond more quickly and effectively when it encounters the microbe in the wild.

In this chapter, we'll talk about immuno-memes that boost the mind's natural capacity to resist pernicious or dangerous memes.

Totalizing Systems

What makes all the examples in this chapter similar is that they are *totalizing systems*. That means, for instance, that science—when taken to an extreme—claims to provide all the answers to life and existence and dismisses as irrelevant the ideas of philosophy or religion. Critics would see this as reductionism—reducing everything to a mere physical formula.

DEFINITION

A **totalizing system** is one that claims to provide all the answers to a complex set of problems without reference to any other system. All issues and facts, therefore, are part of that system regardless of their origin, and if any beliefs don't fit the system, they are dismissed as irrelevant.

Without care, any point of view can become a totalizing system. In this book, we describe a perspective on the world from the point of view of memetics. We think this is important, but we don't claim that memetics is the *only* way to understand the world. Nevertheless, it would be possible to believe that everything can be explained by memes, and that would be a totalizing system.

General Precautions

You'll remember how we talked in Chapter 18 about immuno-depressants—those things such as stress, disorientation, and insecurity that lower a person's immunity to infection by malicious memes. Being aware that these conditions can suppress our meme-immunity is the first step to avoiding infection. We can be on our guard in those situations and take measures not to fall for memes that will get us into trouble. Never sign something when you are tired or distracted; the thing you are thinking of buying will almost certainly still be there tomorrow, after you've slept on the idea; and don't agree to something until you are satisfied that it is to *your* benefit, not just to the benefit of the person who is asking you.

But aside from these natural precautions, there are specific memes that act as immuno-memes and can help inoculate us against passing fads and scams.

Knowledge, the Ultimate Immuno-Meme

In Chapter 18, we discussed disinfecting the contagious meme. You may remember there were two steps to disinfection:

- Awareness

- Knowledge

The first step we mentioned was to become aware of memes and what they can do. This book—along with other popular texts about memetics—is part of the first step toward immunity.

The second step is knowledge. If you understand how something works and know its limitations and effects, you are less likely to fall for its unfounded promises. Those miracle weight-loss programs that promise to drop you three clothing sizes in two weeks without special food or exercise sound too good to be true. (That's because they are.) Anyone with a reasonable amount of knowledge in the areas of medicine or nutrition knows that these claims are unrealistic.

Bill Gates Gives You Money

Back in 1997, an e-mail started circulating claiming to be from a "Bill Gates" whose software company (you might have heard of it) was testing a new e-mail tracking program. "Bill" was promising to give $1,000 to every person who forwarded the e-mail, once the threshold of 1,000 e-mails was passed. According to urban myth–debunking website snopes.com, this same scam has circulated at least 30 times with slightly different details. But the underlying premise is always the same: there is an e-mail tracing program, and Microsoft/Disney/Nike/whoever will pay you money (or a gift voucher, or a copy of Windows 7) if you simply forward the e-mail to all your friends.

PASS IT ON

We talked about the Nigerian e-mail scam in Chapter 12. This famous scam appeals to both a person's greed ("What's in it for me?") and generosity ("How can I help this unfortunate person?") in equal measure. What it doesn't appeal to is his or her sense of logic. Why would a high-placed treasury official (or his wife, in some versions) be contacting a stranger completely at random? If the story were true, they must have friends, family, former colleagues, or professional contacts.

In many cases, poverty or stress reduces a person's meme-immunity, and this sort of scam must seem like an answer to prayer. Hopefully, the immuno-meme of knowledge will protect them in the future.

This is where a little common sense should come into play. People knowledgeable about computers will know that there is no such thing as an "e-mail tracer." Yes, there are ways to see where an e-mail has come from, but the idea that someone— even Microsoft—could trace all the recipients of a chain e-mail is ridiculous. Don't you think if they could, someone would trace all that spam back to its source and shut the spammers down?

Do the Math

Even if you don't know much about computers, think about the implications of the e-mail: $1,000 for everyone once the 1,000 e-mails level is achieved. I have maybe 20 names in my e-mail address book (and that's pretty small by today's standards). If I forward the e-mail to each of them, and they all forward it to their 20 closest friends, we have 400 e-mails—and it's only the second generation. By the third generation, we are up to 8,000 e-mails—well past the threshold, so Bill has to pay up: $8 million so far. What if those 8,000 recipients send it on to their closest friends? That's 160,000 e-mails—and $160,000,000! Even Microsoft can't sustain expenses like that.

A few minutes of thought and the e-mail hoax falls apart. Yet, hundreds of thousands of people fell for it in 1997, and versions of the chain e-mail continue to circulate even today.

The best immuno-meme is good general knowledge and a healthy skepticism. For a refresher on hoaxes, grifts, and other things you should avoid, check out Chapter 12.

Science

Science is the first of the potentially totalizing systems we want to examine.

We are not suggesting that all science is bad or that it is not a good explanatory framework for understanding the world. But some people seem to want to claim that some branches of science provide all the answers to every problem.

Using the Evolution Models

Evolutionary scientists have provided a clear and convincing—if incomplete—theory about the way in which life on Earth developed and evolved. Theories and experiments have shown that when the right chemicals are mixed and subjected to energy in the appropriate form, amino acids start to form. This experiment was first performed convincingly in 1952 by Stanley Miller and Harold Urey, who were bio-chemists at the University of Chicago. They mixed water, methane, ammonia, and hydrogen in the proportions thought to exist on primordial Earth, and applied electricity to the mix to simulate lightning. After one week of operation, about 10 percent of the carbon in the experiment had turned into organic molecules, with about 2 percent of the solution forming amino acids. Miller and Urey didn't create life, but the experiment produced the basic building blocks that are necessary for life.

Scientists have also built a convincing model for the way in which simple organisms evolve into more complex ones: natural selection. They have unearthed a fossil record that provides a partial confirmation of the incomplete evolutionary map.

Still no complete theory about the way in which consciousness evolved has been formulated, but guesses have been made that are starting to form a suggestion.

Spoiled by Acceptance

The problem with all this success is that some people—not necessarily the scientists—claim that's all there is. Life is merely a mechanical process carried on over millennia that results in you and me. All the art, music, philosophy, and other aspects of cultural creation are merely the random outputs of biological machines, with no more significance in the general scheme of the universe than a random comet crashing into a star.

HAVE YOU HEARD?

Despite being an avowed atheist, Richard Dawkins is much less a reductionist than many people think. In the meme chapter of *The Selfish Gene,* he states, "I am an enthusiastic Darwinian, but I think Darwinism is too big a theory to be confined to the narrow context of the gene." That is, he refuses to limit the meaning of what it is to be human to genetics. And that is where meme theory came in.

Because this totalizing theory needs no god to explain anything, it refuses to admit even the possibility of a god. Because a human being can be described in terms of interacting genes, chromosomes, nucleic acids, and so on, some people deny that there can be anything beyond the machine of the human body.

The memes and memeplexes of science are particularly good at rationalizing away problems that cannot be encompassed by their narrow theories. While science is good at answering some questions, it should not be the answer to all of them.

Religion

According to many meme theorists, from Richard Dawkins himself to more recent memeticists such as Susan Blackmore, religion is one of the more insidious meta-memes. Religious memeplexes can form very powerful and very resilient totalizing systems that are immune to many forms of attack.

First, religions possess the ultimate justification: they were designed by God. Anything, including war, can be justified in the name of a deity.

Second, the "god meme" also provides great psychological comfort—an answer to those vexing questions of life and meaning, the promise of an underlying purpose to life, and the promise of life after death.

We provided an overview on religion in Chapter 10, but let's focus on how religion can prevent people from taking on new religious ideas.

The Old Bait and Switch

Religions have highly developed bait and punishment memes that attract hosts with promises of everlasting life or peace and contentment, and sanctions against disbelief—eternal punishment or torment. As we saw in Chapter 14, bait can appeal to both the selfish and the altruistic parts of a host's character.

Again, we stress that just because a structure can be described memetically, it doesn't make it wrong or underhanded. Unlike some other meme theorists, we don't dismiss religion as misguided.

Fundamentalism at Its Finest

But where religion becomes totalizing—or in its own language, fundamentalist—it becomes a memeplex with which we need to be careful. Some people refuse to accept the theory of evolution because it doesn't fit with a literal interpretation of the Bible. If two ideas are incompatible, then one must go, and a totalizing system will always say that the other idea is irrelevant.

PASS IT ON

It is no accident that many of the cults we looked at in Chapter 17 started as fundamentalist sects of existing religions. The fundamentalist meme has something like a siege mentality—it assumes that everyone is attempting to co-opt it or infect it in some way. This is why fundamentalist organizations—not just religious ones—are vigilant about weeding out members who don't hold closely enough to the doctrines of the sect.

This stance can make people say some things that sound pretty crazy. In Chapter 16, we met one-time president of the Flat Earth Society, Charles K. Johnson. One of his main reasons for refusing to accept that the earth was round was because the scriptures say that "Jesus ascended *up* to heaven," and he maintained that you can't go up from a ball. Because Johnson's memeplex refused any explanation from outside his own narrow theory, he was forced into some very strange assertions.

Some very sincere Christians refuse to accept the possibility of manmade global warming because it isn't mentioned in the Bible. This sort of faith has the potential to cause enormous damage to the planet.

Politics

Political ideologies are an area in which intolerance and conflict are a very real danger. For 30 years, the Cold War kept the world in danger of destruction because two different political and economic systems refused to accept that their systems weren't the only ones. Like some religions, some political ideologies come with the meme, "Convert or die."

Political memeplexes don't usually have access to the "special messenger from God" meme but can rely on memes that privilege age and experience and the wisdom that those characteristics bring. The aging oligarchy in China is one of these, and the meme influences people to see value in political stability. In democratic countries, on the other hand, memes for youth and innovation have more hold, and people are more likely to elect a new leader if they are concerned about social problems.

PASS IT ON

There is a reason why potential complex political arguments are often boiled down into sound bites: short, pithy memes are much more "sticky" than difficult reality.

In case you missed it, we go much deeper into the psychology behind political memes in Chapter 11.

A common meme in all political beliefs is one that ridicules the opposition—a far more effective strategy of dismissal than critical argument.

Co-author John Gunders's father used to have a saying about close-minded people: "I've made up my mind: don't confuse me with the facts." A totalizing political system can be summed up in that way. Highly defended memes do not allow the influence of competing memes.

A Taxonomy of Immuno-Memes

As we said earlier, the best defense against malicious memes is a good general knowledge and a healthy skepticism. But there are some specific memes that influence how their host will respond to other memes.

HAVE YOU HEARD?

There are two types of immunization: active and passive. Active immunization is when a mild dose of the disease being inoculated against is injected into the body—usually treated microbes, parts of the microbes, or the toxins they produce. This prompts the body's immune system to react to the microbes and increase its own resistance. Passive immunization is when artificially produced antibodies that directly attack the disease are injected into the body. This form of immunization works faster, but the antibodies break down quickly and the body does not naturally create more.

In 1990, Canadian memeticist Glenn Grant compiled a taxonomy of immuno-memes, which we've slightly modified:

- Conservatism
- Orthodoxy
- Science
- Radicalism
- Nihilism
- Adaptation

Conservatism

This meme automatically resists all innovative memes. The first instinct is that the currently accepted memes are the best for the individual. The problem with this approach is that the individual usually doesn't take the time to actually consider the new meme, despite it possibly being a better fit.

Orthodoxy

A more extreme version of conservatism, this meme automatically rejects all innovative memes. In fact, you'll find the orthodoxy epitaph throughout religious sects. The biggest issue here, in religion, politics, or science, is a zealot mentality that can turn into hatred toward those with different perspectives than one's own.

Science

The most logical approach, science's intent is to test all innovative memes for theoretical consistency and empirical repeatability. This works best if you take "science" in its original sense—from the Latin *scientia*, meaning "knowledge." The process requires the individual to continually re-assess old memes and consider new ones. The challenge with this approach is that the individual can waste time evaluating memes, not because he or she has a true interest in the memes but because he or she must stick to the dogmatic scientific process.

Radicalism

In this approach, the individual embraces one new memeplex and rejects all others. Picture it as the orthodoxy person discovering the memeplex he or she will be committed to for life. The rub here, of course, is that radicalism sounds a bit like the totalizing systems we've been discussing in most of the chapter.

Nihilism

This one has an easy decision process: reject all memeplexes, new and old. Its popularity rises and falls throughout the years, as evidenced by the 1930s Dada art movement or the 1970s punk music revolution. The problem with this approach, as many disillusioned nihilists have discovered, is that not standing for something is a memeplex, too! If there is a label for it, it probably stands for something.

Adaptation

The final approach allows selected innovative memes to infiltrate existing meme-plexes. A good example would be a Spanish speaker who not only learns English but also sprinkles the words within his traditional Spanish speech with other bilingual individuals. The biggest challenge with adaptation is remaining flexible, as human nature tends to gravitate toward security—something this immuno-meme doesn't provide much of.

Be Aware

Regardless of the immuno-meme option you choose, decide with intelligence and wisdom. Remember, not all memes are bad, but even good memes can create problems if they become too powerful or too influential.

INFECTION!

Memes can't be accepted by you without your permission, but they can sneak into your thoughts when you're not paying attention. When it comes to protecting yourself, one of the worst things you can do is focus solely on avoiding one particular meme—because chances are you'll walk right into another one! Fear is definitely not your ally when it comes to navigating memes.

Pernicious memes can only influence your behavior if you don't know that they're there. Be aware of the ideas that you are picking up, and test them against what you already know. Discuss ideas with your friends and colleagues; they'll soon let you know whether you're buying into a conspiracy theory or whether something is starting to swamp your reason.

Don't panic! Remember, memes are tricky replicators that want to spread for their own benefit, not for the benefit of their hosts. But only you can decide what to think and what not to think. The best meme defense is to be in charge of your own destiny.

The Least You Need to Know

- The best defense against a pernicious meme is good general knowledge and a healthy skepticism.
- Even good memeplexes can cause problems if they refuse to acknowledge alternative opinions.

- Remain alert to the memes that you host, and constantly test them against available evidence.

- Science, politics, and religion are meme-based and can be blocked by immuno-memes.

- There are six primary immuno-memes: conservatism, orthodoxy, science, radicalism, nihilism, and adaptation.

The Theories Behind Memes

Memes essentially track our cultural evolution. The modern term "meme" is fewer than four decades old, but we still have a ton of theories as to why certain cultural ideas are passed on. Here, we look at the science and theories behind the meme.

First, we need to go back to the classic theories that came before memes, such as Darwinism, to see what ideas helped create the concept. It makes it easier to know where memes fit within our cultural history.

We can then discuss Richard Dawkins and other luminaries who helped define, promote, and explain the idea of memes in the early '70s.

All the historical knowledge will help us understand the new meme theories. The meme definitions created decades ago haven't remained static, but have evolved and grown over the years. There are even some controversial theorists who argue that memes don't exist at all.

Classic Theories

In This Chapter

- Cultural transmission
- Biological evolution
- Memes and genes
- Theories of cognition
- Theories of culture

We've talked about what memes are, how they spread, and how to recognize them. We've discussed infection and inoculation; we know that memes can be both fun and damaging. And we've laughed at some of the popular and famous memes over the years.

In this chapter, we want to dig a little more deeply into meme theory and look at the way the theory has developed over the years. Some of the theory gets a little dense, but don't worry—we won't get too technical. And we'll provide lots of definitions along the way. If you want to take your knowledge even further, you can go to Appendix C, where we'll point you toward the original sources.

Because meme theory is based on our understanding of genetics, this chapter will also provide a brief outline of the theory of evolution. This might seem a long way from the spread of technology or from RickRolling someone on the Internet, but as you will find, it is impossible to understand the theory behind memes without looking at where it originated. But we promise that we won't get too distracted from our task. If you want to know more, be sure to check out *The Complete Idiot's Guide to Evolution* by Leslie Alan Horvitz.

Early Meme Theories

We said in Chapter 1 that the term "meme" was first used by Richard Dawkins in 1976, but the idea was around before then. The first theory that could loosely be described as memetic was that of German *Lamarckian* biologist Richard Wolfgang Semon in his 1904 publication, *Die Mneme* (translated into English in 1921 as *The Mneme*). Semon's theory was that memory was more than merely remembering facts and events and was also a fundamental biological process in which the effects of experience were encoded in the nervous system of an individual, where they could later be retrieved or even passed on through heredity to later generations. To avoid confusion with the common understanding of memory, he coined the term "mneme" after the muse of memory in Greek mythology to describe this broad construct of ordinary remembering and hereditary memory.

DEFINITION

Lamarckian refers to the work of French naturalist Jean-Baptiste Lamarck, whose early—and now largely discredited—theories on biological evolution included the belief that the environmental development of characteristics, such as the building of muscle tissue, could be passed on to later generations. We will explore these theories in Chapter 22.

Semon's theory was never as influential as he had hoped, and because it relied fundamentally on Lamarck's theory, when the latter was discredited, Semon's work was largely forgotten. It is recognized today mainly through its comparison with the concept of the meme, although despite the coincidence of the names, the similarities between the two theories are mostly superficial.

F. Ted Cloak, Jr.

It wasn't until the early 1970s that theories of culture were proposed that considered learning to be a process of transmitting units of cultural information. One of the first people to fully develop such a theory was American anthropologist F. Ted Cloak, Jr.

Cultural Instructions

Cloak hypothesized that culture was transmitted in small, unrelated snippets, which he called "corpuscles of culture" or "cultural instructions." These instructions could be transmitted across the culture and from generation to generation in a variety of ways, including habituation, conditioning, imitation, or instruction. We would generally call all these types of transmission "learning," but Cloak meant them in quite specific ways. The most interesting of these types of transmission was instruction, which he called "tuition." This occurs when I say to my son, "As soon as the streetlights come on, you must come straight home." There is no demonstration or imitation here—just language carrying the instruction. Cloak maintained that this form of learning was uniquely human.

Two Types of Culture

The important part of Cloak's work in terms of meme theory was that he distinguished between two types of culture: the pictures in our minds, or the cultural instructions, and the external, material expression of those instructions. The mental, cultural instructions are tiny snippets of understanding or belief—the knowledge of how to tie a shoelace, for instance—while the material expressions of those instructions are the physical aspects of our culture: all our interactions, relationships, behaviors, and technologies.

HAVE YOU HEARD?

Cloak had specific names for these two aspects of culture: he called the mental image i-culture and the material structure m-culture.

You can probably see that this breaking of our understanding of culture into two elements is very similar to the way in which we've described memes. The meme is a mental entity that can be carried in material culture, but the meme isn't itself the stone arch, or the YouTube video, but the idea behind those things.

The mental entity is passed from one brain to another—either through imitation or instruction—and if successful, it spreads throughout the society, infecting other carriers. And as it does, it alters the material culture in innumerable ways.

The Goal Is Replication

Cloak maintained that the cultural instructions and their material expressions interact in complicated ways and that each can affect the other—but the heart of his theory is that the ultimate purpose of both the cultural instruction and the material culture is the replication and maintenance of the cultural instruction. Like a flu virus that causes its host to sneeze in order to replicate itself in another host, our cultural instructions control us—we don't control them! From this point of view, we only exist in order to reproduce the cultural instructions.

Cloak went on to say that it wouldn't be very surprising to find behaviors or other material, cultural effects that were irrelevant to, or even destructive of, the individuals who perform them. We saw something of this in our discussion of toxic memes in Chapter 17.

Cavalli-Sforza and Dual-Inheritance Theory

Another theory of cultural transmission developed during the 1970s and in places incorporated Dawkins's work on memes. It is a sub-discipline of cultural anthropology most commonly associated with American biologist E. O. Wilson and Italian geneticist Luigi Luca Cavalli-Sforza and is called gene-culture coevolution or dual-inheritance theory.

Dual-Inheritance Theory

Dual-inheritance theory (DIT) contends that human behavior is influenced by the twin forces of genetic evolution and cultural evolution. Thus, it takes the middle ground in the nature-versus-nurture debates, which seek to determine whether the preprogramming of genetic structures or the influences of external cultural forces are more important in the development of individual consciousness. At the heart of the theory is the concept of *cultural transmission*, which is a Darwinian version of culture that suggests that cultural traits are subject to natural selection.

> **DEFINITION**
>
> **Cultural transmission,** in terms of DIT, means that aspects of culture—thought, speech, action, and artifacts—are transmitted from individual to individual in a way analogous to biological reproduction. In other words, there is the possibility that the reproduction may be imperfect, that a mutation may occur, and that the cultural unit takes on the effects of that mutation, which it passes on when it is next reproduced. It also acknowledges that cultural traits are subject to natural selection—that in a crowded and busy world, some things will prosper and others will be ignored.

Although they acknowledge the role of cultural transmission in their theories, biologists such as E. O. Wilson and Richard Dawkins have been criticized for leaning too heavily on the genetic influences on culture, reducing everything to its essential biology. (You might remember that we quoted Dawkins in Chapter 20, saying that Darwinism was "too big a theory to be confined to the narrow context of the gene," so these claims of reductionism seem to be misplaced, at least in Dawkins's case.) Luigi Cavalli-Sforza, the Italian-born geneticist who spent most of his career at Stanford University, provided one of the first mathematically justified accounts of the way in which knowledge and behavior are transmitted across a culture. His concern was to look at the way in which the transmission of particular cultural traits from parent to child was affected by genetic makeup (and vice-versa).

Three Main Elements

Broadly, the theory developed by Cavalli-Sforza and later picked up by others has three main elements:

- Natural selection

- Evolving culture

- Reaction to the environment

The first maintains that cultural transmission, along with culture itself, arises from a genetically evolved psychological mechanism. That is, our ability to learn from others is an adaptation that has been acquired through natural selection. This Darwinian underpinning leads to the second element, which is that cultures evolve. Although cultural transmission and genetic inheritance are related, they are separate, and both have effects on the culture—producing phenomena that would not occur if there were only one force acting. Finally, this complex of cultural and genetic evolution can result in environmental changes that affect the gene itself.

A good example of how knowledge and behavior are transmitted across a culture is the way in which the culturally learned practice of cooking meat before eating it may have led to the natural selection of genes that shortened the human intestine and changed digestive chemistry to a more energy-efficient model. Similarly, with the rise of agriculture and animal farming and the resulting change in diet, the human genome selected traits that could digest starch and lactose.

Cloak vs. Dawkins

Some people argue that Dawkins deliberately misread Cloak's theory in order to lump it together with other early investigations into cultural transmission, which could then be safely dismissed as not going far enough. And of course, in 1976 the great texts of DIT were yet to be published. While some writers refer to *The Selfish Gene* as one of the early texts of DIT, others cite it as an example of "neo-Darwinian orthodoxy" that doesn't take seriously enough the importance of cultural transmission.

PASS IT ON

The key to Dawkins's theory was that genes were replicators, and that given the right conditions, it was inevitable that they would replicate. As we have already seen, a replicator is an entity that has the remarkable property of being able to create copies of itself. The best-known example—aside from the meme—is the DNA molecule.

Whoever is right about this, the point is that Dawkins wasn't writing a book about theories of cultural transmission; he was writing a book about biology. The main purpose of *The Selfish Gene* was to promote his view of biology as one in which the main drivers of evolution were genes, not species. The invention of the meme was a minor part of the book, intended to clarify his biological theory by pointing out that DNA was not unique as a replicator. To see how he arrived at the concept of the meme, it is necessary to talk about the theory of evolution.

Darwin's Evolution

The belief that species change over time has been held by philosophers and scientists since Greek antiquity, and some ancients—such as pre-Socratic philosopher Anaximander—even considered the possibility that all life sprang from a common ancestor.

The theory of evolution in its modern sense is most commonly attributed to English naturalist Charles Darwin, but there were many other people involved in the discoveries that led to the suite of theories we call Darwinism. Alfred Russel Wallace conducted field work in Central America and Malaysia during the mid-nineteenth century, which led to him proposing a theory of natural selection that greatly inspired Darwin. At that time, Lamarck's work—the first systematic theory of evolution—hadn't fallen completely out of favor.

Today, evolutionary biologists are divided over some of the details of Darwin's theory, and questions remain unanswered about the fossil record—but among scientists and within most of the general community, the principles of evolution are no longer controversial.

Two Major Insights

At the heart of the theory of evolution are Darwin's two great insights that still define it:

- Populations multiply until stopped.

- Only the strong survive.

The first insight was that populations—whether they are microbes, mosquitoes, or humans—will tend to increase at an exponential rate until the environment is unable to sustain the numbers.

The second insight is a consequence of the first and states that given the environmental pressures of population growth, there will be competition between members of that population—and not all of them will survive. Some individuals will, for whatever reason, possess better survival techniques than others, and these individuals will tend to live longer (and, as a consequence, breed more). As their offspring will tend to carry those same advantages, eventually—over many generations—the entire population will carry those genetic advantages. Darwin called this process "natural selection."

Darwinism in Action

One of Darwin's examples, and a favorite of basic naturalist books, is the giraffe. Darwin suggested that in any population of giraffes, some would have necks or forelegs more elongated than the others, and that in times of drought these peculiarities would have been an advantage in allowing those individuals to reach leaves beyond the reaches of their competitors. As the long-necked giraffes would survive to breed for longer and pass on those characteristics to their offspring, so the long-necked giraffe we know today evolved.

INFECTION!

The giraffe example is a great tool for explaining how natural selection might occur, but some biologists have pointed out problems with the theory. First, a taller animal would also have been heavier and required more food to sustain it, so this might actually have been a disadvantage in times of drought. Second, even today female giraffes are about three feet shorter than fully grown males, and if the theory is correct, many females and immature males would have died in drought times—thus condemning the entire population. Finally, giraffes today don't necessarily display a tendency to feed from high branches during times of drought.

Some biological systems are very stable: some species of insects and invertebrates, for instance, have changed very little over the course of millennia, and famously the crocodile shares many of the characteristics of its ancestors in the fossil record.

Requirements for Evolution

For evolution to occur, three pre-conditions are required:

- Variation
- Selection
- Heredity

Variation refers to the fact that individuals within a species will have minor differences: a different height and weight, or maybe slightly greater lung or brain capacity.

Selection describes the way in which some of those variations—like the proto-giraffe's marginally longer neck—may provide a slight survival advantage over other members of the species, and of course living longer means the opportunity to breed more.

And heredity—the way in which the genes of the parents are combined to form the genetic structure of the offspring—means that those characteristics that meant that the parent was able to survive longer to breed are passed on to the offspring so they also have that characteristic.

Proving Evolution Through Genetics

Farmers had long known that there was some mechanism that allowed the transmission of characteristics from parent to offspring, and without necessarily understanding it, they made use of its principles through the selective breeding of plants and animals. The assumptions then were that the characteristics of the mother and father were blended, and the characteristics of the offspring would fall somewhere between the two.

Genetics Chooses Sides

It was not until the mid-nineteenth century that Austrian monk and scientist Gregor Johann Mendel came to realize that this belief was wrong and that there existed somewhere a discrete particle of inheritance. Over seven years, Mendel conducted a series of breeding experiments with pea plants, trying to selectively breed for a number of characteristics, including shape and color of the seed, length of the stem, and flower color. He discovered that the flowers were either white or purple, but never a blend of the two. Inheritance, he hypothesized, was based on a particle received from each parent. We now know that these particles are called genes—a name that didn't exist until British geneticist William Bateson coined it in the early twentieth century. Although Mendel's work was not recognized in his lifetime, the entire science of genetics is based on his pea experiment.

DNA Discovery

By the mid-twentieth century, biologists had recognized that the particle of inheritance was DNA (deoxyribonucleic acid), a substance that exists in the nucleus of every living cell, whether plant or animal. Famously, it was two molecular biologists—American James Watson and Briton Francis Crick—who discovered the structure of DNA in 1953—a discovery that won them the Nobel Prize for Medicine in 1962. They found that DNA was a long complex of molecules called nucleotides, arranged in the form of a double helix or spiral. Along this spiral molecule are arranged a series of smaller molecules called bases, and although there are only four of them (usually identified by the letters A, C, G, and T), the particular order of the bases along the DNA molecule encodes all the information needed to construct the acids and proteins that make up cells—and ultimately, life.

HAVE YOU HEARD?

Although there are only four nucleotide subunits—adenine, cytosine, guanine, and thymine (A, C, G, and T), all arranged in pairs—a human chromosome (a single, coiled piece of DNA containing many genes) can contain as many as 220 million base pairs.

The gene is a particular part of this DNA molecule—a section of the double helix that contains both information about what the gene does and when it should do it, as well as other sequences that scientists still don't understand fully. This building block of life codes for behaviors that cause the host to act in particular ways, as well as the obvious things such as appearance. So I might have dark hair, pale skin, and light-colored eyes because those are the characteristics passed on to me by the genetic material that came from my parents—and in the same way, I might have a particular personality because those same genes predispose me to think in a particular way.

Scientists no longer see the gene as a simple molecule that codes for a single trait—eye color, for instance—but as a much more complicated series of codes that produce overlapping functional products. Fortunately for us, the metaphor of the gene operates perfectly well in its classical formation as a unit of inheritance. Because this book isn't about genetics, the simple definition is adequate for our purposes. Whatever their chemical form, there are two important characteristics of genes: they replicate, and in Dawkins's terms, they replicate for survival.

Richard Dawkins and *The Selfish Gene*

The 1976 book *The Selfish Gene* was in part written to counter a view, popular in biology at the time, that tried to account for certain behaviors in the animal kingdom in terms of "the benefit to the species." Thus, the parent bird that sacrifices its life for its offspring is acting instinctively against its own interests, but in a way that will protect the gene pool or increase the viability of the group as a whole. As attractive as these theories might seem, Dawkins claimed that they were incorrect and that all behaviors were due to genetic programming designed to solely benefit the gene.

The First Replicator

Dawkins hypothesized that somewhere during the birth of life on Earth, there evolved a unique molecule that could replicate itself. We cannot know the properties of that first replicator, however, because it has left no traces. It may have been the precursor to the only biological replicator that exists today—DNA—or it may have been unrelated. It doesn't really matter. What is important is that at some point, self-replicating molecules started building "survival machines"—biological complexes that allowed the molecule to store food and erect defenses. Today, we call those survival machines cells. The replicating molecule, the DNA, lives in the nucleus of the cell, the body of the cell contains cytoplasm that helps to absorb nutrients and give the cell structure, and the outer membrane protects the cell from the environment by allowing some proteins to pass while blocking others.

At this point, it is important to remember that although Dawkins uses language that suggests the replicating molecules have some sort of intention or even consciousness, this is not the case. The replicators are dumb chemicals that operate in the way they do because that is how they are programmed.

The Power of Numbers

In time, those single-celled survival machines—driven by the same natural selection that caused their evolution in the first place—started grouping together in ways that allowed them to share resources and to specialize functions. Multi-celled organisms developed—at first, simple ones such as algae and fungi—and later more complex organisms such as plants and invertebrates (and ultimately, us). In Dawkins's terms, from the point of view of the replicating DNA, we are simply survival machines designed to protect and to aid in replication.

> **HAVE YOU HEARD?**
>
> The idea of humans being the survival machines of their genes might sound shocking and controversial, but even in 1976 when *The Selfish Gene* was first published, this view was not particularly new (and indeed was considered orthodox by many biologists). The new field of sociobiology, largely founded in 1975 with the publication of *Sociobiology: The New Synthesis* by the great American biologist E. O. Wilson, had ensured that these themes were well known in academic circles as well as in the media, and Dawkins's book rode this wave of popularity.

The message to take from *The Selfish Gene* was that simple preconditions can lead to complex results—that the underlying chemical processes that cause the gene to behave in a particular way can account for many of the behaviors that we see in plants and animals (and even in ourselves). Dawkins points out that most organisms will defend and support their kin over other members of the same species and that this altruism is due to the fact that kin carry mostly the same genes. Thirty years since its publication, this scientific principle remains unchallenged.

But Dawkins acknowledges that the gene doesn't have everything its own way and that human intelligence can overcome the insistence of the selfish gene. A good example is contraception, which defeats the gene's attempt to replicate itself.

Memes as the New Replicators

Dawkins used another example. He claimed that a new replicator was evolving that had the power to defeat the dominance of the gene by encouraging people to consciously act against the blind compulsions of that particle. The new replicator was the meme. The selfish gene urges its host to act in a way that ensures the survival of the gene (and the host, obviously). Aside from the kinship example mentioned earlier, this theory doesn't account for altruism very well. Why would a gene's survival machine destroy itself for the benefit of unrelated genes? But people do sacrifice themselves to save others; they do inconvenience or even endanger themselves for a principle or for an ideology. Perhaps someone is inspired by someone's heroic deed to act similarly in the same circumstances. Perhaps a principle such as "The needs of the many outweigh the needs of the few" is recognized and believed and affects the behavior of someone faced by an agonizing decision.

HAVE YOU HEARD?

You might know the phrase "the needs of the many outweigh the needs of the few" from the film *Star Trek 2: The Wrath of Khan,* but the sentiment behind that saying has been around for many years. The ancient Greek philosopher Epicurus taught a doctrine of happiness through the minimization of pain to self and others, and this led to the Utilitarian philosophy of John Stuart Mill, which strove for the "greatest good for the greatest number." There are even echoes of the saying in the Bible when the Jewish High Priest, Caiaphas, justi-fied the execution of Jesus Christ by saying that it was better for one man to die than for the whole nation to be punished (John 11:49–50).

Memes vs. Genes

These are examples of memes that work against the dominance of the gene—something that Dawkins thought would become more prevalent. In Dawkins's formulation, the meme copied the characteristics of the gene almost perfectly. Despite the fact that the gene was a biological entity observable under a microscope and the meme was a purely mental state, their key similarities are the principles of replication and selfishness. In the same way that the gene affects behavior due to its pre-programmed drive to replicate, the meme wants to spread from brain to brain and causes its host to behave in particular ways—from telling a joke to structuring his or her entire life in ways that conform to a particular ideology or belief.

The Birth of Memetics

This section of the chapter has focused on Richard Dawkins and *The Selfish Gene,* but this foundation text is about biology and evolution. And for Dawkins, the meme was only an interesting thought experiment. Indeed, there was very little discussion of the concept in the years following the publication of the book, as most reviewers concentrated, sensibly, on what the book was mainly about.

The Resurrection of the Meme

The concept of the meme—the *meme* meme, if you like—might have faded away if not for the attention of two people. The first was Douglas Hofstadter, who between 1981 and 1983 wrote a column for *Scientific American* called *Metamagical Themas* in which he discussed a broad range of scientific, mathematical, and literary topics. In his January 1983 column on viral sentences and self-replicating structures, he discussed Dawkins's conception of the meme. When the article was reprinted in 1985, in the book that took the name of the column, Hofstadter mentioned receiving a lot of mail concerning the article—including one that suggested that the new science of memes should be called *memetics*. He thoroughly approved of this idea.

The second person was Daniel Dennett, a highly regarded philosopher of the mind at Tufts University in Massachusetts, who found that the concept fitted his developing ideas about the nature of consciousness.

Daniel Dennett and *Consciousness Explained*

In October 1989, Dennett delivered the prestigious Mandel Lecture for the American Society for Aesthetics. The Society asks lecturers to address the question of how art promotes human evolution or development, and Dennett chose to do this by discussing Dawkins's theory of memes. In the lecture, Dennett outlined the theory and emphasized the fact that this wasn't just an analogy—that memes don't just behave *like* genes but that they literally evolve. The two replicators evolve in different media at different rates, but both are subject to the laws of natural selection.

A Higher Consciousness

Dennett incorporated this lecture into his book *Consciousness Explained*, which was an attempt to trace the development of consciousness from an explicitly Darwinian perspective. He saw memetic evolution as the latest in a series of increasingly fast developments, after genetic evolution and *phenotypic plasticity*.

He argued that genetic evolution has taken between three and four billion years to create a brain capable of consciousness. Phenotypic plasticity—the ability of an organism to change its body in reaction to environmental pressures—has been around for some millions of years, but memetic evolution is a recent addition—becoming a powerful force in only the last 100,000 years. The interactions of all these forces have contributed to the design of human consciousness.

Understanding Complex Data for Survival

In the same way that plasticity enhances the ability of an organism to change its body or its behavior to increase its chances of survival, so does the development of memes greatly add to the brain's ability to process increasingly complex data (such as language). Dennett's hypothesis in *Consciousness Explained* was that human consciousness was a huge complex of memes running like a software program on the underlying hardware architecture of a brain that was not designed for any such activities but which owed its development to the way in which its genetic makeup was altered by the "programs" running in its architecture.

This is another version of the gene-culture coevolution we looked at earlier in this chapter. The genetic evolution of the human brain certainly shapes consciousness, but consciousness also has effects on the brain as well as on the entire genome. According to Dennett, the meme is responsible for much of this evolution.

Dennett and *Darwin's Dangerous Idea*

Several years later, Dennett revisited the meme in *Darwin's Dangerous Idea*, a book designed to bring Darwinian theory to an interdisciplinary audience. He again drew on material from the original 1989 Mandel Lecture, adapting and expanding it as he examined how far he could take the identity between genes and memes. If they are identical objects within different media, he pondered, what is to the meme as DNA is to the gene? Can a physiological brain state be found that corresponds exactly to a particular meme? Is there an identical set of chemicals in my brain when I think about spectacles to those in your brain when you think about them?

The answer obviously is no—even if we had the technology to analyze the brain's states that closely. The reason is because genetics is a *syntactic* system. The nucleotide bases (A, C, G, and T) form an alphabet that fits together according to particular rules to form coherent sentences (genes and chromosomes). Memetics, on the other hand, is a *semantic* system; it's about meaning.

DEFINITION

Syntactic and **semantic** are both terms from theoretical linguistics. Syntax is the study of the principles and rules for constructing sentences in language—grammar, in other words. Semantics is the study of the meaning that is produced by those grammatical constructions. Sentences in written English can be incorrect grammatically but still meaningful as well as syntactically correct but meaningless.

Dennett offered an analogy to explain the difference. What do William Shakespeare's *Romeo and Juliet* and Leonard Bernstein's *West Side Story* have in common? (If you are too young to remember *West Side Story*, substitute *The Taming of the Shrew* and Gil Junger's 1999 film *10 Things I Hate About You*.) Syntactically, the answer is nothing—the texts share no common dialogue, the settings are different, and even the genres are different. They do not share a single line of writing. But semantically, we know that the stories are the same—not just because Bernstein told us that he based his musical on the play, but because we can see the similarities in the plot and the characters. The text is different, but the story is the same.

There are other major differences between genetic transcription and memetic transmission. Gene copying is very accurate. It's not perfect of course, or there could be no evolution at all, but there are complex proofreading and duplication routines in DNA to ensure that nearly all the genes are transcribed correctly. Brains, on the other hand, seem to be designed to censor, adapt, interpolate, and otherwise modify any input before it's outputted. Just think of the game Telephone, or the way in which a fishing story tends to get embellished to the point of nonsense. One of the markers of cultural evolution is the extraordinarily high rate of mutation. This means that memes aren't the product of millions of random mutations but of a significantly fewer number of very deliberate mutations.

Dennett doesn't see these problems as terminal (some do, though, and you can read about them in Chapter 22). The connections between the genes and the phenotype are not always apparent, but scientists can extrapolate the genetic structure from the phenotype. A certain type of behavior in animals is assumed to be caused by a particular genetic makeup. It is no different at the memetic level. We do not need to know the particular physiological reasons why an acronym or a clever slogan is easier to remember than a long or random set of words, but we can extrapolate important understandings about human memory because we know that they *are* easier to remember.

In the next chapter, we'll look further at the way in which the concept and theory of the meme was developed further than Dawkins had expected—growing from a theory of cultural transmission to an entire discipline in its own right.

The Least You Need to Know

- The first written mention of memes was by biologist Richard Wolfgang Semon in 1904.
- Anthropologist F. Ted Cloak, Jr. described memelike "cultural instructions," or ideas passed through society.
- Meme theory is based on Darwinism, or the idea that culture naturally evolves based on new needs.
- Richard Dawkins's *The Selfish Gene* focused on evolution and biology but spurred an interest in memes.
- Philosopher Daniel Dennett argued that memes modified themselves as much as genes, through evolution.

New Meme Theories

In This Chapter

- Memetics as a contagion theory
- Memes that tap into belief systems
- Ways in which memes are contagious
- Meme and gene coevolution
- New competing ideas

The work of Richard Dawkins and Daniel Dennett provided a solid theoretical basis for memetics, but it remained little more than an academic curiosity until the work of a number of other writers brought it to the attention of a wider public.

In their own ways, these writers broadened the definitions and meanings of memes. Some simply popularized the science while others moved beyond the limited definitions of Dawkins and even the more completely worked-out version of Dennett, eventually making it the science we recognize today.

In this chapter, we will briefly survey the most important contributions to memetics from this time. The following are certainly not all the books and authors dealing with memetics, but they provide a good overview of the ways in which the science developed.

Richard Brodie's *Virus of the Mind*

One of the first descriptions of memetics designed for a popular audience was Richard Brodie's 1996 book, *Virus of the Mind: The New Science of the Meme*. Brodie was a computer programmer at Microsoft when he became interested in memetics.

The book is really a simple introduction to memetics, broadly speaking from an evolutionary psychology perspective.

Brodie claimed that the book could have been called *Introduction to Memetics* but that the actual title "pushes more buttons: it attracts more attention and more people will read it." This amusing admission illustrates a point that Brodie makes throughout the book: that the most powerful memes are the ones that are based on the primordial human drives of fear, food, and sex, and that in order to have a complete and satisfying life, people need to rid themselves of damaging memes and deliberately choose memes that will benefit them. It is no surprise that Brodie's second book was a self-help guide and that he is popular as a motivational speaker.

What's a Mind Virus?

Psychologists argue that much of human behavior is governed by primordial drives that evolved in the dawn of human development. While our conscious minds can overcome these instinctual motivations, primal urges such as fear, anger, and sex still have an important effect on human behavior. We are often told that "sex sells," but why? Because sex is one of the basic drives, and memes that are attached to that drive tend to be very successful.

PASS IT ON

Have you ever formed an instant dislike of someone or something? Ever said, "That guy really pushes my buttons!"? According to Brodie, this is evidence of prehistoric urges breaking through the civilized veneer of our behavior. Of course, we don't usually act on those urges, but they do take our attention. A "gut feeling" is probably little more than a hidden meme acting on us unconsciously.

While he uses the terminology of the virus throughout the book, for Brodie a mind virus is simply another name for Dawkins's self-replicating meme.

The Five Survival Memes

Because of the underlying drives, memes associated with some sort of fear—fear of contagion, for instance—will be more memorable and more effective. He suggests that the first memes were ones based on those drives. Our distant ancestors—the ones who had to worry about things such as not being eaten by saber-toothed tigers—probably built their worlds on memes that aided in survival.

Brodie theorized that there were five survival memes:

- Crisis

- Mission

- Problem

- Danger

- Opportunity

The "crisis" meme quickly alerted people to danger; the "mission" meme helped groups organize and cooperate to find food or defend the group; the "problem" meme helped to identify issues (such as a lack of food) and organize solutions; the "danger" meme helped groups to understand that dangers existed even in the absence of a specific crisis and to identify those dangers; and the "opportunity" meme reinforced the benefits of quickly acquiring a reward—food or a mate.

Hard-Wired in Humans

Brodie's contention is that these primordial memes continue to influence behavior, and although the crises they warn against might be more sophisticated than "Tiger! Run!", the traces of the memes can still be seen. To illustrate this point, he provides two descriptions of the book: one using neutral language and the other chock-full of words that evoke those five primordial memes:

> *Introduction to Memetics* is a compilation of ideas on the science of memetics. Each chapter summarizes a different topic in this field. Included are examples of how memetics impacts people's lives, illustrates historical data, and offers choices for the future.

> *Virus of the Mind* exposes the imminent crisis of the dangerous new technology known as *memetics*. What is it, and how can we guard against its harmful effects? Our only chance is to have everyone read *Virus of the Mind* before it is too late!

The second blurb reads as more exciting, not just because of the sensationalism but because it taps into those primordial memes that still affect us.

Unconscious Urges

Brodie acknowledges that he had an agenda in writing the book: he wanted to make a difference in people's lives. He sees memes—mind viruses—as (often) unwelcome and unconscious beliefs that add elements of stress and confusion. Each meme programs us in particular ways, and the added stress comes from being infected by contradictory memes at the same time—often with the result of creating new memes to explain away the contradiction.

His solution is to actively choose the memes that will benefit us and lead us in the directions we want to go, and the first step is to become aware of the memes that are currently infecting us. In that regard, *Virus of the Mind* is a sort of self-help book, outlining why we sometimes act the way we do.

Despite the use of the word "virus" in Brodie's book, his definition of memes was much the same as Dawkins's, and he didn't take the metaphor any further. In the next section of this chapter, we'll look at another meme theorist who did explore much further the themes of infection and contagion.

Aaron Lynch and *Thought Contagion*

Aaron Lynch was a mathematics and philosophy major in college when he first started developing his ideas about the transmission of beliefs—a project he continued in his spare time while he worked as an engineer at Fermilab, the U.S. Department of Energy's particle research laboratory.

The book he was writing was tentatively entitled *Abstract Evolution*. In 1983, Douglas Hofstadter mentioned the forthcoming book approvingly in his *Scientific American* column, but Lynch found it hard to get a publisher for this unusual and provocative title. In 1991, he published a paper called "Thought Contagion as Abstract Evolution" in the *Journal of Ideas*, a new memetics journal, but it took five more years and multiple rewriting before his book was finally published in 1996 as *Thought Contagion: How Belief Spreads Through Society: The New Science of Memes*. The book was an immediate best-seller and established Lynch as a leading light in the memetics movement.

Understanding Paradigm Shifts

Lynch describes memetics as a *paradigm shift*—a completely new way of thinking about a subject. Traditionally, people talked about belief in terms of how people acquire ideas: memetics turns the idea on its head and asks how ideas acquire people.

DEFINITION

Paradigm shift is the idea that scientific development continues incrementally, building on previous research and ideas, until the underlying theories and assumptions can no longer support the new evidence and a new way of think-ing is required. The most famous example of a paradigm shift is the Copernican revolution, which placed the sun at the center of the solar system—replacing the Ptolemaic model, which was becoming increasingly over-elaborate in an attempt to match the theory to the observations. The term was coined by American scientist and philosopher Thomas Kuhn in his 1962 book *The Structure of Scientific Revolutions.*

The early chapters of the book look at the ways memetics relates to existing disci-plines with the social sciences, including economics, sociology, cultural anthropology, history, and others. His argument is that memetics offers additional insights into questions that are usually answered by the people-acquiring-ideas paradigm. Thus, in relation to economics, he points out that while economists consider an idea's success in relation to the amount of wealth it generates, memetics is more interested in the number of adherents an idea gathers. His argument is that more people will promote ideas that privilege them personally, and that as capitalism is likely to be more profitable in the long term—despite periods of fast growth of the communism meme—capitalism will eventually become more prevalent.

Similarly, Lynch contends that in history, as it was traditionally practiced, the focus was on prominent people—kings and presidents—and tended to ignore the "little people." Memetics, however, allows historians to look at ideas such as contagion theory to explain how a groundswell of opinion forced the prominent people to make decisions that were acceptable to the populace. While a prominent person's behaviors might be more likely to be imitated, by virtue of their numbers, it is the common people who account for most of a meme's reproduction.

Viral Ideas

While Lynch's application of memetic theory to other disciplines helped to outline its advantages to a growing audience, his main achievement was to add a new dimen-sion to the science of memetics by introducing a new metaphor: contagion. Dawkins himself made reference to this theme by comparing a meme that parasitizes the mind of the host to the way that a virus parasitizes a cell, and you'll remember that F. Ted Cloak, Jr. talked about the flu virus that causes its host to sneeze in order to replicate itself in another host. And of course, Brodie's book explicitly compared memes to viruses.

But Lynch used the metaphor in a much more developed sense than it had been used before. If memes travel virally and increase exponentially, it follows that those that start with a larger population of hosts will tend to be more successful than those that do not. Because many memes are passed from parents to their children, the meme for having a large family will tend to increase the number of people hosting that meme simply through an increased birthrate. Lynch points to the fact that the Amish communities in the United States have a greater birthrate than the general community, and as a result the community can continue to replicate and grow.

In fact, memes can have a significant effect on population growth. Lynch compares the Jehovah's Witness communities with other religious groups in America and finds that the memes for large families (including memes for polygamy), as well as the proselytizing implied in their name, has led the church to become one of the fastest-growing religions in America. On the other hand, the Shakers held a significant influence in American society in the mid-1800s, yet one of their strongest memes was one for celibacy—which led to relatively low birthrates among adherents. With few children joining the movement, outreach and proselytizing was insufficient to match the natural decline in numbers, and the movement is almost extinct today.

Passing On Thoughts

Furthermore, Lynch outlines seven modes of memetic transmission:

- Quantity parental
- Efficiency parental
- Proselytic
- Preservational
- Adversative
- Cognitive advantage
- Motivational

INFECTION!

Lynch is careful to point out that just because memes spread virally, we shouldn't think that they are bad. Most memes are neutral, and the meme that we should love our neighbors is positively good. "Thought contagion" should not carry a negative connotation in relation to memetics.

Lynch's theories of cultural transmission are insightful and complex, and we encourage you to look at the original text, because all we can do here is provide a brief overview of the different modes of transmission.

Quantity Parental

"Quantity parental" pulls on the classic axiom, "Be fruitful and multiply." With a high retention rate for memes passed on by parents, this is an easy way to increase the number of hosts of a particular meme. One of the best examples is in Amish culture, where having large families is highly encouraged—and supported by the necessity for many farm hands in a society that eschews mechanical assistance.

Efficiency Parental

"Efficiency parental" acknowledges that simply having children is no guarantee that they will embrace their parents' beliefs. However, some memes increase their chances of transmission by guiding the method of parenting to include ideas that privilege parents as a source of good ideas. As an example, the saying, "Father knows best" would make sons and daughters consider their dad wise by default.

Proselytic

In "proselytic" mode, hosts actively seek out nonbelievers in order to convince them of the value of the meme. Religions and political ideologies usually grow in this way, and often the form of proselytizing involves fear—fear of punishment in the afterlife, or fear of social decline unless certain political choices are made. More recent religions, such as Scientology, provoke the fear that nonbelievers are not being as successful as they can be.

Preservational

Memes using "preservational" mode protect themselves from disbelief by causing the hosts to avoid activities that might lead to questioning the meme. Thus, there are memes in certain religious communities that warn against higher education, and there is the folkloric injunction not to discuss religion or politics in polite company. An extreme example would be a cult that has a remote compound, forbids interaction with nonmembers, and limits information from the outside world.

Adversative

In "adversative" mode, memes influence their hosts to aggressively attack or sabotage competing memes. This mode has been the basis of the "convert or die" mentality of many religious crusades over the ages. Adversative memes were also the motivation behind the colonization of Africa. Promised riches aside, religious zealots claimed to want to save the natives from damnation—despite their already having an established religion sometimes centuries older than the missionaries.

Cognitive Advantage

In "cognitive advantage" mode, a meme that seems well-founded and cogent will tend to survive longer and spread faster than one founded simply on tradition or superstition. A millennia-old belief system with ancient texts and millions of followers will be more welcomed than a relatively new concept. Who wants to risk investing their lives on a flash in the pan? (Celebrity endorsements help.)

Motivational

Finally, "motivational" mode is evoked when hosts are convinced that adopting a meme will be personally advantageous for them. For instance, some religions teach that the more people you convert, the higher your chances of redemption in the afterlife. It is a brilliant meme that pushes the follower to bring more people into the flock, increasing the power of both the meme itself and the individuals behind it.

Memes Evolve and Cross Categories

This taxonomy—Lynch calls it an epidemiology—is a simplification, and he acknowledges that with any given meme, two or more of these modes may be invoked.

It is also important to note that memes do not remain static but evolve and merge over time. Lynch describes the merging of two particularly virulent memes—the hell meme and the doomsday meme. The doomsday meme is the belief that Earth is in imminent danger of destruction—a theme that was quite prominent at times during the 1980s. The problem for the meme is that the belief doesn't necessarily inspire much proselytism. Many people would rather live in ignorance of the impending doom. On the other hand, the belief that anyone who dies an unbeliever will go to hell inspires a lot of urgent proselytism, as the believer attempts to save the souls of friends and family as well as others. The fact that doomsday will result in the deaths of many unbelievers means that the two memes merge for people who believe in both, and the resulting hell-doomsday meme has much more proselytic drive than either of the memes on their own.

Skepticism with Lynch's Theory

Lynch's book took memetics beyond anything that Dawkins or Dennett had expected in their writing, but it also received a fair amount of criticism.

> **INFECTION!**
>
> As we saw in Chapter 19 in relation to meme allergies, some people have an extreme reaction to particular memes when something they have considered as true and natural are shown to be merely assumptions or convenient fictions.
>
> Something that very much confronts traditional expectations of cultural development and intelligence is meme theory. If you've read this far in the book, you are probably not someone with a strong objection to memetics—but there are many books written dismissing memetics as not having any critical value. As we will see in the following chapter, there are some significant problems with the theory of memes, but many of the objections are not with elements of the theory but rather with the concept as a whole. Even memetics can be a meme allergen. If you're agreeing with this, then we appear to have successfully infected you!

The main problem with the theory is that Lynch's definition of the meme is unclear, and while he acknowledges Dawkins's foundational text, his version of the meme seems to lack all the universal Darwinism specificity that Dawkins spoke about. While he uses the term "replication," it is not at all certain that Lynch means it in the genetic sense. Lynch's meme is of the memes-acquiring-people type, but he never talks about it in terms of the blind autonomy that Dawkins and Dennett saw as its defining characteristic.

Definitions Are Too Broad

Similarly, Lynch seems to be very inclusive in his definition, to the point that almost anything can be a meme. He frequently uses the term "idea" as a synonym for meme, and the reader gets the impression that any idea can be a meme—which is counter to Dawkins's original intention and the more developed definition of Susan Blackmore's, which we will look at in the next section.

Psychologist Paul Marsden, in a scathing review, criticized Lynch for failing to acknowledge the large body of research in evolutionary culture theory that underlies academic studies of memetics and for peppering his book with many unsupported assertions.

A Departure from the Norm

The book is a clear and readable introduction to memetics, but one that departs significantly from the science's origins. But isn't that the point of memes? No one controls them; they control themselves. Once a meme is set free, its original author has no more control over its direction than our earliest human ancestor has over our modern choices and beliefs.

One final author who developed memetics far beyond what Dawkins intended—or even believed—was Susan Blackmore, and we will consider her book *The Meme Machine* in this final section of the chapter.

Blackmore and *The Meme Machine*

If Richard Brodie's intention was to provide a basic overview of memetics, inflected with a self-help agenda, and Aaron Lynch was developing a contagion-based theory of cultural transmission that eventually became a book about memetics, then Susan Blackmore had an altogether more ambitious goal: to codify and develop the growing field of memetics, mapping its outlines and stopping its borders. Published in 1999, *The Meme Machine* has become an important and influential contribution to the field.

Blackmore's fundamental point is that what makes us human is our ability to imitate. When we imitate someone, something is passed on—a meme. As a consequence, unlike Lynch's conflation of "meme" and "idea," for Blackmore not every idea can be a meme—only those ideas that are passed on by imitation.

She also differentiates between contagion as innate behavior—try keeping a straight face in a room of laughing people or not yawning when everyone else is—and contagion as social learning, such as imitated behaviors associated with crazes or fashions. She says the first are not memes, but the second are.

Inspired by Dawkins

Unlike Lynch, Blackmore follows Dawkins's lead in emphasizing the replicator role of memes over the contagion theme. Where her theory differs is that she doesn't see memes as analogous to genes, but that both memes and genes are examples of a "universal replicator." The main characteristics of the universal replicator are that they replicate accurately, make as many copies of themselves as possible, and are long-lived.

HAVE YOU HEARD?

The terms that Blackmore uses to describe the characteristics of the universal replicator are high-fidelity replication, high levels of fecundity, and longevity.

Blackmore also tackles one of the more abiding problems of human evolution: Why did homo sapiens develop such a big brain? The usual answer is that it was forced to grow (over millennia) by the complexities of developing language, which was needed to organize cooperative hunting parties. This can't be right, argues Blackmore, because plenty of predatory animals hunt in packs without the need for syntax. Instead, she proposes the theory that the big brain—which is expensive to run in terms of the energy it consumes—is a result of imitation. Good imitators are seen as good mates (yes, it always comes back to sex!), and this increases their chance of reproducing. As the ability to imitate increases and spreads through the community, there is a drive to imitate better and more often in order to maintain a reproductive advantage. And all this requires a big brain to maintain.

So homo sapiens have a big brain because the memes needed it in order to reproduce themselves!

This is a version of meme-gene coevolution theory—a variation of the gene-culture coevolution or dual-inheritance theories we looked at in Chapter 21. In Blackmore's version, memes and genes work together to benefit each other. Memes needed a large brain in order to replicate effectively, and the genes provided it. In return, memes improve the reproductive capacity of the genes by selecting for mates who are good at imitation.

Memes vs. Lamarckism

There is one other area of Blackmore's theory of memetics that is worth examining. In Chapter 21, we mentioned French naturalist Jean-Baptiste Lamarck and his theories that environmentally developed characteristics—such as the over-developed muscles of a blacksmith—could be passed on to his progeny.

Lamarck was a member of the French Academy of Sciences and professor of zoology at the Musée National d'Histoire Naturelle from 1793 to 1829. His was the first systematic theory of biological evolution based on natural selection, in which he hypothesized two competing forces—a "complexifying force" and an "adaptive force"—as the drivers of evolution. Since Darwin, these forces have been dismissed in favor of genetic mutation as the underlying principle.

However, it was for another aspect of his evolutionary theory that he became better known: the principle of the inheritance of acquired characteristics. This principle stated that physical characteristics of an individual acquired during his or her lifetime could be passed on to his or her progeny. Thus, to use an example that Darwin would return to years later, the giraffe, compelled by the harshness of the environment to strain to reach the upper leaves of trees, imperceptibly stretches its neck, causing a physiological adaptation that can be passed on to its progeny. This principle is what is called "soft inheritance"—transmission across generations without DNA modification. Today, apart from some tantalizing experiments with bacteria, Lamarckism is dismissed by biologists.

There is one area, however, where Lamarckism—or at least, neo-Lamarckism—is gaining some ground: cultural evolution. Blackmore argues that while genetic evolution can only progress through Darwinian processes, memetic evolution can show both Darwinian and Lamarckian traits. While she would deny that learned characteristics can be passed on genetically, she distinguishes two types of meme inheritance through imitation. The first is Darwinian imitation, which is "copying the instructions." This happens when someone gives you a recipe or a sheet of musical notation and you follow the written steps to produce the dish or play the song. The second type of imitation is "copying the product," and this happens when you watch someone prepare the dish or play the song, and Blackmore describes this as a form of Lamarckian imitation.

The Least You Need to Know

- Memetics has developed far beyond the speculations of Richard Dawkins and Daniel Dennett.
- Newer theories have emphasized different aspects of memetics, such as the focus on contagion.

- An understanding of memetics is crucial for a full understanding of human evolution.

- Susan Blackmore, Aaron Lynch, and Richard Brodie all propose different meme theories.

- The newer theories are still trying to reconcile cultural and genetic evolutions.

Alternative Theories

In This Chapter

- Anti-meme theorists
- Plato and memes
- The problem with metaphors
- Darwinism's incompatibility with memes
- Evolutionary culture theory

This far into the book, you might be thinking that memetics is the best way—maybe the only way—to explain how ideas are spread across society. But that would be to overstate the success of the theory. There are a number of competing theories that differ in a number of ways from memetics, and there are some theorists who object to memes on various grounds.

In this final chapter, we will look at several alternative theories of cultural transmission as well as consider some of the objections to the theory.

Challenges to Meme Ideas

Despite the efforts of Dawkins, Dennett, Blackmore, and others, the proponents of meme theory don't have everything their own way. There are some significant objections to both the science of memetics and the underlying conception of universal Darwinism, and there are some high-profile thinkers who disagree with it on a number of issues.

Platonic Essentialism

We have described the meme as "a unit of culture," the smallest identifiable "idea" that can be transmitted from mind to mind. We also suggested that minor differences in the expression of the meme (its memotype) were insignificant—the "arch" meme remains consistent regardless of the way in which it is described or whether its concrete example is wooden or stone. Because the meme is the mental entity that refers to some sort of example in the physical world, it can encompass differences between its expressions. Some people have claimed that this is an example of *Platonic essentialism*.

DEFINITION

Platonic essentialism is the principle that there exists a perfect version of every physical object and human idea in an inaccessible, metaphysical realm and that objects and ideas in the physical realm are mere copies or representations of this ideal form.

This is a principle first proposed by the Greek philosopher Plato. It is also referred to as the "Doctrine of the Forms." Plato believed that all objects and ideas in the physical realm were merely shadows of an ideal form that existed concretely in the metaphysical realm. Thus, a triangle—whether it is scratched roughly in the sand or carefully calculated and carved into stone—is still just an imperfect copy of its metaphysical ideal. Similarly, human love is merely an imperfect expression of the metaphysical ideal of love. An echo of this idea continues in the Christian doctrine that separates imperfect human love (*phileo*) from the perfect love of God (*agape*). The ideal or the Form is then the perfect essence of the object or idea.

Later philosophers (starting with Aristotle) took issue with some of the implications of Plato's doctrine, but in modern times philosophers and theorists have moved away from the idea that all entities in human existence contain some sort of intrinsic essence that defines their identity, preferring to define types of entity in relation to their environmental or social context.

By referring to memetics as an essentialist science, its opponents are dismissing it as outdated and based in a mystical philosophy. Some proponents of memetics have attempted to offer a way out of this bind, but the charge of essentialism remains a difficulty for the philosophical analysis of memes.

Metaphor Gone Mad

Another objection to memetics lies in the science's basis in genetics. Dawkins, Dennett, and other proponents of memetics claimed that memes were not just analogous with genes, that they were entities that actually followed the same rules—they were not just *like* genes, they *were* the genes of a different but comparable system. It was a system that was conceptual, rather than organic, but as it was subject to the same pressures and influences, it should be considered in the same terms.

Some opponents find this idea impossible to accept. Sure, they say, memes act *like* genes, but that doesn't make them actual replicators. It is still nothing more than an elaborate metaphor—and, subject to all the problems of metaphors, sooner or later the analogy will break down and the theory will fail.

They point to the fact that genes are physical particles that carry within them the replicating molecule (DNA). Memes are mental entities, and the replicating agency is external—it is the unique capacity of humans to imitate behavior. Also, if memetics is completely analogous to genetics, its proponents should be able to point to other parallels between the two. Where are the meme's chromosomes, cells, organelles, and other biological parts? What is the memetic equivalent of the genome?

They claim that the cultural influences on ideas are simply too complex to be analogous to genes. You will remember from the section on evolution in Chapter 21 that Gregor Mendel found that heredity was particulate; that is, inherited characteristics were based on a transmitted particle, rather than the blending of parental essences. Some of meme theory's opponents claim that cultural influences are too complex to be considered particulate and that ideas and other cultural entities act more like the pre-Mendel idea of the blending of characteristics. Kate Distin has tried to address this criticism by suggesting that memes are particles that can fit together in different ways to create different wholes.

HAVE YOU HEARD?

An England-based scholar, Kate Distin wrote a 2005 book called *The Selfish Meme* that took Richard Dawkins's genetic philosophies in *The Selfish Gene* and expanded them further into the realm of ideas.

A related criticism is that the gene is far from the simple unit of heredity that Mendel envisaged. Individual genes don't necessarily begin and end along the length of the chromosome, but some of them overlap or blend into each other, forming supergene complexes that are less clearly defined than smaller units. If the genetic structure is far from clear, it is argued, how can the analogous structure be trusted?

Objections to Universal Darwinism

As we all know, Darwinism in some parts of the world is a controversial theory. Some people think that by accepting that life evolved from simple replicating amino acids into the complexity we see all around us, we must deny belief in God. And it is true that many of the proponents of Darwinism that we have discussed in this book—Dawkins, Dennett, and others—are atheists. On the other hand, many people are happy to reconcile their religious or spiritual beliefs with organic evolution.

We do not make any comment either way, because that's not what this book is about. But there are some problems with Universal Darwinism aside from religious ones, and these have implications for memetics.

Stephen Jay Gould, the paleontologist and science writer, was involved in a long-running controversy with Dawkins and Dennett about gene-culture coevolution. His first objection was that the claims for cultural evolution were based on analogy and metaphor. It couldn't be actual evolution because cultural transmission lacks a particle of heredity, and the mechanisms of transmission are nothing like those of the sexual reproduction that defines organic evolution. Gould argued that those who claimed that cultural evolution was a mechanism subject to natural selection were misrepresenting Darwinian evolution.

But his main objection was with what he saw as a reduction of Darwinian evolution to the principle of adaptation—that the natural selection of genes was responsible for all the diversity of life on Earth. In fact, Gould went so far as to claim that Dawkins, Dennett, and others were Darwinian fundamentalists, taking the idea of natural selection much further than even Darwin himself suggested. Gould strongly believed that there were forces—directionless and materialist, to be sure—other than natural selection that explained the complexity and diversity of life on Earth.

Some of these objections can be easily answered; others are more difficult to ignore. Like any theory, meme theory is only as good as its ability to explain phenomena and can only maintain its influence until a better explanatory mechanism arrives.

But many people maintain that meme theory has developed for good reasons.

The Purpose of Meme Theory

The reason for having a meme theory is embedded in the broader question of why we have theories for anything. In the humanities and social sciences over the last 20 years, there have been many debates about theory, with some people arguing that theory provides a critical and overarching view of the practices being observed. Others argue that theory simply ends up talking about itself and ignoring the object of study.

The argument is more than a century old, but this debate reached the level of controversy starting in the 1970s, when a number of key works by (usually) French philosophers and theorists were translated into English for the first time. The views on culture and knowledge by thinkers such as Jacques Derrida, Jean Baudrillard, and Jacques Lacan took the academy by storm and in a short time became very influential. It was the reliance on work by these and other theorists that led to the rise of a raft of views and theories that we now call *postmodernism*.

DEFINITION

Postmodernism, as it is popularly understood, is a complex of theories derived from philosophy, literary criticism, linguistics, and other disciplines, which share a general suspicion of "grand narratives" such as progress and reason, and which claim that what classical philosophy saw as an external reality is merely a baseless layering of culturally defined and arbitrary meanings. There is no "truth"; there is only spectacle.

Let's take a look at postmodernism.

Postmodernism

It's not hard to see how postmodernism fits with Darwinian theories of evolution. Traditional philosophies saw human progress as a purpose-filled journey to some sort of ultimate end—civilization, or enlightenment, perhaps—and this journey, as well as life itself, was subject to the guiding hand of God. Darwinism says that there isn't (necessarily) the intervention of God in creation, but rather the interactions of pre-programmed molecules which, over millennia, create the complexity we see around us. Similarly, postmodernism denies that there is any underlying metaphysical purpose or meaning to life—just the cultural interactions of people struggling to live in a complex world of competing forces.

The theory of memetics which says that ideas spread not because they are good or bad, but simply because they are programmed to spread, has some resonances with postmodern theory.

For some people, postmodernism was a fresh and valuable way of explaining a culture obsessed with appearance and spectacle; for others, it was a deliberately incomprehensible and self-indulgent case of theory for its own sake, rather than as a way of explaining what it set out to explain.

These debates have now largely died down, but they have left a legacy in some places that includes a suspicion of theory and a tendency to ignore not just the extravagant theories of postmodernism but all theory.

Arguments for Theory

The proponents of theory argue that it provides a way to extrapolate from the specific to the general so that a properly grounded theory is a systematic way of accounting for new phenomena that fits the theoretical outline.

This is true for meme theory, in that a general theory of culture that is grounded in biological evolution should be able to describe things that were never considered in the first place. A good example is the way in which meme theory seems to describe exactly what happens on the Internet, despite the fact that in 1976 the Internet was known to few people outside the U.S. military and several major universities—and the World Wide Web was still 13 years away.

PASS IT ON

Meme theory is so well tuned to the Internet that many people assume that Internet memes are the only type we have. When we started writing this book, we made a point of asking friends and family what, in their opinion, was the most influential meme. The answer was almost invariably "RickRolling"! A good answer, but from our perspective it's a meme that is not as influential as the discovery of fire or the invention of the wheel!

Meme theory tries to provide a general theory of cultural transmission that is not reliant on a medium. The vector could be an e-mail, a Web page, a photocopy, or a conversation, but the underlying theory remains the same.

It also has a related purpose: to demonstrate that Universal Darwinism, which is itself a theory based on general principles, is similarly coherent across different media.

Universal Darwinism claims that the principles of natural selection apply to nonbiological as well as biological entities, and many argue that meme theory confirms this claim.

Other Evolving Ideas

In our estimation, meme theory provides a good way to explain a significant and widespread cultural practice. In spite of the objections discussed earlier, the theory is rigorous and seems to accurately explain cultural activities.

But that is not to say that there aren't competing theories, and in this final section we will look at some other theories behind the cultural transmission of ideas.

E. O. Wilson and the Culturgen

In Chapter 21, we talked about the biologist E. O. Wilson and his theory of sociobiology. This was a coevolution theory that said human culture had to be understood as a combination of genetic evolution and cultural evolution, with each influencing the other. His 1975 book, *Sociobiology: The New Synthesis*, outlined the terrain of the new discipline, arguing for a biological basis for behaviors such as altruism and aggression. With Charles Lumsden, he later refined the theory to draw on data from developmental psychology, cognitive science, population genetics, and mathematical physics to create an underlying, predictive theory of human culture.

Wilson's work, along with other versions of sociobiology, have been criticized as too reliant on the biological base—some critics going as far as accusing him of biological determinism (the principle that all animal behavior, including human, is determined at the genetic level).

The Culturgen

There were a number of similarities between Wilson's and Dawkins's theories, notably the importance of biological evolution and natural selection. But the most striking was the creation of a unit of culture similar to the meme: the *culturgen*. Like the meme, the culturgen is transmitted by imitation and is subject to the laws of natural selection. Wilson based the culturgen on the "artifact type" or "social artifact" of archaeology—a product of a social group or individual, whether physical or mental.

> **DEFINITION**
>
> A **culturgen** is an idea, historical within a social group or advanced by an indi-
> vidual, that is passed on physically or mentally. Coined by biologist E. O. Wilson,
> it is comparable to a meme.

In this formation, the culturgen is not subject to natural selection itself but is evidence
of the biological and cultural pressures on the group or individual who produces the
culturgen. Thus, a particular style of cooking pot might be able to provide evidence
of the environmental pressures on the people who designed and made it, and if the
design is transmitted to another group with different pressures, the design will evolve
in accordance with those pressures.

An Important Study

In spite of the controversies, sociobiology remains an important discipline in the
study of culture—and one that has a greater depth of theoretical structure than
memetics. Its aspirations are also greater, seeking to trace and classify the full history of human sociality—something that memetics does not seek to do, even in the
grander versions of Susan Blackmore and others.

Richerson and Boyd

Sociobiology is a coevolution theory. Proponents of the dual-inheritance theories we
looked at in Chapter 21 differentiate themselves from sociobiology by claiming that
it has too great a reliance on biological factors. Peter Richerson and Robert Boyd
have produced a significant contribution to cultural understanding with their work,
which moves away from what they see as biological determinism to a system that sees
culture itself as a system of inheritance. Their ideas were first proposed in 1976 and
then expanded in 2005 as *Not by Genes Alone*, which was a much more accessible book
for general audiences.

Like Dawkins and other proponents of memetics, Richerson and Boyd believe in
the mutual influence of biological and cultural factors in human evolution and that
these factors are transmitted through imitation, teaching, and other means. The
information that is passed in these ways is any mental state that affects behavior, such
as ideas, beliefs, values, skills, or attitudes. Where their theory differs from memetics
is that they do not insist that there needs to be a discrete, genelike particle of culture.
They contend that sometimes the transmitted information can look somewhat genelike, but at other times it is decidedly not.

Their word for the unit of culture is *cultural variant*, and the important distinction between this and a meme is that a cultural variant is not a replicator. Instead, the cultural variant in someone's brain produces in them a certain behavior that is observed by someone else, who then creates another cultural variant in their own brain, which produces more or less the same behavior they observed. Richerson and Boyd, therefore, talk about cultural variants from a population perspective as similar, but not necessarily identical, learned representations.

> **DEFINITION**
>
> A **cultural variant** is a human behavior that, unlike a meme, isn't passed on but is simply observed by another individual. The individual then comes up with his or her own version of the behavior. Biologists Peter Richerson and Robert Boyd observed similar patterns with people in a group, but patterns that were not necessarily exactly alike.

Culture is therefore the accumulation of learned behaviors, passed on for multiple generations. Learning occurs in two ways:

- Biased transmission
- Guided variation

The biased transmission of cultural variants is a process subject to natural selection and refers to the way in which competing ideas are selected by the group or individuals. Guided variation refers to variations incorporated during learning and is not subject to natural selection, because the mutations are actually conscious improvements that tend to enhance the value of the cultural variant.

Richerson's and Boyd's theories continue to be influential in areas as diverse as psychology and economics. Time will tell whether they become as influential with a popular audience as well.

Evolutionary Culture Theory

The last theory we want to look at in this chapter is less well known than the other theories of cultural transmission, but it offers some important differences.

The main proponent of the evolutionary culture theory is William Durham, professor of anthropology at Stanford University, and it was most fully worked out in his 1992 book, *Coevolution: Genes, Culture, and Human Diversity*. Its main point of distinction is that it claims that all cultures on Earth, through a complex system of transformation and diversification, have descended from a common ancestor culture—referred to as "descent with modification." While the full path of this descent has not been worked out (nor, probably, can it), the evidence is based on the commonality of certain beliefs and practices in disparate cultures: for example, funeral rites, incest taboos, and inheritance rules. While it is possible that some of these practices could have evolved independently, Durham argues, it is against the laws of probability for all of them to have done so.

INFECTION!

All the theories we've discussed in this and earlier chapters—coevolution theory, dual-inheritance theory, and so on—are part of the ongoing controversy known as the "nature versus nurture" debate. This debate is over the relative influences of biology (nature) and social and cultural pressures (nurture). While most scientists and theorists agree that both contribute to the formation of human personality, they disagree on the proportions, and the other side of the debate is always ready to point the finger. Too close to the nature end, and proponents are accused of biological determinism; too far the other way leads to social determinism. While it's a cliché, a healthy balance between the two is probably the correct position.

The other main area of difference is that Durham argues for a theory of cultural transmission that does not rely on the biological underpinning of sociobiology and other coevolution theories. He claims that those neo-Darwinian theories see biological evolution as the underlying cause of cultural evolution, whereas Evolutionary Culture Theory takes organic and cultural evolution as parallel, but unconnected, processes. Of course, he admits, there are many analogies between the two, but that's because there is evolutionary change in both fields—not because evolutionary biology is applied to cultural change.

Where Theories Are Headed

All these competing theories of cultural transmission have key differences as well as significant similarities with memetics, and only time will tell whether one of them will defeat the others or whether all will continue to coexist.

One thing is certain: the pressures that will tend to select one theory over the others are already coded in our genes and in the way in which we understand society. Each theory is a memeplex that is competing for dominance, and if one survives the others, it is not because it is necessarily most correct but because it is the best at replicating.

The Least You Need to Know

- Some theorists have pointed out problems with memetics.
- The theory of Universal Darwinism is opposed by some biologists.
- Meme theory is still worth pursuing.
- Several competing theories exist with both similarities and differences.
- Because they are conceptual, theories supporting and arguing against memes are hard to prove.

Glossary

Know your memes! Here's a breakdown of the terms you need to understand the wonderful world of memes.

abacus   The first known device made specifically for counting. It was invented in China.

adversative   Based on the memetic transmission theories of Aaron Lynch, memes influence their hosts to aggressively attack or sabotage competing memes. This idea has been the basis of the "convert or die" mentality of many religious crusades over the ages. Adversative memes were also the motivation behind the colonization of Africa.

alarm calls   Common in animals, when one member of the herd shouts when a predator is in the group's area; one type of expression that is comparable to gossip among humans. Richard Dawkins and others argued that it wasn't a purely altruistic act.

arch   Popularized by the ancient Romans, the shape enabled stones to fit snugly overhead, accomplishing seemingly magical physics; each hanging block would be secured by the two adjacent hanging blocks.

astroturfing   The act of making a professionally done marketing campaign look like a grassroots movement. The assumption is that people will be more receptive to the message if they believe it happened organically.

auto-defense   Usually found in memeplexes, a meme that carries within itself its own defense. Most religions teach that they alone carry the truth. If they are challenged by an alternative belief system, they have already dismissed it as false.

auto-toxic   An auto-toxic meme is one that encourages behavior that is dangerous, or even fatal, to its hosts. It can be a meme that encourages suicide, reckless behavior, or delusions of invulnerability.

bait   The desired result promised by the meme.

BBS   Short for bulletin board service; an online posting program that was a precursor to the Internet.

casual Friday   Also called dress-down Friday, it is a day when the company's dress code is relaxed and is seen as a morale-building exercise for workers in carefully managed situations. It is an interesting meme because psychologists tell us that happy workers are more productive, so it really is for the benefit of the company. Common in many U.S. and Canadian businesses, the tradition is slowly spreading to other countries.

censorship   An attempt to stop a meme by blocking its vectors or controlling its hosts; generally tends to be unsuccessful.

co-meme   A type of retromeme in which two memes have coevolved, forming a symbiotic relationship that benefits both. It is also known as a symmeme.

coevolution   This term can have two meanings: one, the principle from memetics and cultural transmission that genes and memes evolve together, each influencing the development of the other; two, in memetics, when two memes evolve together, each modifying the other. *See also* co-meme and memeplex.

cognitive advantage   Based on the memetic transmission theories of Aaron Lynch, a meme that seems well-founded and cogent will tend to last longer than one founded simply on tradition or superstition. A millennia-old belief system with ancient texts and millions of followers will be more welcomed than a relatively new concept.

connectors   According to Malcolm Gladwell's *The Tipping Point*, these are individuals who are great at networking. Their communication and people skills are essential to creating a buzz. When it comes to memes, this is the equivalent of the host, the deliverer of the information. These hosts instinctively know the right sociotype, or group of people, for whom the meme would be most effective.

conspicuous consumption   Buying goods, services, and other related items to prove an equal or superior social status to peers. When two connected individuals or groups accept this meme, the never-ending battle can drive them to spend more than they can actually afford. It will only end when one stops believing in the meme.

conspiracy theory   A particular type of meme-complex in which different memes work together to protect and help replicate the meme. In other words, the number of active memes helps keep the entire memeplex alive.

copycat crime   A crime that mimics the technique, or signature, of another individual. Copycat crimes are exo-toxic memes that tend to use the mass media as a vector—inspired by newspaper reports, television newscasts, and so forth—although the original criminal may commit a false copycat crime to create confusion.

cults   In memetic terms, a cult is a memeplex with a particularly resistant auto-defense system.

cultural currency   The respect a potential meme receiver has for the deliverer. The level of the deliverer's cultural currency is just as relevant as the appeal of the meme itself.

cultural transmission   A dual-inheritance theory term, it means that aspects of culture—thought, speech, action, and artifacts—are transmitted from individual to individual in a way analogous to biological reproduction. That is, there's the possibility that the reproduction may be imperfect; that a mutation may occur; and that the cultural unit takes on the effects of that mutation, which it passes on when it is next reproduced. It also acknowledges that cultural traits are subject to natural selection—that in a crowded and busy world, some traits will prosper and others will be ignored.

cultural variant   A human behavior that, unlike a meme, isn't passed on but is simply observed by another individual. The individual then comes up with his or her own version of the behavior. Biologists Peter Richerson and Robert Boyd observed similar patterns with people in a group—but patterns not necessarily exactly alike.

culturgen   An idea, historical within a social group or individual, that is passed on physically or mentally. Coined by biologist E. O. Wilson, it is comparable to a meme.

Darwinism   The Charles Darwin theory that argued creations evolved through natural selection.

dead language   An entire collection of words rarely spoken or written or forgotten entirely.

doomsday meme   The idea that most, if not all, of the human race will die from a particular event at a specific time. This meme can be passed around like an urban legend, described in a religious form or declared by a leader.

dormant meme   A meme left with no host because the last carrier either died or stopped believing in the idea. It can be resurrected, however, usually through another, active meme.

dual-inheritance theory   The philosophy that human behavior is influenced by the twin forces of genetic evolution and cultural evolution.

dumb replicators   Also known as genes. Coined by *The Selfish Gene* author Richard Dawkins, they are called "dumb" because they don't make judgments, only replicate.

earworm   A song or a portion of a song that gets stuck in your head.

efficiency parental   Based on the memetic transmission theories of Aaron Lynch, parents will acknowledge that simply having children is no guarantee that the children will embrace the parents' beliefs. However, some memes increase their chances of transmission by guiding the method of parenting to include ideas that privilege parents as a source of good ideas.

exo-toxic   An exo-toxic meme is dangerous or fatal to people other than the host. For instance, a cult leader spreading an exo-toxic meme could hurt others while he or she remained safe.

fashion-forward   Something or someone that has a good instinct for the next couture trend and is secure enough to dress like it.

fundamentalism   A religious, political, or scientific memeplex that relies on a totalizing system to shut down other competing memeplexes.

gene   A piece of DNA that holds a particular physical trait. *The Selfish Gene* author Richard Dawkins compares memes to genes in that they hold a particular piece of cultural information.

genotype   The specific genetic constitution of an organism; its genetic fingerprint. In memes, it is analogous to memotype.

glass ceiling   The limit to how high a person is allowed to climb the corporate ladder because of demographic or cultural differences. The term is usually used in reference to women in a male-dominated environment.

gossip   A meme that isn't necessarily malicious but does imply personal gain. It is traditionally passed via word of mouth.

grassroots   A social movement that naturally comes from the people, not from a corporate entity. Marketing teams sometimes try to make advertising seem like a grassroots effort, which is called astroturfing.

groupthink   When a crowd makes decisions that the individuals within the group would not commit to on their own. The group usually emphasizes swift action over rational discussion and judgment.

histameme   Memes that act to immunize us against other memes; also called immuno-memes or vaccimes.

hook   The connector that attracts us to memes. It is a common term in advertising.

host   The carrier that sends the meme. If the meme vector is viewed as mail, the host is the mail deliverer.

immunization   Memetically, immunization is something that protects a host against pernicious memes. The best immunization is a good general knowledge and a healthy skepticism.

immuno-depressant   Medically, an immuno-depressant is an agent that suppresses the body's immune response—but a meme immuno-depressant makes a host more susceptible to infection, such as tiredness, disorientation, stress, or distraction.

immuno-memes   Memes that act to immunize us against other memes; also called vaccimes or histamemes.

Lamarckian   The work of French naturalist Jean-Baptiste Lamarck, whose early and now largely discredited theories on biological evolution included the belief that the environmental development of characteristics, such as the building of muscle tissue, could be passed on to later generations.

mavens   According to Malcolm Gladwell's *The Tipping Point*, people with a deep knowledge base—something that is both recognized and respected by the general public. They like to be of service and to provide people with the most reliable information. They could be considered the equivalent of a memetic engineer, recognizing patterns and ideas and creating memes.

meme   A cultural expression that is passed on to another person or group. It was first popularized in Richard Dawkins's 1976 best-seller *The Selfish Gene*, calling it a cultural unit of measure.

meme complex   A collection of memes; also known as a memeplex.

meme-allergen   From the medical term "allergen," which is any foreign substance that causes an extreme reaction in the body's immune system. A meme-allergen may cause surprising and excessive responses that seem completely out of proportion to the stimulus.

memebot   A person completely controlled by a meme. It is an obsession with a particular cultural idea.

memeoid   A host who has become completely consumed by a meme. Unlike a memebot, who is obsessed with a particular meme, a memeoid is connected to a meme that can definitely harm them.

memeplex   A collection of memes; also known as a meme complex.

memetic drift   The way in which memes change meaning through incremental mistranslations as they are passed from host to host. A good analogy is the child's game Telephone.

memetic engineer   The creator of the meme itself. The actual meme creation doesn't have to be a conscious act, and the memetic engineer doesn't even have to be human.

memotype   The actual expression of a meme. In organic evolution, it would be called a genotype.

meta-meme   A type of memeplex, a meta-meme is a meme about memes. This term can also refer to memes that influence the acceptance of other memes, such as the "tolerance" meme.

motivational   Based on the memetic transmission theories of Aaron Lynch, hosts are convinced that adopting a meme will be personally advantageous for them. For instance, some religions teach that the more people you convert, the higher your chances of redemption in the afterlife. It is a brilliant meme that pushes the follower to bring more people into the flock, increasing the power of both the meme itself and the individuals behind it.

natural selection   The biological evolution theory. It requires three preconditions: variation, selection, and retention.

obsessed with youth   Limited growth opportunities at a young adult–run organization for a person older than a certain age. It is inspired by the term "glass ceiling."

old boys' club   Limited growth opportunities at an older male–run organization for a female or racial minority. It is inspired by the term "glass ceiling."

paradigm shift   The idea that scientific development continues incrementally, building on previous research and ideas, until the underlying theories and assumptions can no longer support the new evidence and a new way of thinking is required. The most famous example of a paradigm shift is the Copernican revolution, which placed the sun at the center of the solar system—replacing the Ptolemaic model, which was becoming increasingly over-elaborate in an attempt to match the theory to the observations. The term was coined by American scientist and philosopher Thomas Kuhn in his 1962 book *The Structure of Scientific Revolutions.*

pay it forward   The act of repaying a good deed done for you by performing a good deed for another person. One particular philosophy, popularized in the movie adaptation of the book *Pay It Forward*, is that one good deed should be repaid with three good ones.

phenotype   The observable characteristics of an organism—its physiology, appearance, and behavior. In memes, it is analogous to the sociotype.

phenotypic plasticity   The way an organism can alter its behavior, physical shape, growth, or population characteristics in reaction to certain environmental pressures. It can be expressed either across generations of a species or in a single individual. A good example is the way in which frog tadpoles forage less and grow larger tails (for speed in escaping) in the presence of predators, at the cost of slower growth, while foraging more and growing faster in the presence of competitors, at the cost of being more vulnerable should those predators show up.

Platonic essentialism   The principle that there exists a perfect version of every physical object and human idea in an inaccessible, metaphysical realm and that objects and ideas in the physical realm are mere copies or representations of this ideal form.

postmodernism   Any new set of ideas, usually radical compared to the long-established theories. With regard to memes, postmodernism refers to any theories varying from earlier work—particularly from modern-meme forefathers Richard Dawkins and Daniel Dennett.

preservational   Based on the memetic transmission theories of Aaron Lynch, memes protect themselves from disbelief by causing the hosts to avoid activities that might lead to questioning the meme. Thus, there are memes in certain religious communities that warn against higher education, and there is the folkloric injunction not to discuss religion or politics in polite company.

proselytic   Based on the memetic transmission theories of Aaron Lynch, hosts actively seek out nonbelievers to convince them of the value of the meme. Religions and political ideologies usually grow in this way, and often the form of proselytizing involves fear—of punishment in the afterlife or social decline unless certain political choices are made.

quantity parental   Based on the theories of Aaron Lynch, parents will have multiple children to increase their chances of memetic transmission. With a high retention rate for memes passed on by parents, this is an easy way to increase the number of hosts of a particular meme. One of the best examples of this transmission is in Amish culture, where having large families is highly encouraged—and supported by the necessity for many farmhands in a society that eschews mechanical assistance.

retention   The idea that characteristics of a particular entity will be passed on to others. In organic evolution, this idea is called heredity—characteristics of your parents are passed on to you—but retention can refer to any form of information transmission. It is part of the natural selection theory.

retromeme   A meme that transcribes a bit of itself into an existing meme, attempting to commandeer the original meme for its own purposes.

reverse racism   Limited growth opportunities at a minority-run organization for a person in the majority population. It is inspired by the term "glass ceiling."

salespeople   According to Malcolm Gladwell's *The Tipping Point*, salespeople are charismatic, persuasive folks with the ability to get the general public to see things their way. In the meme world, these would be the curators of the hook and the bait—the intended message and the implied reward.

sampling   Taking a portion of a song and modifying it in some way to create a new song. The process began in hip-hop music and was later picked up by pop, rock, and country artists.

selection   The idea that if entities are subject to environmental pressure—and diminishing resources, perhaps—only some will survive. Furthermore, the ones that do survive would have been better suited for the environmental conditions, albeit in different ways. It is part of the natural selection theory.

semantics   The study of the meaning that is produced by grammatical constructions. Sentences in written English can be grammatically incorrect but still meaningful, as well as syntactically correct but meaningless.

signature   A distinct action a criminal creates at a crime scene. It comes from a need to be recognized for his or her work. Criminal psychologists claim that nearly every "bad guy" has one. In fact, a copycat crime is defined by the signature or signatures of an act—the duplication of the original meme.

soapbox   The collection of ideas a politician stands for during a particular campaign. The most successful soapboxes have memes that create a particular overarching theme.

social artifact   From archaeology, a product of a social group or individual, either physical or mental; the underlying definition of a culturgen.

sociotype   The meme's expression within the social and cultural environment in which the memotype exists. It's the way a meme is understood and applied in a particular situation. In organic evolution, it would be called a phenotype.

symbiotic   The relationship between two things (usually beneficial). In memes, the term describes the co-meme or symmeme relationship, when two ideas build and feed off each other.

symmeme   A type of retromeme in which two memes have coevolved, forming a symbiotic relationship that benefits both. It is also known as a co-meme.

syntax   The study of the principles and rules for constructing sentences in language; in other words, grammar.

Telephone   A classic grade-school game. A group of kids are lined up next to each other and the teacher whispers a short but complex sentence in the ear of one child at either end. The child then turns to the next child and whispers the phrase in his or her ear, and so on, until it reaches the final child. The last person says out loud what he or she was told—which is usually quite different than what was initially said. It is an example of how a meme, specifically gossip, is transformed by the deliverer.

tipping point   The moment when a trend becomes popular among the mainstream; when a meme becomes both public and viral. It is based on Malcolm Gladwell's best-selling book of the same name.

totalizing system   A memeplex that claims to provide all the answers to a complex set of problems, without reference to any other system.

Trojan horse   Familiar from computer viruses, in memetic terms a Trojan horse is a meme that piggybacks on another meme. A blonde joke might be replicated because the host thinks it is funny, but it also passes on the nasty tinge of sexism.

Universal Darwinism   The principle that natural selection does not necessarily have to apply only to organic evolution but can describe equally well things as diverse as economics, linguistics, and computer algorithms. It was inspired by the evolution theories of Charles Darwin.

vaccimes   Memes that act to immunize us against other memes; also called immuno-memes or histamemes.

variation   The idea that there will be slight differences between individuals within the same group of entities. It is part of the natural selection theory.

vector   The impartial medium used to transport the meme to others. Think of the vector as a carrier, or a messenger, such as a book or a television show delivering the cultural idea to the masses.

viral marketing   Creating an advertisement or message so powerful that the recipient will tell everyone in his or her social circle about the product.

viral video   A film, usually on the Internet, that is so good it's passed along to others in the recipient's social circle.

virus   A small, malicious program that enters computers and self-replicates—usually until it takes over the machine or the machine dies.

wheel   A revolutionary device invented around the fourth millennium B.C.E.

White Man's Burden   The belief that the race in power must help the "less-sophisticated" race with the socio-economic and/or intellectual disadvantage. The term comes from an 1899 Rudyard Kipling poem of the same name. The poem pushed for colonization of "lesser" cultures, and it's still unclear whether the English *The Jungle Book* author meant it as satire or truth. But, like most popular memes, it doesn't really matter; the idea has taken a life of its own, and believers apply it as they see fit.

Y2K bug   The theory that computers would go haywire on January 1, 2000, because programmers a decade earlier didn't have the forethought to prepare for years in the next century. Registering only the last two zeros, the computer would believe it was the year 1900 instead of 2000, and our technology-dependent society would be paralyzed. The meme was extremely popular in the 1990s, particularly in 1999, but the bug itself had very little—if any—impact on the computers throughout society.

Questions and Answers

Memes can be conceptually complicated. Here are some answers to commonly asked questions.

Okay ... I guess I should read Chapter 1, but first, tell me what a meme is.

A meme is a cultural unit of measure. It can be a thought, a phrase, a style, or any other cultural expression that can be imitated by individuals. More important, a meme is a replicator; that is, a particle of culture that strives to get itself copied as many times as possible. (And yes, you should read Chapter 1.)

Why are memes important?

Cultural ideas that can be passed to others, memes are the fabric with which society is constructed. A meme can be as relatively superficial as fashion trends and pop-music hits, but even these "lighter" memes represent markers in our history. The heavier memes, such as views on the death penalty or modern opinions of sex, affect people and all the generations that follow.

Are memes good or bad?

Neither; memes are completely neutral. They replicate through imitation because human minds are great imitators, and it is our nature to repeat things we find interesting. There is no moral value to a meme; it is simply a unit of culture.

Memes can, however, carry meaning that can have moral value. The old saying, "Love your neighbor" is a meme, and so is racism.

Who actually first discovered memes?

Biologist Richard Dawkins is often credited with popularizing the term in his 1976 best-seller *The Selfish Gene*, but the first mention of the concept goes back nearly a century earlier to another biologist, Richard Wolfgang Semon, in 1904. Semon argued that our memories were actually a biological event "remembered" within the nervous system and passed on to later generations. Semon's ideas weren't furthered until the early seventies, prior to *The Selfish Gene*, by anthropologist F. Ted Cloak, Jr. Cloak argued that ideas were moved via small "corpuscles of culture" passed from generation to generation via imitation, conditioning, and other methods. Leaning on biology, Dawkins's *The Selfish Gene* popularized similar ideas.

"Meme" is a weird name. Where did it come from?

Biologist Richard Dawkins coined it from the Greek word *mimeme*, meaning "imitated." He shortened the word to *meme* so that it would resemble the word *gene*—its closest biological analogue. It is very similar to the term coined by turn-of-the-century German biologist Richard Wolfgang Semon, "Mneme," from the Greek muse of memory. Dawkins claims he was unaware of Semon's usage.

Did memes exist before the Internet?

Definitely. In fact, one of the oldest memes we know of is the discovery of fire! There were countless memes happening within the world before our recent information age. Technology is a popular meme medium, but so are word of mouth, advertising, and other methods of transmission.

That said, the Internet certainly changed not only the speed with which memes spread but also the types of memes capable of being created easily. As an example, a video-related meme would traditionally have to be broadcast through a television station or physically passed from person to person, but the early Internet (and later, video upload websites such as YouTube) democratized the process and made it easier for more memes to find other parties.

Why do the silliest things, like dancing babies and keyboard cats, become the most popular Internet memes?

In history, even the most "sophisticated" societies have gained pleasure from sophomoric acts. Plays during Shakespeare's era were punctuated with fart jokes while the walls of Pompeii were covered with crude sexual humor.

When it comes to the Internet, it is important to remember the wide audience. A complicated thought may require knowing another language, a deep understanding of a foreign culture, and other skills to create the right context. For every major international meme, there are countless memes that remain confined within a country, a city, or even a family. Watching achingly cute puppies snuggle in a basket, however, is adorable in any language. No interpretation is necessary.

I have this great idea for a meme. How can I guarantee that it will spread?

You can't. Once released into "the wild," there is no way to predict what will happen to a meme. Many memes fail to get copied and die immediately. Others change their meaning and become unrecognizable—or worse, become something you really regret.

Ever tell a joke that turned out to be exactly the wrong thing to say at that time? Context and the influence of other memes can alter a meme's meaning, turning it into something that you'd really prefer had stayed hidden.

What does Charles Darwin, who studied physical evolution, have to do with the transfer of ideas?

Most major meme theorists, such as Richard Dawkins and Daniel Dennett, studied Darwin heavily. Furthermore, in 1976's *The Selfish Gene*, Dawkins argued that perhaps the physical evolution of humans was over and that any further evolving would happen through the mind—an idea pushed further in Dennett's 1995 book *Darwin's Dangerous Idea*.

A meme isn't really alive, so why do you keep talking about it as if it has an intention and goals?

The precursor is Richard Dawkins's *The Selfish Gene*, which applies a metaphorical intentionality to genes throughout.

But you're right—memes don't really *want* to replicate; they replicate because that is what they do. Think of it as a chemical reaction. If you mix hydrogen and nitrogen in the correct ratios, they form ammonia—not because they *want* to, but because that is their nature. Memes replicate because that is how they exist in the world.

Resources

Books and Articles

Check out the following books and articles for more information on memes.

Cultural Transmission

Cavalli-Sforza, Luigi L., and Marcus W. Feldman. *Cultural Transmission and Evolution: A Quantitative Approach.* Princeton: Princeton University Press, 1981. Cloak, F. Ted Jr. "Is a Cultural Ethology Possible?" *Human Ecology* 3 (3): 161–182, 1975.

Hofstadter, Douglas. *Metamagical Themas: Questing for the Essence of Mind and Pattern.* New York: Basic Books, 1996.

Lumsdon, Charles J., and Edward O. Wilson. *Genes, Minds, and Culture: The Coevolutionary Process.* Cambridge: Harvard University Press, 1981.

McElreath, Richard, and Joseph Henrich. "Dual Inheritance Theory: The evolution of human cultural capacities and cultural evolution." In R. Dunbar and L. Barrett (Eds.), *Oxford Handbook of Evolutionary Psychology.* Oxford: Oxford University Press, 2007.

Schacter, Daniel. *Forgotten Ideas, Neglected Pioneers: Richard Semon and the Story of Memory.* Philadelphia: Psychology Press, 2001.

Evolution

Gould, Stephen Jay. *The Structure of Evolutionary Theory.* Cambridge, Massachusetts: Belknap Press of Harvard University Press, 2002.

Miner, Benjamin G., et al. "Ecological Consequences of Phenotypic Plasticity." *Trends in Ecology and Evolution* 20 (12): 685–692, 2005.

Genetics

Bronowski, Jacob. *The Ascent of Man*. London: British Broadcasting Corporation, 1973.

Dawkins, Richard. *The Extended Phenotype*. Oxford: W. H. Freeman, 1982.

———. *The Selfish Gene*. New York: Oxford University Press, 1976.

Horvitz, Leslie Alan. *The Complete Idiot's Guide to Evolution*. Indianapolis: Alpha Books, 2002.

Simmons, Robert, and Lue Scheepers. "Winning By a Neck: Sexual Selection in the Evolution of Giraffe." *American Naturalist* 148 (5): 771–786, 1996.

Watson, James D. *Double Helix: A Personal Account of the Discovery of the Structure of DNA*. New York: Scribner, 1968.

Memes

Aunger, Robert. *The Electric Meme: A New Theory of How We Think*. New York: Free Press, 2002.

Blackmore, Susan. *The Meme Machine*. Oxford: Oxford University Press, 1999.

Brodie, Richard. *Virus of the Mind: The New Science of the Meme*. Seattle: Integral Press, 1996.

Dawkins, Richard. *The Selfish Gene*. New York: Oxford University Press, 1976.

Dennett, Daniel. *Consciousness Explained*. London: Allen Lane, 1991.

———. *Darwin's Dangerous Idea: Evolution and the Meanings of Life*. New York: Simon & Schuster, 1995.

———. "Memes and the Exploitation of Imagination." *Journal of Aesthetics and Art Criticism* 48: 127–135, 1990.

Distin, Kate. *The Selfish Meme: A Critical Reassessment*. Cambridge: Cambridge University Press, 2004.

Lynch, Aaron. *Thought Contagion: How Belief Spreads Through Society*. New York: Basic Books, 1996.

Marsden, Paul. Review of *Thought Contagion: How Belief Spreads Through Society* by Aaron Lynch. *Journal of Artificial Societies and Social Simulation* 2 (2), available at http://jasss.soc.surrey.ac.uk/2/2/review4.html, 1996.

Objections to Meme Theory

Gould, Stephen Jay. "Darwinian Fundamentalism." *New York Review of Books*, Volume 44, Number 10, June 12, 1997.

Psychology and Sociology

Greene, Robert, and Joost Elffers. *The 48 Laws of Power*. New York: Viking Press, 1998.

Johnson, Joni E. *The Complete Idiot's Guide to Psychology*. Indianapolis: Alpha Books, 2009.

Miscellaneous

Andrews, Synthia, and Colin Andrews. *The Complete Idiot's Guide to 2012*. Indianapolis: Alpha Books, 2008.

Brown, Damon. *Porn & Pong: How Grand Theft Auto, Tomb Raider, and Other Sexy Games Changed Our Culture*. Seattle: Feral House Publishing, 2008.

Channer, Cecily, and Damon Brown. *The Complete Idiot's Guide to Connecting with Your Angels*. Indianapolis: Alpha Books, 2009.

Herek, Gregory M., Jeanine C. Cogan, and J. Roy Gillis. "Victim Experiences in Hate Crimes Based on Sexual Orientation." *Journal of Social Issues* 58.2, 319–339, 2002.

Websites

The Memes of Production

thememesofproduction.org

Cultural studies discussion group with *The Complete Idiot's Guide to Memes* co-author John Gunders, Ph.D.

DamonBrown.net

www.damonbrown.net

Writings of *The Complete Idiot's Guide to Memes* co-author Damon Brown.

Dipity

www.dipity.com/tatercakes/Internet_Memes

An interactive timeline of the Internet's viral video memes.

Journal of Memetics

pcp.vub.ac.be/jom-emit/

A defunct science journal now available online in its entirety.

Snopes

snopes.com

Urban legends described and verified or refuted.

Know Your Meme

knowyourmeme.com

Launched in 2007, Know Your Meme video documents the latest Internet memes.

Memes.org

memes.org

A blog community with meme postings.

RichardDawkins.net

richarddawkins.net

The official site of *The Selfish Gene* author Richard Dawkins.

E. O. Wilson Biodiversity Foundation

www.eowilson.org

The foundation launched by biologist, theorist, and two-time Pulitzer Prize winner E. O. Wilson.

The Daily Meme

thedailymeme.com

A new meme every day.

The Lifecycle of Memes

www.aleph.se/Trans/Cultural/Memetics/memecycle.html

A scientific meme discussion by Henrik Bjarneskans, Bjarne Gronnevik, and Anders Sandberg.

Memetic Lexicon

www.lucifer.com/virus/memlex.html

An extensive meme term dictionary.

The Seven Most Influential Memes

As we've learned, memes aren't anything new—they have helped our world run forever. Here is a concise, albeit narrow, rundown of the seven most influential memes in known history.

Discovery of Fire

Memes are ideas that are passed along to others, and two of the earliest in human history are the discovery of fire and—much later—the invention of the wheel.

Believed to be discovered in the early Stone Age, fire allowed further expansion by moving to colder climates, presumably lower death rates during winters, and the ability to cook foods easily—killing more dangerous bacteria and adding variety to what could be considered nourishment. As we saw in Chapter 22, the eating of cooked meat even led to changes in the human body itself, because humans didn't need such a large and energy-inefficient digestive system if the food was already partially broken down.

The meme of fire moved quickly, never was replaced, and passed on easily from generation to generation for millennia.

The Invention of the Wheel

Arguably invented in the fourth millennium B.C.E., the wheel enabled easier, faster transportation of not only people and goods but also of the wheel meme itself as people saw this strange new device and decided to copy it.

Like fire, the wheel led to the creation and passing on of other memes, because both gave humans the ability to spread their ideas faster. The wheel itself is a meme, but the wheel became the foundation for the wheelbarrow, the carriage, the train, the car, and so on—enabling memes to travel more easily and to farther distances.

Religion

It may be hard to imagine something as personal and as sacred as one's religious interior as a meme, but beliefs, customs, and traditions—which by definition create a religion—are memes themselves.

Not to be confused with spirituality, religion is something that is passed on through families, through sects, and through communities. The practice of praying, for example, the Hail Mary originated somewhere, and even if it was divine intervention, it was a human's job to pass on the idea. A perfect example would be Moses, who—according to the King James Bible—was given 10 commandments to pass on to others in his community. From Taoism to Catholicism, religion is given, taught, and spread—as are other memes.

For further proof of religion as meme, look toward meme pioneer Richard Dawkins. The self-professed skeptic followed up the meme-birthing *The Selfish Gene* with *God Is Not Great* and other atheist-focused treatises. For Dawkins, the line between memes and religion was a short one.

The Arch

We choose the arch because it is a very obvious architectural feature, but we could as easily have chosen buttresses, glass windows, or even scientific discoveries such as the lever or telescope. What these things share is their ability to be copied by an observer.

The arch solved a particular problem for builders in early Rome—how to create a wide opening in a wall without having to put supports in the way. While it seems obvious now, it must have come as quite a surprise to the first person who discovered that such a large pile of stone held itself up instead of crashing to the ground.

But once the principle was discovered and developed, the idea was easily spread. You only have to look at an arch to understand how it works, and then you can build your own (maybe after one or two false starts). The physical arch becomes the vector of the arch meme—visitors to Rome could see the way it worked and take it back to their own buildings, where in turn others could see it and try out the idea.

In time, the concept evolved further, with more efficient designs and other developments. Arches were joined together to form aqueducts and bridges, and the vaulted ceiling is basically a series of arches at right angles to each other that allowed builders to span an entire room, not just a doorway. But behind all these constructions is the simple meme of the arch.

The Confidence Scam

Whether it is the pyramid, the Ponzi scheme, or the currently popular Nigerian Scam, any of these confidence scam variants make up one of the most important memes of human time. It also conveys a clear message: no matter how much humans have, we always want more.

In its most modern premise, a con person tells the mark (the potential victim) that a high-ranking international official has a large sum of money coming to him, but an immigration policy is preventing the official from actually accessing the money. The con person asks the mark to help—usually in the form of money required to transfer the money—in exchange for a percentage of the bounty. Of course, there is no bounty, and the con person is that much richer from the mark's "investment."

Named because it usually involves an African prince, the Nigerian Scam is important in that it reflects human foibles, including greed and deception, and that these weaknesses have not changed since the beginning of recorded history. Because it is based on basic human values, the Nigerian Scam and its ancestors are truly the memes that will never die.

Memes

No typo here—the idea of memes is actually one of the most important memes in history.

Coming into prominence with Richard Dawkins's book *The Selfish Gene* and exploding with the advent of the Internet, the concept of memes has helped us articulate the flow of modern culture. It is the blood-revealing Luminal in the landmark TV show *CSI* or the black light at a nightclub: an easy way to trace the path of our current situation, which would otherwise be nearly untraceable.

Memes allow us to categorize and describe the exponentially increasing flow of ideas. In a truly meta moment, defining memes has helped us recognize more memes—and if perception is reality, our acceptance of memes has actually increased the number of memes seen, created, and passed along.

The Internet Meme

It's a broad category that is named after the medium, not the meme itself. But without the Internet, many memes wouldn't be popular—or even possible.

Emoticons, a new language that has been embraced by several generations, would not have taken off without online discussions, and social networking would be impossible without the Internet as its backbone. LOLCats, RickRolling, and countless other ideas work only within the context of the World Wide Web.

Biggest Internet Memes

The Internet didn't create the meme, but it sure did speed up the spreading process. There are also some memes that would only be possible with the still-young World Wide Web. Here are some of the notable ones.

Images

Peanut Butter Jelly Time

www.youtube.com/watch?v=Z3ZAGBL6UBA

One of the first visual Internet memes, "Peanut Butter Jelly Time" is a moving image of a dancing banana (with legs and arms). Originally passed along via e-mail, later videos put the dancing banana to music. The most famous was the southern staple "Peanut Butter Jelly Time," from one-hit wonders Buckwheat Boyz.

Dancing Baby

www.youtube.com/watch?v=-5x5OXfe9KY

A landmark visual meme, 1996's "Dancing Baby" showed off the latest in 3D animation. The diaper-clad child danced joyously to no particular music, but viewers quickly modified and added their own soundtrack to the baby. And, like "RickRolling," it became a bigger meme through television, starring as a regular hallucination in the hit comedy *Ally McBeal*.

Bert Is Evil

www.bertisevil.tv/

In 1998, Dino Ignacio, Wout J. Reinders, and Jasper Hulshoff Pol won a Webby Award and the People's Voice Award for Best Weird Website for their collection of manipulated photos of the popular *Sesame Street* character apparently consorting with various villains and in incriminating positions. One favorite shows Bert apparently watching the passing motorcade minutes before the assassination of President John F. Kennedy.

In a particularly appropriate twist, proving that memes are impossible to control, in 2001 a Bangladeshi protester at a pro–Osama bin Laden rally held up a poster with a photo of the terrorist leader, unaware of the small image of Bert beside him. He had downloaded the image from the "Bert Is Evil" site without realizing its significance.

Hope

obamiconme.pastemagazine.com/

In 2008, as Illinois Senator Barack Obama ran for U.S. president, pop artist Shepard Fairley created a stunning Obama profile from an Associated Press photo. The intense, polarizing image in red, white, and blue was simply titled "Hope." The picture became a popular poster—and arguably helped Obama get to the White House—but it spawned parody upon parody on the Web. The online images mocked icons as varied as Darth Vader, Apple head Steve Jobs, and the Cookie Monster.

Phrases

The "O RLY?" Owl

Usually accompanied by a photograph of a snowy owl with an expression that could be interpreted as sarcastic, the words "O RLY?" ("Oh, really?") have become Internet shorthand for a reply to a statement that the user thinks is obvious, self-evident, or clearly false. Often used on discussion lists, the usual reply is "YA RLY!" ("Yeah, really!").

I Did It for the Lulz

The term "laughing out loud," or LOL, goes back at least a decade and became mainstream as text messaging—and the character restrictions of the medium—became commonplace, something that increased even more with Twitter. "I Did It for the Lulz" is a derivative meaning ("Well, I did it just for a laugh"). We can consider "lulz" a past tense of LOL—"I did it so I could laugh out loud."

It is usually used when someone defends performing an evil, usually unnecessary deed, such as Darth Vader destroying the planet Alderaan with the Death Star. Internet denizens have created some truly gruesome uses of the term with regard to the Holocaust, the events of September 11, 2001, and other large-scale tragedies.

FIRST!

Blogging culture became ultra-mainstream in the mid-2000s, and unlike the static stories of the past, the comment section—and the commenters themselves—became as important as the post writer. "FIRST!" became a point of pride, something written by the first person to comment on a blog. Ironically, "FIRST!" is usually the entire comment, which makes it both annoying and useless. It tapered in the late 2000s as the practice became heavily discouraged. At its peak, there would be multiple commentators posting "FIRST!"—when, because of Internet lag, he or she would be second, third, or eighth.

Owned/Pwned

Owned means totally winning or dominating something—or, more often, someone (as in, "I owned you guys in that last hand of poker"). In tech culture, it's often spelled "Pwned." The origins of the alternative spelling are fuzzy, but the website "Know Your Meme" says it may have come from chess terminology—"pwn" is likely short for pawn, the weakest piece in the ancient game.

Om Nom Nom Nom

From unknown beginnings, "Om Nom Nom Nom" means eating something really, really tasty—usually without hesitation. Online, the "Om" is usually dropped and it's just "Nom Nom Nom."

Concepts

Ninjas Versus Pirates

Started in 2003, the concept is simple: Who would win in a battle between the two most lauded adventurers in history, stealthy ninjas or ruthless pirates? The website "Know Your Meme" attributes the well-trodden idea to Robert Hamburger of the humor website RealUltimatePower (realultimatepower.net).

The concept revived interest in ninjas, including ninja-themed T-shirts, mugs, and other accessories. Pirates also regained popularity with the billion-grossing *Pirates of the Caribbean* movie trilogy—coincidently beginning in 2003—and, more importantly, "Talk Like a Pirate Day" every September 19 (www.talklikeapirate.com).

Flash Mob

A flash mob is a large group of people who organize a seemingly chaotic, but actually choreographed, public event for spectacle. For instance, hundreds of people may agree to meet in Central Park in New York City at a particular time and do a five-minute dance routine.

Flash mobs may have existed before the Internet, but the speedy communication among literally billions of people made them more commonplace. Experts say they started in earnest around 2003. An excellent recent example was the dozens of flash mobs happening worldwide after pop star Michael Jackson's death, usually to perform his famous 1982 "Thriller" music video dance routine.

Videos

RickRoll'D

www.youtube.com/watch?v=oHg5SJYRHA0

The Rick Astley '80s video "Never Gonna Give You Up" was used to "RickRoll" unsuspecting victims. To RickRoll, you promise an important link and send the mark to this video instead. Since 2007, more than 20 million have been served.

Apparently, the meme started in 2007 when the first release of the *Grand Theft Auto IV* trailer became unavailable due to heavy traffic, and people were sent to the YouTube site instead. Since then, there have been numerous examples of RickRolling—not necessarily confined to the Internet, such as Astley's surprise appearance in the 2008 Macy's Thanksgiving Day Parade.

Tay Zonday's "Chocolate Rain"

www.youtube.com/watch?v=EwTZ2xpQwpA

Uploaded in 2007, amateur singer Tay Zonday's "Chocolate Rain" was about racism, but the 45 million viewers probably watched it to understand the dense lyrics, catch the funny melody, or listen to Zonday's awkward singing style ("I move away from the mic to breathe in"). It was popular enough to spawn T-shirts, late-show appearances, and a Dr. Pepper commercial featuring Zonday himself.

"Leave Britney Alone!"

www.youtube.com/watch?v=kHmvkRoEowc

By summer 2007, young, meme-worthy pop singer Britney Spears had shaved her head, gone to rehab, and lost custody of her children—and began the fall with a heavily criticized "comeback" on the MTV Video Music Awards. Britney fan Chris Crocker uploaded a manic, eyeliner-smeared video yelling, "Leave Britney alone!" The disturbing two-minute clip became arguably the pop-cultural meme of the year, with people randomly yelling, "Leave [fill in the blank] alone!" online and off. The 28 million views also encouraged Crocker to start selling songs through iTunes.

All Your Base Are Belong to Us

www.youtube.com/watch?v=qItugh-fFgg

Like many Japanese games in the '80s, the sleeper video game "Zero Wing" had awful English translations. In a key scene, an evil alien leader threatens the human hero with seeming gibberish; particularly, "All your base are belong to us." Dug up a decade later, the bad English became a funny online threat used in different contexts. The advent of YouTube popularized the actual video game clip and started several websites, including Engrish—a site dedicated to bad Japanese-to-English translations.

Keyboard Cat

www.youtube.com/watch?v=J---aiyznGQ

It's not clear who first decided to have his or her cat try to play the piano, but the most notable one was "Keyboard Cat." Filmed by Charlie Schmidt, "Keyboard Cat" features a chubby cat slamming its paws on an '80s Casio keyboard in a fitted Hawaiian shirt. It was bizarre, even by Internet standards. The one-minute, off-beat tune spawned dozens, if not hundreds, of imitators and was part of the bigger LOLCat phenomenon.

Badger Badger

www.badgerbadgerbadger.com/

One of the most bizarre Internet memes, this is a flash animation of dancing badgers accompanying a highly repetitive dance song whose words consist mainly of "badger badger badger badger," with occasional references to mushrooms and a snake. It's incredibly pointless but strangely compelling.

Back Dorm Boys

www.youtube.com/watch?v=N2rZxCrb7iU

In late 2005, Chinese students Wei Wei and Huang Yuxin set up a camera in a bedroom, put on matching Houston Rockets basketball jerseys, and excitedly lip synced to the Backstreet Boys pop hit "I Want It That Way."

The exuberant performance, made even more special because they didn't seem to know English, became one of the first major hits on YouTube. Nicknamed the Back Dorm Boys, the duo uploaded many other improvisations and inspired dozens and dozens of parodies, including Back Dorm Boys clones in other Asian countries. The original cover of "I Want It That Way" has still racked up the most views, hitting 11 million in early 2010.

Downfall Parodies

www.youtube.com/view_play_list?p=A20DAC818C423798&search_query=downfall

Oliver Hirschbiegel's 2004 film *Der Untergang*—known in English-speaking countries as *Downfall*—about the final days of Adolph Hitler has had a surprising second life as the source of a persistent meme in which a key scene in the film is shown, complete with original audio (in German), but with subtitles referring to contemporary popular cultural events, such as the release of the iPad, accessibility problems with Twitter, Michael Jackson's death, and the correct use of English grammar.

Perhaps surprisingly, Hirschbiegel has spoken approvingly about the parodies, accepting that people are able to do whatever they like with the material.

However, in spring 2010, *Downfall* distributor Constantin Films had the YouTube videos blocked because of copyright violation. Co-author Damon Brown discussed the dilemma on one of his blogs: industry.bnet.com/media/10007945/movie-distributor-bans-popular-hitler-parodies-shoots-itself-in-foot/.

The Evolution of Dance

www.youtube.com/watch?v=dMH0bHeiRNg

One of the first major video memes on YouTube, stand-up comedian Judson Laipply spends six minutes performing major dance crazes. Uploaded in 2006, the universally funny video has racked up nearly 140 million views in four years. The real funny part is that the Twist, the Robot, and other cultural touchstones are memes themselves. "The Evolution of Dance" is not only a memeplex—that is, a collection of memes—but also a reviver of memes long forgotten, if not dead.

OK Go's "Here It Goes Again"

www.youtube.com/watch?v=pv5zWaTEVkI

In 2006, the indie pop group OK Go uploaded a video directed by the frontman's sister, Trish Sie. Set to its song "Here It Goes Again," the short video has the quartet dancing on treadmills in unison.

The quirky video made the song a hit, scoring the small band a performance spot at the MTV Music Video Awards and a major deal with EMI. In 2007 the video won the Grammy for "Best Short Form Music Video." By 2010, there were just under 50 million views on YouTube alone.

Dramatic Prairie Dog/Chipmunk/Squirrel

www.youtube.com/watch?v=a1Y73sPHKxw

One of the shortest video memes ever, the five-second clip is of an animal with its back turned and, suddenly, turning its face to the camera with an expression worthy of a film noir (the dramatic music helps). According to the website "Know Your Meme" (www.knowyourmeme.com), the brief clip is from a longer video excerpt of a 2001 Japanese game show. An ingenious 4chan (www.4chan.com) user cut it down to a five-second animated graphic—one that would later make its way to YouTube.

It is best known as "Dramatic Chipmunk" or "Dramatic Squirrel," but the little guy (or gal) is actually a Dramatic Prairie Dog—the least-popular video name of the three on YouTube. The video website has dozens of "Dramatic Prairie Dog" parodies featuring Chihuahuas, cats, and lizards as well as Prairie Dog homages to *Star Wars*, *Family Guy*, and James Bond films.

The video meme also spawned a text companion of equal import, with e-mails, blog posts, and other digital communications punctuated with "*queue dramatic squirrel*."

Websites

Know Your Meme

www.knowyourmeme.com

An excellent resource for the latest memes, "Know Your Meme" is a massive repository of trending Internet videos and images. The visitors can nominate certain ideas for meme status, and other visitors—through commentary and voting—decide whether or not they qualify. There are thousands of items cataloged as confirmed memes, submitted memes, or deadpool (rejected) memes.

Memes are public by nature, and "Know Your Meme" takes advantage of the Internet and the democratic process it creates. The judging process also proves that the most popular idea isn't the same as a strong meme, because the ability to be known isn't the same as the ability to be spread, accepted, and passed on.

4chan

www.4chan.org

"4chan" is one of the few websites that retains the Wild West energy of the early Internet. Essentially an elaborate message board, the virtually uncensored content and commentary are fertile ground for some of the biggest memes, such as "O RLY?", "Dramatic Prairie Dog," and "LOLCats/I Can Haz Cheezeburger," the latter of which spawned its own site.

Meme Generator

memegenerator.net

Talk about an enabler. "Meme Generator" takes the most popular visuals and makes it easy to create overlay text, modifying the iconic picture and transforming the meme's original meaning.

"Meme Generator" proves that, on the Internet, the image itself and its original meaning becomes secondary to the inspired memes it creates.

I Can Haz Cheezburger?

icanhascheezburger.com

Launched in 2007 by Eric Nakagawa, "I Can Haz Cheezburger?" features cute animal pictures—usually of cats—with funny, slightly misspelled captions representative of what the animal is doing. It spawned the term LOLCats, or "laugh-out-loud cats."

The first recorded use of the term LOLCat was on a discussion board in 2005, although the idea of attaching captions to amusing photos of animals has been around for decades. Nakagawa's site became so popular that it eventually started offering ways in which people could create their own LOLCats.

FAILBlog

failblog.org

"FAILBlog" displays a combination of pictures and videos showing people failing, such as a handle-less car door shut with duct tape or a football quarterback running in the wrong direction. It is a domain established as early as Alan Funt's *Candid Camera* TV show in the '60s, but the audience participation and the broader access via the Internet spawned an entire fail culture—including the term "FAIL" into the Internet nomenclature.

The blog is a close relative of the "Darwin Awards" (www.darwinawards.com/), a website by Wendy Northcutt that "honors those who improve the gene pool by accidentally removing themselves from it." The Darwin Awards have been around since at least 1985, circulating first as photocopies then as e-mails.

Chuck Norris Facts

www.chucknorrisfacts.com/

Since 2005, Chuck Norris facts—over-the-top claims about the abilities of the martial artist and television star—have gained popularity. Based on a genre of sketches popular on late-night television, the "facts" tend to be based around the popular "Russian Reversal" joke: "In Soviet Russia, you don't drive car; the car drives you."

Some famous examples are:

- When Chuck Norris falls in water, Chuck Norris doesn't get wet. Water gets Chuck Norris.

- Chuck Norris does not get frostbite. Chuck Norris bites frost.

- There is no theory of evolution. Just a list of animals Chuck Norris allows to live.

Interviews with Meme Originators

"Chocolate Rain." LOLCats. Certain ideas have made a huge impact on Internet culture—and in turn have penetrated greater pop culture.

We've delved into the makeup of a meme, how it is spread, and why it is important. But what do three of the major meme originators themselves have to say?

They were nice enough to talk to co-author Damon Brown about their influence, their inspiration, and their unexpected fame.

Erik Nakagawa, Co-Founder of "I Can Haz Cheezburger?"

Have you ever been online and stumbled upon one of those cute kitten pictures with a funny, misspelled caption? Erik Nakagawa didn't invent adorable animal pictures, but his website "I Can Haz Cheezburger?" definitely made them popular on the Internet.

Inspired by a cat picture with the aforementioned caption, Erik Nakagawa and his partner, Kari Unebasami, created a simple website for people to upload their own funny photos and sayings. It was instantly popular. They launched the site in January 2007 and sold it to Ben Huh of Pet Holdings, Inc., the following September for an estimated $2 million.

Damon Brown: Number one, do you even like animals?

Erik Nakagawa: I like animals. Who doesn't like puppies and kittens?

Damon: Do you have any pets now?

Erik: We currently do not have any pets. We do have a little baby—and are interviewing puppy candidates.

Damon: How did "I Can Haz Cheezburger?" come about?

Erik: It started as a collection of cute and funny photos as an interruption in your workday.

Damon: Who was the co-founder?

Erik: Kari Unebasami and I created the site in 2007.

Damon: Why the misspelled statements? Is there a story behind why Hi became Hai?

Erik: Buy our book *I Can Haz Cheezburger?* to find out more (at en.wikipedia.org/wiki/Lolspeak).

Damon: Why cheeseburger and not, say, fish or chicken?

Erik: It started with the first misspelled photo. I had never seen the photo before. To this day, it still makes me smile.

Damon: What were the approximate number of visitors your first month?

Erik: A couple hundred thousand.

Damon: When did you realize it was taking off?

Erik: When you receive 100k hits in a couple weeks, you have something hot/addictive/fun/viral.

Damon: Were you surprised when someone wanted to buy the site?

Erik: We had been working with Ben [Huh] previously. He's done an amazing job growing the site into a media empire.

Damon: What did you do with all that Cheezburger money?

Erik: Working on a time-traveling De Lorean.

Damon: Do you still visit every day?

Erik: I visit every week. Or … when I am stressed out. Or worse … when I see something that must be unseen.

Damon: There were plenty of cute animal sites, even back in 2007. What made "I Can Haz Cheezburger?" stick?

Erik: Curated photos, constant attention to our fans, always trying to make people laugh, attention to detail, and keeping in touch with who and what is said and posted about us.

Damon: What are you working on now?

Erik: Mobile app development at my company App Dev + Mktg.

Damon: What memetic trend is your favorite right now?

Erik: I love the memes of Reddit (www.reddit.com). My current right-before-bedtime addiction.

Chris Menning of Know Your Meme

If Internet memes were in the Olympics, then Know Your Meme would be the official judging committee. Home of a savvy, passionate audience, the young website has new ideas daily that are ranked, debated, and tossed based on their memetic quality.

Everyone may be talking about the Grammys' outfits the night after the event, but will people remember Bjork's dead swan dress years after the ceremony? The Know Your Meme audience decides what will stick and what won't.

Chris Menning of Know Your Meme talked about how the website came to be.

Damon Brown: Why are memes important?

Chris Menning: In essence, a meme is a self-empowering concept. It lends us a fresh perspective on how popular information travels, grows, and mutates through the medium from the information's point of view, rather than those who participate in enriching and spreading it. In simple words, it gives information a "face" of its own. By studying a meme's history from origin to current day, we can draw bigger cultural implications and social trends that may reflect our own times, in a somewhat objective fashion.

Damon: How many items are on the website?

Chris: So far, we've had a total of 2,060 submissions, 560 confirmed entries.

Damon: Do you remember the first meme posted?

Chris: The first entry posted on Know Your Meme, it was FAIL (at knowyourmeme. com/memes/fail).

Damon: What was the initial response to Know Your Meme? Did most visitors know what a meme was?

Chris: At first, there were many users who joined the site with a lot of misconceptions about memes, such as, "they have to be funny" or "if everyone knows about it, then it's not a meme." Many people have made the mistake of confusing an inside joke with a meme. Even though many memes start as a joke, there are countless memes that are anything but insider knowledge. Susan Blackmore said it best when she said, "A meme is that which is imitated."

There are also those who rush to call something a meme because it might look like other memes, confusing the format of the content for a meme rather than identifying a trend of participatory content creation. There are people still making this mistake today.

Damon: Memes aren't limited to the Internet, but how did the Internet change memes?

Chris: Internet memes can be distinguished by a list of characteristics (check out the Know Your Meme FAQ at knowyourmeme.com/forums/general/topics/ 3937-frequently-asked-questions), but one of the most unique elements is its material document-ability. Because info exchange on the Web typically leaves some sort of meta-information accessible to most Internet users, we can use these clues to chart a tangible map of a digital territory unseen as a whole.

Damon: What are the more controversial memes on the site?

Chris: Oh, there are a lot! Racism, sexism, homophobia, pedophilia, you name it! One very important thing to understand about memes is that they don't spread because they are inherently good, cute, or funny. There are plenty of memes that spread simply because they are effective at evoking an emotionally charged response from those who come in contact with them.

The practice of saying or doing things to incite anger from someone else for your own enjoyment, even if you are portraying a viewpoint that you might not personally agree with, is called trolling. A troll might otherwise be a decent human being, but under the cover of anonymity provided by the Internet, there are plenty of people who might pretend to be more ignorant than they really are—with the hopes that someone will get upset and waste their own time involving themselves in a heated moral debate.

And then there are those who are genuinely racist, sexist, or otherwise hateful, and they truly believe the views they present. Given the faceless nature of sites like 4chan, differentiating one from the other is very difficult and sometimes impossible.

Some other sites might be quick to delete this kind of content. But pretending that this kind of thing doesn't occur doesn't make it go away. Instead, we address these memes for what they are. Condemning them only "feeds the trolls," so we try our best to objectively state what the memes are and why they behave the ways that they do.

Damon: The discussions are pretty passionate. Why do people argue about the importance of one meme versus another?

Chris: The arguments about the importance of one meme over another usually arise because so many people have such deep feelings invested in different memes. Some people try desperately to create a brand new meme, proclaiming that "this is the next big new meme to take over the Internet" when it hasn't actually appeared anywhere else online. That's mostly what you'll find in the "Deadpool" section of our site.

Others may be personally offended by a meme and attempt to downplay its importance, allowing their feelings to cloud their objectivity.

Damon: 4chan and geek culture have understood memes for a while, but now it seems more mainstream. Did YouTube make memes more well-known, or was there another tipping point?

Chris: I would argue that only a small number of people on 4chan really understand memes. We actually have to deal with lots of others who claim to be upset over what they refer to as "stolen memes" completely ignorant of the mechanics of memetics, not to mention the fact that we aim to link to every place where a meme is found, track down the originators if possible, and give credit where credit is due.

To be brutally honest, the word "meme" gets bandied about as a buzzword way too often. I think that tipping point you refer to is yet to come.

Damon: We have recent trends, like Epic Beard Man (a winter 2010 meme inspired by a brutal recorded fight on a moving bus), and lasting ones like "O RLY." Have you guys figured out why certain memes stick and others don't?

Chris: Generally, when a meme gains mainstream recognition as quickly as Epic Beard Man did (at knowyourmeme.com/memes/epic-beard-man), it tends to lose its appeal. The great memes that last the longest generally start out as small inside jokes that slowly rise to national attention through legitimate person-to-person contact. Whenever you see, say, something like, "This is the fastest growing meme ever," you can be sure it won't last very long. As soon as mainstream media picks up on the joke and starts contributing to it, those who enjoyed it initially will feel like it has lost its value—much like having one's favorite band "sell out."

This is what we've started to refer to as "The Benjamin Button Effect"—when a meme is already old at birth. Although the meme itself seeks to propagate, it's how the meme is perceived by its potential hosts that ultimately decides how far a meme will go.

Tay Zonday, Singer of "Chocolate Rain"

"Chocolate Rain" was one of the first major hits on YouTube, notable for the nebulous lyrics, monotone vocals, and most importantly the singer Tay Zonday. A Ph.D. candidate who sang as a hobby, Zonday recorded the simple video of him performing in the studio—and his odd habit of turning away from the mic when he wasn't singing.

"Chocolate Rain" racked up millions of YouTube views, was featured in commercials, and created a ton of clones, parodies, and homages—a good indicator of its meme power.

Damon Brown: When did you write/record "Chocolate Rain"?

Tay Zonday: The melody for "Chocolate Rain" first came together circa 1999 or 2000. The lyrics for "Chocolate Rain" were written in March and April of 2007. The song was recorded in April of 2007. The version I recorded was experimental, and I had never intended for it to be a "final" product. I posted it on YouTube to get feedback on what was, essentially, a prototype.

Damon: When did you realize that it was taking off?

Tay: The song gained attention on Digg.com during the second week of July 2007. Someone saw it there and posted it on 4chan, a large anime board, where it became a popular joke. It was part of a prank called into Tom Green's Internet show, where the caller suddenly broke into singing "Chocolate Rain." Soon the combined attention led to major media mentions like Carson Daly's show on NBC. This snowballed into a national news story where I did roughly 40 radio interviews in mid-July 2007 and eventually made the front page of Sunday's *Los Angeles Times* and did live interviews on CNN and G4TV.

Damon: How did the Dr. Pepper commercial come about?

Tay: Representatives from the ad agency responsible for designing a promotional campaign for Cadbury Schweppes (now Dr. Pepper Snapple Group) contacted me to express interest, and it went from there.

Damon: What is the oddest promotional thing you've done with "Chocolate Rain"?

Tay: I would not call any paid work "odd" because it might offend whoever had paid for it.

Damon: What is the oddest promotional thing you've been asked to do but *didn't* do with "Chocolate Rain"?

Tay: These are very "Chocolate Rain"-centric questions, maybe because this is a book on memes. I've been approached to do many odd promotions as Tay Zonday nonspecific to "Chocolate Rain." I wish I could name-drop or break NDAs (nondisclosure agreements), because some proposals have been quite humorous, but it would be impolite.

Damon: Do you ever get tired of singing "Chocolate Rain"?

Tay: No, I don't. But I do think I had a lot of growth to do as a singer, performer, and entertainer in 2007 and still have a lot to learn. In the same way that "Chocolate Rain" was a prototype song that got big, I was a novice entertainer who got big. It is exciting to try to do everything that I do better.

Damon: What is your favorite post–"Chocolate Rain" song right now?

Tay: The media loves absolute qualifiers. "Most," "best," "favorite," "oddest," "greatest," "worst." Truth is never so obvious, binary, and uninflected. Truth is contingent, gradated, duplicitous, vexed, and changing—or you don't dig deep enough.

Damon: There are plenty of people singing on YouTube, even back in 2007. What makes "Chocolate Rain" special?

Tay: Some people said I had a voice-body mismatch because I looked young and am not a large person. Others said the melody was catchy. Still others said that my mannerisms were humorous. Sometimes people were moved by the song's deep politics or what they saw as a cryptic message. But above all else, the song was a very easy song to parody. People could loop the melody and make their own versions and lyrics. This allowed people to sing humorous rewrites like "Menstrual Pain." Many of these rewrites imitated the artistic style of the original, filming in front of a bed sheet with a microphone.

After all these factors, there might be room to opine that I was talented and different, but I wouldn't have the hubris to do so.

Damon: What kind of "Chocolate Rain" merchandise do you have available?

Tay: There are T-shirts linked from my website, www.tayzonday.com.

Damon: Could you see yourself living off of "Chocolate Rain"?

Tay: "Living off" sounds so vulgar and parasitic. I guess Don McLean "lives off" "American Pie" and Gloria Gaynor "lives off" "I Will Survive" in the same way that Bill Gates "lives off" of Microsoft—but that's really a question of whether one has multiple commercially successful brands. I'm just happy to make a living period, whether it's from one thing like J. D. Salinger or a catalog of things like Shel Silverstein.

Damon: I read in previous interviews that you look at "Chocolate Rain" more as poetry, as in it doesn't have to have a specific meaning. What is the funniest interpretation you've heard from others?

Tay: I said that? I don't like to be polemic about the meaning of music, because if you can say what it means, why sing it?

"Funniest" is another absolute, and I spoke about my discomfort with absolutes earlier. I have laughed at many "Chocolate Rain" interpretations.

Damon: Did you wrap grad school? What's the next step for you?

Tay: I dropped out of my Ph.D. program at the University of Minnesota with a Master's degree in 2008. Since then, and as of this writing, I have been a self-employed independent musician.

Damon: What do you think the next memetic trend will be?

Tay: Now isn't that oxymoronic? You deploy the term "memetic trend," but meme and trend are different. A "trend" represents the cutting edge of things that will someday be conventional. You monetize a trend by developing that cutting edge before competitors. A "meme" is something to be imitated. It orbits convention. You monetize a meme by knowing its predictable and permanent result. Gilbert Gottfried's loud and annoying character is a meme that has become synonymous with him. It has survived many entertainment trends and remains predictable, unique, and fun to imitate. Maybe I should write a book.

Index

  consciousness development ideas, 231
  gene-culture coevolution, 232
  genetic transcription and memetic transmission theory, 232-234
  meme evolution ideas, 231
dual-inheritance, 222
  Cloak versus Dawkins, 223-224
  cultural transmission, 222-223
  main elements, 223
Lynch's *Thought Contagion*, 238
  broad meme definition, 243
  criticism, 243
  departing from science origins, 244
  merging memes, 242
  modes of spreading memes, 240-242
  paradigm shifts, 238-239
  viral ideas, 239-240
postmodernism, 253-254
proving evolution through genetics, 226
  DNA discovery, 227-228
  inheritance, 226
purpose, 253-254
resurrecting memes, 231-232
Semon, Richard Wolfgang, 220

Thought Contagion: How Belief Spreads Through Society: The New Science of Memes, 190, 238
  broad meme definition, 243
  criticism, 243
  departing from science origins, 244
  merging memes, 242
  modes of spreading memes, 240-241
    adversative, 242
    cognitive advantage, 242
    efficiency parental, 241
    motivational, 242
    preservational, 241
    proselytic, 241
    quantity parental, 241
  paradigm shifts, 238-239
  viral ideas, 239-240
Tipping Point, The, 31
tipping points, 31
  connectors, 31
  criticism, 32
  mavens, 32
  salesmen, 32
  social shifts, 33
  timing, 33
tolerance, 149
totalizing systems
  defined, 206
  politics, 211-212
  religion, 210
    bait and punishment memes, 210
    fundamentalism, 210-211
  science
    acceptance, 209-210
    evolution models, 208-209

toxic memes
  auto-toxic, 174
    defined, 174
    recklessness, 175
    signs, 174
    suicide, 174-175
    terrorism, 179
  copycat crimes, 180
    being a part of something bigger, 181
    covering tracks, 180-181
  cults, 177-178
  exo-toxic, 176
    copycat crimes, 180-181
    defined, 176
    Nazism, 176
    terrorism, 179
  memeoids, 177
  terrorism, 179
    auto-toxic, 179
    conscious self-sacrifice, 179
    exo-toxic, 179
    immune to logic, 180
    religious or political memeplex links, 179
  types, 173
traditions, 85-86
Trojan horses, 186
Truman, Harry S., 110
Trump, Donald, 19
Twitter, 55
types
  cultures, 221
  immuno-memes, 212
    adaptation, 214
    conservatism, 213
    nihilism, 213
    orthodoxy, 213
    radicalism, 213
    science, 213